V

THE YEAR LEFT 2

An American Socialist Yearbook

Edited by
Mike Davis, Manning Marable,
Fred Pfeil, and Michael Sprinker

Verso is the imprint of New Left Books.

The Year Left is an annual publication.

Editorial correspondence should be directed to:

The Year Left
c/o English Department
SUNY-Stony Brook
Stony Brook, NY 11794–5350

First published 1987
© Verso, 1987

Verso
15 Greek Street, London W1

Filmset in Ehrhardt by
Pentacor Ltd, High Wycombe, Bucks

Printed by Thetford Press Limited
Thetford, Norfolk

ISBN 0 86091 171 3
ISBN 0 86091 883 1 Pbk

British Library
Cataloguing in Publication Data

The Year Left: an American socialist yearbook.
   Volume 2.
   1. Socialism — United States
   335′.00973   HX86

Contents

SECTION TWO
The Culture of Color

SECTION THREE
Crisis in the Hemisphere

The Haymarket Series

General Editor, Michael Sprinker

The Haymarket Series is a new publishing initiative by Verso offering original studies of politics, history and culture focused on North America. The series presents innovative but representative views from across the American left on a wide range of topics of current and continuing interest to socialists in North America and throughout the world. A century after the first May Day, the American left remains in the shadow of those martyrs whom this series honours and commemorates. The studies in the Haymarket Series testify to the living legacy of activism and political commitment for which they gave up their lives.

Already Published

BLACK AMERICAN POLITICS: From the Washington Marches to Jesse Jackson by *Manning Marable*

PRISONERS OF THE AMERICAN DREAM: Politics and Economy in the History of the U.S. Working Class by *Mike Davis*

MARXISM IN THE U.S.: Remapping the History of the American Left *by Paul Buhle*

THE YEAR LEFT: *Volume One*: 1984 U.S. Elections; Politics and Culture in Central America.

Forthcoming

MECHANIC ACCENTS: Dime Novels and Working-Class
Culture in 19th-Century America by *Michael Denning*

ORIGINS OF THE AMERICAN FAMILY
by *Stephanie Coontz*

YOUTH, IDENTITY, POWER: The Chicano Generation
by *Carlos Muñoz, Jr.*

LABORING ON: The U.S. Working Class Since 1960
by *Kim Moody*

THE PARADOX OF AMERICAN SOCIAL DEMOCRACY
by *Robert Brenner*

THE CALIFORNIA MIRACLE: Capitalism's Fertile Land
by *Dick Walker, Ed Soja, Mike Davis, and Alan Scott*

THE YEAR LEFT: *Volume Three*: Reshaping the American
Left; Media Politics.

Themes

This second volume of *The Year Left* focuses on questions of race and ethnicity across a wide range of social practices in several nations and regions throughout the Americas. It takes up one of the central topics announced in our Statement of Purpose—the functional specificities of white racism, and the political articulations and disarticulations among racial minorities—and thus contributes to the long labor of understanding and ultimately transforming the major structures of oppression in the heartlands of the American imperium.

Section One consists of seven essays on the politics and theory of racial and ethnic minorities in the United States. It opens with an overview of the current political situation on the Black left by *Manning Marable*, author of the widely admired *Black American Politics: From the Washington Marches to Jesse Jackson* (Verso, 1985), and general editor of this group of essays. Marable's contribution is by way of updating the conditions and directions in progressive Black politics which are situated historically and explained theoretically in his book. That account had stopped with the moment of Jesse Jackson's Rainbow Coalition and its failure to transcend the electoralism which had been its inaugural premise. Despite the seemingly bleak outcome of the 1984 national elections (chronicled in Marable's contribution to the first volume of *The Year Left*), Marable had ended his study on an upbeat and future-directed note: 'The next stage in the struggle to uproot racism, gender oppression, and social class inequality, requires that Afro-Americans and other oppressed sectors begin to think of politics in a new way, and perceive that the power to transform capitalist society is already in their hands.' The present essay outlines some of the strategies immediately available for such struggles, while remaining conscious of the constraints of white racism and the renascent illusions of 'Black capitalism'.

Complementing Marable's analysis and projection, *Herb Boyd* chronicles grassroots resistance to the current epidemic of racist violence spurred by Reaganism's attempted roll-back of civil rights reforms. He reveals a pattern of militancy and tenacity that challenges the stereotypes of post–1960s passivity or the 'end of the Movement'. At the same time he shows how the repeated failure of the Black left to overcome residual sectarianism and particularism has made it more difficult for valiant local efforts to coalesce into a national fight-back. The strategic key, for Boyd as for Marable, is the alliance of Black liberation with other oppressed groups in a 'broad class movement'.

To the extent that the Rainbow Coalition offers the actual possibility of such a movement, much depends on its ability to encompass the specific historical experiences and programmatic demands of a variegated Latino working class. *Carlos Muñoz*, a founder of the 1960s Chicano Power Movement and its principal historian (*Youth, Identity, Power: The Chicano Generation*—forthcoming in the Haymarket series from Verso), debunks the mistaken assumption that there exists an ethnically unified constituency of 'Hispanics'. The national, regional, class and cultural divisions differentiating Latino communities must figure heavily in any calculation of the potential for a new 'Rainbow socialism'. Focusing on Chicano politics, Muñoz describes how traditional pro-business groups have reasserted their leadership through the manipulation of patriotic symbols and family-centered values. If the Chicano left's immediate task is 'ideological guerrilla warfare' against these conservative forces, its longer-term perspective must be based on the search for the broadest unity against epidemic racism and Anglo-nativism.

Julianne Malveaux's eye-opening critique of the current literature on the 'feminization of poverty' points out how the appeal to 'common gender interests' often obscures the differential situations of Black and white women. Extensive empirical research demonstrates that the economic position of Black women cannot be understood apart from the overall crisis of the Black community, in particular the increasing economic marginalization of Black men— a fact that is sometimes ignored or downplayed in white feminist analysis. Given that Black and white women occupy different positions in the marketplace and occupational structure, she argues that women of color may come off second-best from ameliorative strategies that focus exclusively on gender equality. To build a 'truly powerful coalition of all women who suffer the effects of an inhuman capitalist marketplace', the specific interests of Black women—encompassing class and race, as well as gender—need to be acknowledged at every level of discussion and action.

No issue is more charged for Marxists, none more centrally implicated in the historic struggles of Black peoples, than the relationship between race and class. Our section on the politics and theory of race and ethnicity culminates with three contributions to this still unsettled debate, each of which asserts the obvious starting point for any Marxist accounting: the differential causality and effects of racial and class oppression. *Cornel West* offers a broad overview of conservative and liberal views of Afro-American oppression before considering specifically Marxist theories of race and class. He criticizes the inadequacies of an ethnocentric class reductionism as well as of the 'class nationalism' espoused by Haywood, Forman, Baraka, Cruse and Allen. Instead, he proposes a 'genealogical materialism' which recognizes that racism is not only rooted in the relations of production but also in autonomous cultural practices, including Judeo-Christian religions and Western psycho-sexual anxieties. In his view, a comprehensive theory of Black oppression must assume discursive and micro-institutional perspectives, utilizing Nietzsche, Althusser and Foucault, as well as a more orthordox Marxist attention to the infrastructure of class conflict and production.

Leonard Harris's point of departure is a careful analysis of recent books by Philip Foner (*American Socialism and Black Americans*) and Cedric Robinson (*Black Marxism*). He argues that the Left in the United States has been misguided by a false universalism—the postulate of an undifferentiated material interest of the proletariat—that has occluded the real historical needs of Black people. For *Lucius Outlaw*, writing as both a Marxist and nationalist, the central, irreducible interest is the right 'to live distinctively and self-consciously as people of African descent'. He argues that it is precisely the left nationalist tradition which has been most radical at the grassroots, with its emphases on self-emancipation and a humanistic Africanity. Like Muñoz, Outlaw asserts that US socialism must become a real rainbow of diversity, validating and defending the cultural and 'ontological' aspirations of people of color.

Section Two carries this thematic focus on race and ethnicity onto the terrain of cultural production. It opens with two essays surveying the history of postwar Black film. *David James* concentrates primarily on the turbulent 1960s, especially on the impact of Black political militancy on the representation of Blacks in film. Given the position of Black people in American society, and given the monopoly power of Hollywood over mass film distribution, attempts by Black filmmakers to overcome racial stereotyping were bound to be entangled in contradictions. Thus, films like *Sweet Sweetback's Baadasss Song* and the documentaries on the Black Panthers reflected the very marginalization of Blacks which they struggled to overcome. As James argues in conclusion, the project of a Black cinema must confront not only endemic white racism, but also, like other ethnic cultural production, the absence of a working-class cinema.

Carrying the history of Blacks in film forward from the emergence of Sidney Poitier in the 1950s down to the recent commercial success of *The Color Purple*, *James Miller* analyzes Hollywood's successive attempts to exploit a growing Black film market. From the emollient, integrationist Poitier to the super-macho caricatures of early 1970s 'blaxploitation' films, Hollywood relentlessly and parasitically distorted the changing self-image of Blacks in popular culture. Then in the middle 1970s, after the repression of much of the Black liberation movement, it seized upon the lucrative formula of the 'crossover': a comic Black character with enormous box office appeal for white as well as Black audiences. Although the genre was launched by the early films of Richard Pryor, it has been his recent successor Eddie Murphy who has taken the 'crossover' to new commercial heights—and new ideological depths. The name of the game for Blacks in films of the 1980s, as *A Soldier's Story* and *The Color Purple* amply illustrate in other modes, is assimilation.

Both James and Miller contrast the cultural assimilation (i.e. stereotyped degradation) of Blacks in Hollywood with the indigenous cultural practices produced and consumed by Blacks themselves, notably (although not exclusively) jazz. *Nancy Guevara's* investigation of three contemporary modes of ghetto art—graffiti writing, rap music, and breakdancing—testifies to the rich ingenuity and imaginative energy of urban popular culture. More than that, she shows how these particular forms, which have been portrayed in the mass media as exclusively male preserves, are significantly inflected by female artists.

Women's interventions in 'hip-hop' culture have been invariably contradictory, tending often to reproduce the images of patriarchal hierarchy that their activity seeks ultimately to subvert, but what remains most significant is the assertion of their right to participate fully in all the arenas where public identities are made and social power is contested.

In a different register and on the seemingly unrelated terrain of American national mythology, *Hortense Spillers* examines the intercalation of racial and sexual domination in the figures of the mulatto and the mulatta. Focusing primarily on two canonized texts,

Faulkner's *Absalom, Absalom!* and *Light in August*, but also drawing upon slave narratives, Spillers tentatively proposes a theory of race and gender in the national symbolism of the United States which challenges facile notions about the discrete features defining these characters, and thus segregating absolutely white from Black, male from female. The mulatto/mulatta, as the very type of the liminal character, provides a key to the explosive contradictions inherent in the dominant structures of racial and gender discrimination.

Section Three continues, from our first volume, the survey of the current crisis in Central America and the Caribbean. Amplifying the discussion of class and ethnicity, *Carol Smith* draws from her wideranging knowledge of Guatemalan Indian cultures to mount a sustained critique of the applicability of classical Marxist notions to the political struggle in Guatemala. Her theoretical point of departure is the well-known debate among Edward Thompson, Gareth Stedman Jones and Perry Anderson over the meaning of class in English popular history. Smith's essentially Thompsonian view is that the economic aspects of class formation are insufficient to account for the empirical realities of political conflict and cultural identity in societies like Guatemala, where indigenous culture maintains a corporate identity over and against forced assimilation and proletarianization. According to her, Guatemalan Indians have been surprisingly successful in sustaining a powerful communal solidarity, transcending their own incipient class divisions. The state, rather than the 'rich', is perceived as the main exploiter, and social conflict is structured along ethnic, i.e., Ladino-versus-Indian, lines. The tendency of leftists to minimize ethnic fragmentation in Guatemala, and to ignore the Indians' tenacious struggle for cultural survival, has contributed, in Smith's view, to recent defeats of the popular revolutionary forces.

Taking the entire Caribbean Basin as their empirical instance, *Marc Herold* and *Nicholas Kozlov* weigh the evidence of a 'new international division of labor' involving a major shift of manufacturing capacity to third-world nations. Far from a revolutionary new epoch of capitalism in the Caribbean, they discover familiar forces at work in Jamaica, the Dominican Republic, Haiti, and the smaller nations of the region, as investors take advantage of tax havens, tariff exemptions and low-wage labor forces. Although the aggregate of new production is relatively insignificant from the standpoint of the overall pattern of US investment, the local effects are very considerable.

The ultimate logic of this dependent, off-shore industrialization is exemplified by the crisis of the Caribbean's most 'developed' society: Puerto Rico. We conclude with a sobering overview by *Aline*

Frambes–Buxeda of recent developments in the USA's major colony. Soaring unemployment and further deterioration of the island's social fabric have only aroused authorities in San Juan and Washington to greater repression against local nationalist and militant labor movements. At the same time, under the 'Reagan Doctrine', Puerto Rico has acquired exceptional strategic importance as the main staging area for Yanqui interventionism in Central America and the Caribbean Basin. As Frambes emphasizes, Puerto Rico has in many ways become the crux for anti-imperialist movements in North America. Support for Puerto Rican independence remains a touchstone of progressive politics inside the United States.

We encourage readers to send their comments and criticisms, as well as proposals for future articles, to the editorial committee of *The Year Left:* c/o Sprinker, Department of English, SUNY-Stony Brook, Stony Brook, New York, 11794–5350.

SECTION ONE
Politics and Theory of Race and Ethnicity

1

The Contradictory Contours of Black Political Culture

Manning Marable

Over the past two years, the political mood across Black America has grown more pessimistic. Allies of the Black freedom struggle have abandoned their previous support for affirmative action and expanded civil rights legislation. Among Blacks there is a deepening sense of social alienation and political frustration, generated partially by the continued popularity of President Reagan, the conservative trend in the Democratic party, and the intense economic chaos which plagues Black inner cities despite three years of national economic 'recovery'. The contours of the contemporary crisis within Afro-American political culture and some tentative proposals for resolving it are my topics here.

The most fundamental characteristics of modern Black political life derive from a single historical cause: Afro-Americans have never been fully integrated within the national public-sector and civic discourse in the United States. The essential duality of Black America, described in the classic 1903 statement of W.E.B. Du Bois, remains largely valid: 'One ever feels his two-ness', Du Bois observed, 'an American, a Negro; two souls, two thoughts, two unreconciled strivings; two warring ideals in one dark body, whose dogged strength alone keeps it from being torn asunder.'[1] Afro-Americans do not comprise a nation, yet they remain a distinctive national minority oppressed by the traditional boundaries of institutional racism, residential segregation, educational and social inequality, and class exploitation.

Several variables should be considered in any analysis of 'Black political culture'. First, there is the factor of civil society, or what could be termed civic socialization. Black political behavior is conditioned by the long-term patterns of family development, schooling, religion, cultural and social association as well as by the role of the Black intelligentsia. These structures and individuals fashion generational values, language, and normative civic judgments, and largely determine Black public conduct as a whole. A second factor, more abstract yet vitally important, may be described as either 'Black political history' or Blacks' collective experiences in relation to capitalist state power. These are the repetitious patterns of leadership, political organization and strategy which have usually emerged over several generations. There are several powerful and competing traditions within the Black national minority with different definitions of what constitutes 'politics'. Moreover each tradition tends to be associated with a specific mode of leadership and mass mobilization. A familiar example is the Messianic leadership model: an articulate, charismatic figure, usually associated with religion, who dominates a loosely-structured political organization composed largely of working-class, poor and unemployed Black people. Moreover the forms of Black organization are mediated by the intensity of white racism fostered by the state at given historical moments as well as by the relative position of most Blacks within the political economy.

Materially the economic status of the majority of Black America has continued to deteriorate. About one-half of all Afro-American children 18 years and under live in households below the poverty level. Since 1973, the level of Black median income in relation to white median income has fallen from 63 percent to 55 percent, while the number of Blacks living below the poverty threshold has increased from eight to ten million. This climate of economic austerity has also had a negative impact upon Black educational and social prospects. In 1977, 50 percent of all Black high school graduates enrolled in college or some form of post-secondary education; by 1984, the figure had dropped to 36 percent. Only 29 percent of all Black high school graduates currently enroll directly into college. Although Blacks have made notable gains in some middle-class professions, the overall trend in many jobs is toward greater racial segregation. In education, for instance, according to the Department of Education's Office of Civil Rights, the number of minority undergraduates receiving bachelor's degrees in education has declined from 14,209 in 1975 to 6,792 in 1983. In a recent study of eleven Southern states, a decline of 6.4 percent was noted in the total number of black teachers. By the year 2000, it is estimated that 'the percentage of minorities in the teaching force of the United States could be cut almost in half'.[2]

Both political parties are increasingly viewed by Blacks as being at best apathetic about their declining economic and social conditions. The general orientation of the Reagan administration towards race relations can be termed a 'non-racist racism'. The administration's social and economic policies hurt Blacks dispro- portionately, since larger percentages of Afro-Americans are among the working poor and unemployed. Administration officials pre- sume that political and civil inequities between whites and Blacks that were a legacy of Jim Crow segregation no longer exist. Thus, there is no need for race-sensitive policies targeted to assist the victims of racism. Affirmative action therefore is seen as 'reverse discrimination' against innocent white victims. Bureaucratically, the administration has tried to stop the collection of data 'on the participation of Blacks and other minorities in employment, housing and education'. The coordinated effort is undoubtedly 'linked to the administration's fervent opposition to policies, particularly involving numerical goals and quotas, that give preference to individual members of minorities based on past discrimination'.[3]

Nor is the Democratic Party's national leadership more enlight- ened towards Blacks' perceived policy interests. Since the Mondale defeat in 1984, the Democratic National Committee has taken steps to reduce the Rainbow Coalition's potential leverage in the 1988 presidential primaries. In March 1986, the DNC ruled that a presidential candidate was required to win at least 15 percent of the vote in a Congressional district's primary or caucus in order to qualify for a proportional share of national convention delegates. While this threshold is less than the 20 percent figure of 1984, it still effectively discriminates against minority challengers. Neither frontrunner for the 1988 Democratic nomination, Senator Gary Hart of Colorado nor New York Governor Mario Cuomo, has extensive political ties with civil rights organizations, Black politic- ians or other minority constituencies.[4]

Electoral Disenchantment

There is nothing new in the retreat from racial equality expressed by Reaganism as well as by the Democratic Party's neo-liberal trend. What is particularly striking, however, is the perception among many Afro-Americans that activism within bourgeois democratic structures cannot really address the economic and social problems in a fundamental way. This is not a proto-revolutionary realization among the Black working classes that the electoral system must be radically transformed to empower the proletariat. Rather, it is a profound disillusionment with the pace of dese- gregation in the political system as well as with reformist Black politicians who frequently promise much but who deliver remarkably little. First, the total number of Afro-Americans in elective and appointive offices still remains surprisingly small. As of January 1985, there were 6,056 Black elected officials, only 1.2 percent of the 490,800 elective offices in the USA. The vast majority exercise marginal influence within the electoral system. Most are either members of local public school boards (1,368, or 22.6 percent of all Black officials), or town council-persons (2,189, or 36.1 percent). Only five public officials elected on a statewide basis are Black; there are only eight Black judges on state courts of last resort, and fewer than one hundred Black state senators. Despite the November 1985 election of Democratic State Senator Douglas Wilder as Virginia's lieutenant governor, the general pattern in American politics is towards further Black marginality. Blacks comprise substantial electoral blocs in Alabama (23 percent of the voting age population), Florida (11 percent), Louisiana (27 percent), Arkansas (14 percent), North Carolina (20 percent), and South Carolina (27 percent)—but not a single Afro-American has been elected to Congress from these states since the Reconstruction period nearly a century ago.[5]

In numerous instances where Blacks have successfully mobilized to elect Afro-American politicians, the actual public policy consequences have contributed little to the improvement of socioeconomic or political conditions. Perhaps the best examples are provided by the Black mayors of major cities. In Philadelphia in 1983 a massive organizing effort culminated in the election of Black Mayor Wilson Goode. But from the outset, Goode was the obedient representative of corporate and financial interests. In 1984, Goode vocally opposed the Rainbow Coalition, despite the fact that over 75 percent of all Black Philadelphians voted for Jackson in the Democratic primary. Police brutality against Blacks was left unchecked. The logical culmination of Goode's policies occurred on 13 May 1985, when the Philadelphia police attempted to evict an Afro-American naturalist group, MOVE, from its residence in the Black community. The confrontation resulted in a firestorm, as police unleashed more than seven thousand rounds of ammunition into the MOVE residence. In the aftermath of the assault, which culminated in the police bombing the building (with the mayor's consent), six adults and five children died. Sixty-one homes were destroyed by fires sparked by the bomb, and over 250 Blacks were left homeless for more than one year.

Few Black Americans believed that police anywhere in the USA would have firebombed any home containing whites, or would have permitted a massive fire to rage in a residential area for more than one hour before the fire department began to combat the blaze. But there was a singular difficulty: Goode was Black, and the established Black petty-bourgeois leadership, which shared the Philadelphia mayor's political instincts and outlook, refused to condemn the MOVE incident. The Congressional Black Caucus, vocal against the many crimes of Reaganism, fell into a numbing quiescence. Most national civil rights leaders and Black officials had little to say on the matter. Only Jesse Jackson seemed to comprehend that the MOVE bombing was 'not a Philadelphia matter. Racists in this country are delighted with this situation and a lot of police chiefs throughout the country might follow Philadelphia's lead.' One year after the MOVE siege, an investigatory panel appointed by Goode declared that the mayor was 'grossly negligent', and had displayed a 'reckless disregard for life and property'. Hundreds of local Black religious leaders and community organizers continue today to campaign for Goode's resignation.[6]

A slightly different example is provided by Newark. In 1970 Kenneth A. Gibson became the first Black mayor of any Northeastern city. During his sixteen years in office, Gibson was able to provide marked improvements in some aspects of the Black community's life. Municipal resources were used to improve public health, and as a result, Black infant mortality rates declined sharply. With limited federal funds, the city of Newark was able to renovate or construct almost 11,000 apartments for families and the elderly. Crime also dropped slightly under Gibson, but only about six percent between 1970 and 1985. Gibson unsuccessfully sought the Democratic nomination for New Jersey governor, and became a prominent advocate for a domestic 'Marshall Plan' to revive American cities. But Gibson did little to promote visible economic development in the city, and rapidly Newark became something of a disaster area. The number of restaurants in the city fell from 937 in 1970 to 246 in 1986; retail stores dropped from 3,869 to 1,794; hotels, 32 to 16; drug stores, 205 to 59. In a city of over 316,000, there is only one large supermarket. Most of the problems Gibson faced could have been addressed by vigorous leadership and strong initiatives in grassroots organization among the Black and Hispanic communities. Instead, the Gibson administration turned increasingly corrupt, becoming notorious for its graft, clientage system, and isolation from the Black working class. In May 1986, Gibson was soundly defeated in his reelection campaign by Sharpe James, a Black college professor and city councilman. Ingenuously, Gibson declared that he 'never saw it coming'.[7]

Some evidence suggests that the presence of a Black Democrat on the ballot will no longer guarantee a strong voter turnout by Blacks. In 1985 Herman Farrell ran a largely symbolic campaign against incumbent mayor Ed Koch in New York City, and only 38 percent of all Black registered voters cast ballots. In the election of Wilder in Virginia, 'Black turnout was estimated at 12 percent of the total turnout—3 percent less than in the previous gubernatorial election'.[8]

Even the traditional civil rights organizations have experienced a loss of prestige and credibility among Blacks. The National Association for the Advancement of Colored People (NAACP), the oldest and largest anti-racist formation in the USA, is currently in the midst of its most severe crisis in decades. Founded in 1909, the NAACP still maintains 1,700 branch offices across the country, and it periodically mobilizes Blacks against public policy initiatives of the Reagan administration. However, the organization is plagued by declining membership, a sharp loss of income, and a high staff turnover rate. In 1983, NAACP president Margaret Bush Wilson was ousted from her post in a public feud with the Association's executive secretary Benjamin Hooks. In 1984, the NAACP's general counsel Thomas I. Atkins left the organization, charging that Hooks had 'taken the Association in circles' and 'abandoned one approach after another'. In mid-1986, the Association's director of voter education Joseph Madison also resigned. Hooks's political credibility first began to erode in 1980, when he volunteered to enter the Black Miami community in order to 'cool off' rebellious Black youth. His stock fell even further in 1984 when he strongly attacked Jesse Jackson's presidential campaign: 'Afro-Americans are too sophisticated to need a Black presidential candidate to stimulate their going to the polls . . . A Black person [hasn't] a ghost of a chance of winning in 1984'. In the wake of these policies, NAACP membership has plummetted from 550,000 during the mid-1970s, to approximately 150,000 today.[9]

Are Blacks Becoming More Conservative?

Several conservative political scientists have argued that this tendential erosion of community support for traditional Black petty-bourgeois leaders reflects an ideological division inside the Afro-American community: that Black elected officials hold generally a 'liberal' political orientation, while the majority of Blacks are more 'conservative'. The Center for Media and Public Affairs, a nonprofit organization, randomly surveyed the opinions of 600 Blacks and collected the responses of 105 leaders from the Congressional Black Caucus, Operation PUSH, the NAACP, Urban League, National Conference of Black Mayors, and the

Southern Christian Leadership Conference. The 1986 surveys revealed, according to the Center, 'a surprising divergence between Black leaders and the average Black American on a broad spectrum of concerns, including some at the very heart of race relations'. The study claimed that 77 percent of the Black leaders 'favor minority preferences in hiring and college placement, while 77 percent of all Blacks oppose them'. Sixty-eight percent of the leaders reportedly favored busing to promote school desegregation, while 53 percent of all Blacks surveyed opposed busing. Forty percent of the Black leaders support religious prayer in public schools, while school prayer was endorsed by 83 percent of all Blacks. Only 14 percent of the Black leaders supported a legal ban on all abortions, while 43 percent of all Blacks supported outlawing abortions. Sixty percent of Blacks 'oppose letting homosexuals teach in public schools; three in five leaders favor it'. Politically, 68 percent of Black leaders refer to themselves as 'liberals', compared to but 27 percent of all Blacks. Most significantly, the surveys note, 'a bare majority—52 percent— of all Blacks say that the Black leaders they see on TV newscasts and read about . . . speak for a majority of Black people'.[10]

This curious thesis that Afro-Americans are moving to the ideological right superficially has been reinforced by several gubernatorial and municipal elections in 1985, and by several public opinion polls. In Cleveland's recent mayoral election, 85 percent of the Black precincts supported incumbent Republican Mayor George Voinovich. Three out of five New Jersey Black voters endorsed incumbent Republican Governor Thomas Kean. Throughout 1982–83, only about 10 percent of all Blacks questioned in opinion polls gave their 'approval' for President Reagan's job 'performance'. But in late December, 1985, the *New York Times* conducted a controversial poll which asserted that 56 percent of all Blacks endorsed Reagan! Skeptics, questioned the results, especially when the *Times* admitted that only 103 Blacks were interviewed. In January 1986, the *Times* interviewed 1,022 Blacks, and produced a slightly lower approval rating for Reagan of 37 percent. A more broadly representative Black opinion poll, commissioned by the *Washington Post* in January 1986, gave the president a 23 percent approval rating.

Is Black political culture becoming more aligned with Reaganite policies? Since Afro-Americans are the principal victims of the Reagan agenda, this seems most unlikely. As Black political scientist Linda F. Williams has observed, the 'improvement in Black ratings of Reagan . . . has more to do with the president's personal style and political success than with his political philosophy. When Blacks were asked about Reagan's handling of particular economic and race-specific policies and about their own political philosophies, they distanced themselves from the president by exceptionally wide margins'. In the *Washington Post* poll, for example, 49 percent of the Blacks stated that Reagan's policies 'held them back', 33 percent stated Reagan's policies 'made no difference', and only 11 percent said that the policies 'helped'. Only 14 percent of all Blacks endorsed Reagan's 'handling [of] unemployment'; and 56 percent affirmed that 'Ronald Reagan was a racist'. The *Washington Post* poll directly contradicts some of the findings of the less scientific Center for Media and Public Affairs survey. Forty-one percent of all Blacks in the former poll identified themselves 'liberal' and only 23 percent claimed to be 'conservatives'. A clear majority of Blacks also supported affirmative action programs.[11]

A more accurate reading of the 1985–86 Black political surveys would suggest that while there is no visible 'Reaganization' of the Black electorate there is indeed a degree of alienation between Blacks and their petty-bourgeois leaders. This gap represents in part the persistence of conservative *cultural* values among most working-class and low-income Blacks. Profoundly religious in their outlook and civic socialization, the majority of Afro-American working people have no difficulty in accepting legislation to permit prayer in public schools. This cultural conservatism extends to social relations and, to some degree, law enforcement. Undoubtedly, most Blacks outside of the middle class would probably oppose abortion rights and legislation to protect the civil rights of homosexuals, and would not support federally-mandated school desegregation. A majority of Afro-Americans support the death penalty, despite its systemic racist application against Black prisoners. However culturally conservative Black working-class people may be, this fact has never translated into an ideological or *political* conservatism. Since the Great Depression, only a tiny minority of Blacks have identified with the Republican Party. Most Blacks have distinctly left-liberal opinions on foreign policy matters, strongly oppose US intervention into peripheral societies, and favor the destruction of the apartheid regime. Afro-Americans have a healthy dislike for the structual inequalities of America's advanced capitalist system, and are more favorable towards trade unionism than any other major group.

As William observes: 'In 1972, when 68 percent of the Black population was affiliated with the Democrats, 37 percent of all Blacks considered themselves strong Democrats while another 31 percent considered themselves weak Democrats. By 1984, the proportion of Blacks identifying themselves as Democrats climbed to 76 percent, with 55 percent viewing themselves as strong Democrats and 21 percent as weak Democrats.' According to the January 1986 *Washington Post* poll, 87 percent of all Afro-Americans interviewed viewed Jesse Jackson favorably. More importantly, 66 percent of all Blacks supported a second Jackson presidential campaign in 1988, while 53 percent thought that Jackson could run as an independent.[12] The data reveals that the Black working class favors an insurgent electoral strategy, and despite the relative cultural orthodoxy of Afro-American civil society on some important issues, it remains the most ideologically advanced major political bloc within US electoral politics.

Waiting for the Rainbow

Unfortunately, despite the Rainbow Coalition's unprecedented achievements in the 1984 presidential primaries, neither Jackson nor the more progressive forces surrounding his campaign have taken the initiative to consolidate their previous gains. The first national Rainbow Coalition founding convention was not held until April 1986. The convention, held in Washington D.C., attracted several groups, notably farmers' organizations and organized labor, which were previously under-represented in the Rainbow Coalition. The Coalition's 'statement of purpose' also defined the formation in dynamic terms, as 'a new political movement, dedicated to healing the nation by implementing a program of human priorities at home and peace and human rights abroad, seeking to achieve social, political and economic justice'. Jackson clearly placed himself at odds with the dominant trend of anti-Sovietism within both major capitalist parties, insisting that 'we cannot be blinded by anticommunist obsession'.

Conversely, the convention's chief failure was in ratifying a strictly centralist structure. Jackson and his closest lieutenants selected the Rainbow's board, which in turn was empowered to credential all state groups seeking to join the coalition. Jackson personally reserved the right to select each state's chairperson. Locally, Rainbow Coalition branches are to be organized along Congressional district lines, a decision which may reinforce the narrow inclination to perceive 'politics' in strictly partisan electoral terms. Jackson did little to distance himself from the Democratic Party, in any event. 'We have too much invested in the Democratic Party', he explained at the convention. 'When you have money in the bank you don't walk away from it.' More disturbing was his justification for a top-down centralism within what was theoretically to have been a mass-based formation. The Rainbow Coalition was only 'an embryo . . . more democracy [will] come later'. In effect, what Jackson had done was to extrapolate the Rainbow's structure largely from the centralized apparatuses of many civil rights formations, such as the NAACP and his own group, Operation PUSH. The national organization of the Rainbow Coalition could discourage the broadest possible participation of the Black masses, and concentrate power in the hands of a well-meaning but still demonstrably petty-bourgeois elite.[13]

Part of the reason for the Rainbow Coalition's hesitancy in mapping a coherent national strategy is to be found in the racial polarization in American politics. Since 1984, a majority of whites—well over 66 percent—have consistently voiced 'approval' of President Reagan in public opinion polls. Since 1968, white voters have supported Republican presidential candidates by strong majorities; in 1984, white women and men supported Reagan by 64 and 68 percent, respectively. The political terrain for a left social democratic agenda represented by the Rainbow Coalition is not at all substantial. Statistically, Jackson's electoral totals in the 1984 Democratic primaries were often low: 2 percent of the white electorate in Florida, 3 percent in Georgia, 4 percent in Pennsylvania, and less than 1 percent in Alabama. Even as the campaign progressed, and as Jackson began to overcome the negative media and racial stereotyping of his candidacy, the totals for white voters improved only slightly—10 percent in California, for instance. Considering the profound depths of racism in American political culture, and the stampede to the right of the political spectrum by both capitalist parties, it seems highly unlikely that the Rainbow Coalition will attract any significant numbers of whites, surely not beyond the levels of roughly ten to twenty percent. Some white constituencies will be more likely to join a multiracial coalition than others: anti-nuclear activists, feminists, small farmers, militant labor union leaders, and left-liberals for instance. But the bulk of the white working class has historically resisted appeals for a multiracial, progressive alliance, except in periods of severe economic depression.

The most important political bloc sharing a substantially common agenda with Afro-Americans is the Latino community. Between 1980 and 1985, the Mexican American population grew from 8.7 million to 10.3 million. The Puerto Rican population in the mainland USA was up from 2 million to 2.6 million; Cuban Americans grew from 800,000 to 1 million. There are also approximately 1.7 million Spanish-speakers in the USA from Central and South America. If one also counts the 3.3 million people living in Puerto Rico, there are over 20 million Latinos in the USA over 8.5 percent of the total population. The parallels between Black Americans and Latinos in economy, education, and other social categories are striking. In 1984, 25 percent of all Latinos lived in poverty, compared to 10 percent of all whites and 36.3 percent of all Blacks. Notably, 42 percent of all Puerto Ricans were below the poverty line. In terms of median family income, Latinos earned an average of only $18,800, compared to $15,000 for Blacks and $27,000 for white Americans. Educationally, only 42 percent of all Mexican-Americans were high school graduates, and barely 5.5 percent graduated from college. Blacks and Latinos share a common racial and economic distribution. Common political activities, therefore, with the notable exception of the heavily anti-Communist Cubans, would seem to be in the interest of both groups.

With rare local exceptions, however, a Black-Latino alliance has not generally materialized. A majority of Latino Democratic voters supported Mondale over Jackson in 1984 by a two-to-one margin. In no primary did Jackson receive more than 35 percent of the Latino vote. In New York City, Puerto Rican and Black politicians failed to find a consensus mayoral candidate to run against Koch in 1985, and divided bitterly when Farrell ran for the office. In Albany's state legislature, the twenty-five member Black and Puerto Rican caucus has declined in influence and suffered deep divisions in its ranks. Members openly criticized the caucus's financial dealings and its inability to secure meaningful legislation. At one point, Jackson was brought to Albany in a futile effort to 're-energize' the caucus's members.[14] But even Jackson himself has failed to develop serious ties with broad sectors of the Latino liberal-left. For example, in the May 1986 Democratic primary for a state legislative seat in Dallas, Domingo Garcia, a Jackson delegate at the 1984 convention, challenged a conservative white incumbent. The district's population was 23 percent Black and 43 percent Chicano. Jackson was asked by Garcia's supporters 'to come down and campaign or at least to cut a radio tape for Garcia,' in order to increase Black voter turnout. Jackson did neither, and Garcia lost by several hundred votes.[15]

The Revival of Black Capitalism

The absence of a coherent Black left program and strategy, and the contradictory and sometimes antagonistic relationship between Black elected officials and their constituents, has created a political vacuum within Black America. Within this space, the older organic elements of Black political culture have reemerged with a striking suddenness. The innovative and forward-looking political currents, reinforced by the Harold Washington mayoral movement in Chicago in 1983, and by the Jackson campaign, have given ground to more inward-looking, nativist trends since Reagan's reelection. One does not have to look hard for appropriate historical parallels. A period of Black political retrenchment occurred a century ago, on the heels of the demise of the Reconstruction, the Compromise of 1877, and the Supreme Court's overturning of the Civil Rights Act in 1883. The basic response of the Negro petty bourgeoisie was summarized in the slogan, 'racial self help'. Government could not be expected to intercede to protect the political and civil rights of Blacks. The white electorate, North and South, was hostile to the concept of Black equality. Black Americans recognized their political isolation and attempted to fashion a strategy of group advancement on the parochial margins of capitalism. As a people apart, Blacks had to devise methods to build their schools, businesses, farms, and communities without the assistance of whites.

'The Negro confronts destiny', observed Black attorney J. Madison Vance in 1894. 'He must be the architect of his own fortune. He must demonstrate capacity and independence . . . Let us stand on our own racial pride and prove our equality by showing the fruits of thrift, talent and frugality.' A leader of Black Chicagoans, Ferdinand Barnett—the husband of noted anti-lynching activist Ida B. Wells-Barnett—shared these sentiments. 'We must help one another', Barnett insisted. 'We are laboring for race elevation and race unity is the all-important factor.' The chief architect of the Black self-help political philosophy was, of course, Booker T. Washington, founder of Tuskegee Institute and the National Negro Business League. 'No race that has anything to contribute to the markets of the world is long in any degree ostracized,' Washington declared. 'An inch of progress is worth more than a yard of complaint . . . no race of people ever got upon its feet without severe and constant struggle, often in the face of the greatest disappointment.'[16] Self-help meant a retreat from multi-racial political coalitions, and a concerted effort to promote capital accumulation among the Black petty bourgeoisie. This pessimistic strategy was veiled in the language of racial self-sufficiency and nationalism. Few among its advocates understood that the crooked road of Black petty capitalism and self-help led ultimately to a dead end for the Black masses.

The tradition of Black self-help and entrepreneurialism still palpably exists. Black politicians who supported both Mondale and Jackson in 1984 have returned to this century-old rhetoric. At the 1986 National Conference of Black Mayors, Washington D.C. Mayor Marion Berry declared:'We are going to make it despite the federal government's breaking of its social contract.' Barry called for Blacks to become less dependent on federal social programs and more 'self-reliant.' Gary, Indiana Mayor Richard Hatcher, Jackson's principal adviser, went even further. Hatcher urged Black mayors to 'stop begging the federal government for funds' and encouraged them to promote 'other sources of income'.[17] The Black Leadership Family, led by Congressmen Walter Fauntroy and Parren Mitchell, established the U.S. Investment Company in November 1985, with the hope to increase the power of the Black private sector. The Company will 'provide funds for Black businesses, along with expert managerial guidance.' According to Mitchell, 'these Black businesses will greatly alleviate unemployment among Blacks'. More ambitious are the efforts of the Black Leadership Roundtable, a coalition of 300 Afro-American organizations. The Roundtable recently established a 'national Black capital fund', with an initial amount of $200,000 as of December 1985. The fund is designed to 'create the capital base and facilities necessary for the economic development of Black people and to provide the enterprises and means whereby we become the employers of our own people'.[18]

The most obvious contradiction in these attempts at Black self-help is the inexplicable separation between politics and economics. Since the 1960, Black private-sector growth has not been possible without minority set-aside programs, which establish specific percentages of money or work for businesses owned by women, Blacks, Latinos and other national minorities. In 1985 alone, $5 billion in federal contracts were awarded to women and national minorities. However, in April 1986, Clarence Pendleton, chairman of the US Civil Rights Commission, called for the temporary suspension of minority set-asides, on the grounds that there was 'rampant corruption' in such programs. Pendleton's draft criticized 'group remedies such as set-asides' as 'over-inconclusive in that they confer a remedy for discrimination on some who have not been affected by discrimination'. But even Black Reaganites who favor the self-help approach were unwilling to go as far as Pendleton. Thirty Black Republicans, including Fred Brown, an executive member of the Republican National Committee, and Frank Kent, publisher of *Black Family* magazine, immediately called for Pendleton's resignation. Although Attorney General Edwin Meese backs Pendleton's position, President Reagan was pressured to voice support for minority set-aside programs. Many civil rights leaders, including the NAACP, bitterly accused Pendleton of 'Out-Reaganing Reagan'. But few recognized that their entire approach to Black private-sector growth was almost fully dependent on political rather than market forces.[19]

The Farrakhan Phenomenon

A different self-help strategy built along Black nationalist lines has been promoted by Louis Farrakhan, leader of the Nation of Islam religious sect. The group started a network termed POWER— 'People Organized and Working for Economic Rebirth'. Essentially a strategy to promote Black petty capitalism, POWER projects a system of cooperation between Black-owned firms which would sell personal services and household items to Black consumers. The capital accumulated from sales would be used to start small manufacturing companies. POWER received an interest-free loan of $5 million from Libyan leader Muammar Kaddafi in May 1985, and hundreds of Black would-be capitalists have applauded the concept. Even civil rights matron Coretta Scott King, who has characterized Farrakhan's political rhetoric as 'extremely harmful', supports the POWER approach to Black economic development. Farrakhan has urged Blacks to seize any opportunities to develop their own private enterprises. Thus, he encourages Afro-Americans to purchase land for rural-based production from bankrupt Western farmers.[20]

Any petty entrepreneurial class learns its nationalism in the marketplace. To develop a self-contained, highly motivated Black consumer market, Farrakhan and his vocal supporters have resorted to narrow racial chauvinism and anti-Semitism. Although blatant anti-Semitism has never had a mass appeal among Black workers, Farrakhan was successful in developing a substantial base in 1985. On 22 July, 10,000 Blacks attended his public address in Washington, D.C. As white media criticism of Farrakhan was magnified, his audiences and popularity among Black workers increased. On 14 September, 17,000 people gathered at the Los Angeles Forum to hear him speak. And on 7 October, Farrakhan attracted over 20,000 Blacks to New York City's Madison Square Garden, while another 5,000 people watched his speech live on closed-circuit television in another building. On the basis of his published statements, it was not difficult for many observers to dismiss Farrakhan as an anti-semitic fanatic. He first received national notoriety during Jesse Jackson's 1984 campaign for the

Democratic presidential nomination by reportedly terming Judaism a 'gutter religion,' and by later describing Hitler as 'a (evilly) great man'. Farrakhan's more recent statements have been equally repugnant. At his Washington, D.C. rally, he lumped all American Jews together in the politics of Zionism: 'I'm not backing down from the Jews because I know their wickedness. I'm not separating just Zionists out, because the Zionists are the outgrowth of Jewish transgression.' Even when Farrakhan has attempted to qualify his previous remarks, an inevitable strain of anti-Semitism seems apparent. During one 1985 press conference, for instance, he declared: 'I said the state of Israel has not had any peace in 40 years; that's true. And I said the state of Israel will not have any peace; that is also true. And then I made mention that the name of God was used to shield a dirty religion—and when I say dirty, I mean the practice of displacing millions of people from their homeland.'[21]

But the Farrakhan phenomenon is far more complex than the rubric of 'Black anti-semitism' allows. Farrakhan first entered Black political life a quarter century ago as the young protege of Malcolm X. Farrakhan was named the minister of the Black Muslims' Boston mosque, and he acquired a substantial following even among Black militants and working people who had no relationship with the Nation of Islam. In 1964, Malcolm X broke from the Nation of Islam, and moved rapidly in a socialist and internationalist political direction. But Farrakhan remained loyal to the sect's conservative mentor, the aged Elijah Muhammad. After Elijah Muhammad's death in 1975, the Nation of Islam was radically transformed by its new leader, Wallace D. Muhammad. The sect's anti-white dogmas were summarily dropped, and the theological basis of the organization was made to conform closely to orthodox Sunni Islam. Farrakhan broke from the reformed group in 1978, and in January 1981, announced the 'rebirth' of the 'Nation of Islam' under his leadership. During the early 1980s, Farrakhan recruited about ten thousand Blacks into his sect, which espoused the Black nationalist creed of the late Elijah Mohammad. But unlike the 'old' Nation of Islam, which eschewed electoral political involvement, Farrakhan and his lieutenants have become active participants in contemporary Black struggles. Farrakhan was a major speaker at the August 1983 'March on Washington' mobilization, which attacked the Reagan administration's domestic and foreign policies. Farrakhan was of course one of the earliest Black national leaders to endorse Jackson's presidential candidacy, and his followers provided campaign workers and security personnel for the electoral mobilization.

To the masses of unemployed and working-class Afro-Americans, Farrakhan's message represents a cathartic release from their deteriorating economic and social conditions under the aegis of Reaganism. Instinctively, they recognize that *any* Black public leader who evokes such harsh condemnation from white religious leaders and the politicians of both capitalist parties must have something in his program for them. And indeed, a careful analysis of Farrakhan's public addresses reveals a strong commitment to anti-racist and anti-imperialist politics which parallels the later social thought of Malcolm X. In his Los Angeles Forum speech, for example, Farrakhan echoed Jackson's call for a 'Rainbow coalition' of the dispossessed to coalesce against the dominant political and corporate establishment. In the tradition of W.E.B. Du Bois, Martin Luther King, Jr., and earlier Black peace activists, he challenged the Reagan administration's adventurist foreign policies. Black Americans should never participate in 'any US war against Black Africans'. He made common cause with the revolutionaries in Central America: 'We will not invade Nicaragua!' This ambiguity in Farrakhan's rhetoric has made it difficult for Black progressives to attack the Muslim leader in unqualified terms. The Reverend Benjamin Chavis, leader of the United Church of Christ's Commission on Racial Justice and a Rainbow Coalition activist, for example, has declared that Farrakhan's 'primary message is about self-determination'.

Farrakhan's racially based appeals for petty capitalism, alone with the less nationalist-oriented efforts of Black politicians, are all part of the same problem in Afro-American political culture. Systemic racism retards the development of an indigenous bourgeois class among Blacks. Thus 'Buy Black' campaigns and other entrepreneurial efforts can be viewed as effectively 'progressive' by those who exercise no power in corporate circles. The ideological dominance of Reaganism within the national political culture plays a role as well. If Blacks cannot expect expanded federal funding for public housing, food stamps, health care, and other essentials, they must somehow provide their own resources without state intervention. Yet, as previously noted, it is only through the progressive intervention of the capitalist state—through affirmative action programs, minority set-asides, and so on—that the Black middle class has historically been able to consolidate and expand its gains. The more pervasive problem in contemporary Black politics is that there remains no formation with a working-class base which is capable of articulating a more advanced public policy program in economics, domestic and international politics. The Rainbow Coalition has the capacity in the late 1980s to evolve toward this point. But if it is to be successful, it must challenge the more conservative elements within Black political culture, and nurture a more progressive cadre of leaders at the grass-roots level. Only then will Black politics begin to transcend its past and create a new social history of struggle capable of overthrowing both the racial and the economic structures of oppression which have held Blacks in thrall since the advent of chattel slavery.

2

The Black Left in Struggle: 1980–85

Herb Boyd

No matter what the political stripe, ideological perspective or class outlook, for Black Americans the 1970s was a decade of setbacks and devastation. According to a National Urban League report, the Black community during the seventies was severely afflicted by record unemployment, wholesale cutbacks in social services and resurgent racism. The civil rights organization charged that the rise in racism was attended by many acts of violence directed against Black people. When seventy-five Klansmen and Nazis attacked a group of anti-racist demonstrators in Greensboro, North Carolina in November, 1979, killing five protestors and wounding eleven, the decade was moving toward a fitting close. The incident was also a harbinger of the reaction and retrenchment that would typify the political environment during the early 1980s.[1]

To combat the mounting racial violence, police brutality and terrorist attacks, hundreds of rallies, protest demonstrations and meetings were held. In several sectors of the radical community, fight-back organizations were formed by the summer of 1980. A broad spectrum of Black activists, espousing a variety of political tendencies, gathered in Brooklyn to discuss tactics and outline strategies to oppose the growing repression. 'We have produced here,' said Reverend Herbert Daughtry, one of the event's coordinators and a National Black United Front leader, 'a mass-based, independent, active and progressive national organization.' It was an organization of great potential, commented Phil Gardiner of the National Anti-Racist Organizing Committee. 'But the organization must also struggle against narrowing its base by breaking eventually with the petty-bourgeois nationalism that characterizes some aspects of the group.'

Another hopeful sign during these dark days of transition from the 1970s to the 1980s occurred with the release of Rev. Ben Chavis from prison. Chavis, the last of the Wilmington 10 to be freed, emerged in December 1979, after serving four years on a trumped-up charge of firebombing a white grocery during the siege of the Black community in Wilmington, N.C. by white vigilantes in 1971. By the fall of 1980, Chavis was again in the forefront of the struggle for social and political justice. At a Congressional Black Caucus meeting held in September in Washington, D.C., Chavis gave the only militant address. Speaking to a group of 350 Black youngsters and jobs advocates, Chavis, who now heads the United Church of Christ's Commission for Racial Justice, deplored 'the lack of organization and the lack of leadership among Black people in the United States. It is time for Black Americans to declare their independence from the two parties that never had the interests of Black liberation in mind . . . there is a problem of exploitation that is caused by the very nature of the capitalist system. Racism has its roots in that system.'

Chavis also alluded to some of the turbulence which had occurred the spring and summer before when Liberty City, a Black enclave in Miami, exploded in one of the largest rebellions since the 1960s. It took 7,000 troops, including national guardsmen, state troopers, local and metropolitan police forces, to quell the disturbance, which left in its wake 16 people killed, hundreds injured, 1100 arrested and more than $100 million in property damage. In July, like an aftershock, Miami experienced another riot in which 40 people were injured.

The upheaval in Liberty City was triggered when an all-white jury acquitted four white police in the brutal murder of Archie McDuffie, a Black insurance executive from Miami. McDuffie was just one of several Blacks slain by overzealous police officers. In Philadelphia a young Black man, William Green, was gunned down; in New Orleans, Lawrence Lewis was a victim of police brutality; in Boston, Brooklyn and Wrightsville, Georgia, young Blacks were being deliberately killed by law enforcement officers. The daily atrocities committed by the police and rightist terror were key issues on the agenda when the National Black Political Assembly (NBPA) met in August 1980 in New Orleans. The NBPA, which came into existence in 1972 in Gary, and peaked as an organization in 1974, was now being revived. More than 196 delegates attended the meeting, but no principles of unity or strategy for the party were drafted. It was reported that such issues would be discussed at the convention that coming November.

But for the left, Black and white, there was a much more significant political event scheduled for November: the presidential election. In October, Black disenchantment with President Jimmy Carter began to surface—this time, however, from the bourgeois nationalist sector of the Black community. Two former civil rights leaders from the Southern Christian Leadership Council, Reverends Ralph Abernathy and Hosea Williams, after declaring that Carter had not kept his campaign promises, openly endorsed Ronald Reagan's candidacy.

As Reagan's campaign gathered momentum and the prospect of victory became virtually assured, the Black left (a category loosely composed of revolutionary nationalists, Marxists, socialists, and other anti-capitalist radicals), as well as thousands of progressives from around the world received some more bad news, this time from the Caribbean. In Jamaica, Michael Manley's eight-year old anti-imperialist government was defeated, and his CIA-backed opponent was installed as prime minister. Manley's principled and uncompromising stance against the dreadnought of US imperialism was a vital source of strength and guidance for the Black left, if only from an ideological standpoint. Within a few days of this gloomy report, the socialist government of Grenada arrested 12 in a plot to overthrow Prime Minister Maurice Bishop. The government announced that three separate landings were to be made on the island. This operation was one of several dress rehearsals for that ultimate bloodbath. Not since the murder of Walter Rodney in a bomb blast the previous summer was there such disturbing news for the Black left from the international front.

Black Independent Politics

For the left, Reagan and Carter presented a Hobson's Choice— i.e., no choice at all. In the eyes of most Black activists, Reagan and Carter were equally dangerous, and so many began to consider the possibility of undertaking independent political actions as an alternative. The Oakland-based African People's Socialist Party, through its publication *Burning Spear*, offered one possibility: they called for a boycott of the elections.

When the votes were finally tallied, Reagan had won by the barest of majorities, commanding only 50.7 percent of the votes. Moreover, only 54 percent of the voting age population went to the polls, so that, of the total who were eligible to vote, 27 percent voted for Reagan. As political scientist and election specialist Walter Dean Burnham observed, the largest party in the election was 'the party of non-voters.' The voting total from the Black community illustrated this trend most graphically: three million Blacks who voted in the 1976 elections did not vote in 1980.

With Reagan's victory fresh in mind, some 1300 Blacks

assembled in Philadelphia at the end of November to form the National Black Independent Political Party (NBIPP), an outgrowth of the National Black Political Assembly. According to a statement issued by the party, its goal was to 'advance a new Black politics of social transformation and self-determination for the Black nation.' Speakers at the convention included: Rev. Ben Chavis, Haki Madhubuti, Manning Marable, NBIPP Steering Committee members Ron Daniels and Barbara Sizemore, and nationalist figure Queen Mother Moore. Daniels, who chairs the NBPA, said that the first order of business, once the party was firmly established, was to set up local chapters and develop local leadership committees.

Simultaneously, at another gathering, the National Black United Front (NBUF) was struggling valiantly to expand its political base. If there was any hint of possible alliance between the NBPA and NBUF, it was put to rest before the NBIPP convened. In a *Guardian* interview Rev. Herbert Daughtry stated that the position of the leadership of NBPA was opposed to the idea 'of the NBPA devoting its energies to developing a Black independent political party and we being the mass-based movement . . . they said they understood politics in the more comprehensive sense to the extent of doing really what NBUF is doing.' Daughtry did express that his organization, NBUF, planned to support the political aims of the NBPA.

On another front, such prominent activists of the Black liberation movement as Jamil Abdullah al Min (H. Rap Brown), Kwame Toure (Stokely Carmichael) and Afeni Shakur, a New York City Black Panther who was framed on bomb conspiracy charges, called on the Congressional Black Caucus to initiate congressional hearings on the FBI's domestic 'Counter-Intelligence Program'— COINTELPRO. Assisted by famed radical attorney William Kunstler, the activists charged that the FBI campaigns were responsible for the decimation of Black leadership and organizations in the 60s and the 70s. Much of the impetus for this new appeal for investigation of COINTELPRO stemmed from the release of FBI documents in the frame-up of former New York City Black Panther leader Richard (Dhoruba) Moore, who remains incarcerated. The documents revealed a campaign of forged letters, anonymous telephone calls and other illegal tactics that were designed to undermine the New York Panther chapter.

The year 1981 was hardly a month old when it was reported that three Black youths in Miami had been convicted of beating three whites to death during that city's rebellion. By spring, more disturbing news came from the tense communities of Atlanta and Buffalo, where Blacks were being mysteriously abducted and killed.

But bad as this news was, it was comparatively less ominous than the mean-spirited message from the White House. In rapid succession, the Reagan administration eliminated the Comprehensive Employment Training Act program, which had been originally funded at $3.1 billion, thereby summarily ending more than 150,000 federally supported jobs; then cut by $1.7 billion the child nutrition program, designed to feed hungry urban children; and to top things off, it was rumored they were planning to cut nearly a half million families from the welfare rolls. The rollback and retrenchment plans of the Reagan administration were thus fully underway.

Responding to Reagan's rollbacks, on September 19 more than 300,000 demonstrators from labor and civil rights organizations protested the social policies of the Reagan administration in a Solidarity Day march on Washington, D.C. A month before in Chicago, the NBIPP held its first convention under the banner of a similar theme: 'Fight Reaganism, Racism and Economic Reaction!' The 800 delegates representing 3,000 members in 58 chapters were also concerned about 'reawakening the freedom struggle throughout the Black community.' One of the key issues raised at their convention centered on the participation of other organizations and their leaders in NBIPP. It was finally decided to bar national leaders of other organizations from serving as leaders in NBIPP. The following day the motion was amended to allow anyone willing to carry out NBIPP policies to become a leader. To some degree this was essentially a rift between the cultural nationalist wing and the Marxist tendency among the delegates. This ideological split was by no means new, but unlike the splintering effects which a comparable rift had caused during the 1960s, the difference here was at least temporarily resolved when a large centrist group of delegates voted to join in a compromise motion proposed by delegates associated with the Marxist tendency. Ron Daniels of Youngstown, Ohio and Elsa Brown of Charlottesville, Virginia were elected to head the convention.

While some activists were busy conferring and mapping out strategy, others were marching: in Selma, Alabama, an old civil rights battleground, 5,000 marched in support of voting rights extension, another gain threatened by the Reagan administration; in Mobile, some 100 miles to the south, 9,000 marched for the same cause; in Harlem, 20,000 people took to the streets against Reaganism; 7,000 rallied in Jersey City, 5,000 in Washington, D.C.; and in Milwaukee, 10,000 marched in opposition to the police murder of Ernest Lacy on July 9.

Fighting Back against Racist Violence

All the marching, however, did little to halt the escalating racial violence which was spreading like an epidemic across the United States. Some of this violence was clearly random, but a disturbingly large proportion of it was deliberately carried out by white supremacist groups, which were in many instances aided and abetted by law enforcement officers.

The FBI, instead of investigating these numerous attacks upon Black youths and the Black community, was busy launching search and destroy missions against the Republic of New Afrika (RNA), which it characterized as a 'terrorist organization.' On October 27, 200 FBI and S.W.A.T. team officers surrounded Sunni Ali's house in Gallman, Mississippi, armed with high-powered rifles and backed up by four Army tanks. The FBI claimed that Ali, through her husband, was linked to the attempted Brinks robbery the previous week in Nyack, New York. Ms. Ali was arrested and her attorney Chokwe Lumumba, vice-president and grand counsel for the RNA, was initially not allowed to visit her. This attack was but the first of many to be directed at militant Black nationalists and so-called members of the Black Liberation Army.

But revolutionary nationalist groups would scarcely sit passively by as the FBI stepped up its campaign of violence and harassment. A National Plenary Conference on Self-Determination was convened in December in New York City, attended by a number of groups, including representatives from NBIPP, NBUF, RNA, the African People's Party, the Patricia Lumumba Coalition, the All-African People's Revolutionary Party, the National Black Communicators and the National Conference of Black Lawyers. No common strategy or program was formulated at this meeting, but the gathering itself was a step toward the revitalization of the revolutionary Black nationalist movement.

At the end of the year and into 1982, one vital wing of the movement was active in Milwaukee, with noted revolutionary Owusu Sadaukai (Howard Fuller) playing a key role in the Coalition for Justice for Earnest Lacy, the young Black man slain in the summer of 1981. Speaking at a February 7 rally, Sadaukai described the continuing mood of resistance in Milwaukee's Black community. 'Wrong and injustice must be fought; they must be fought with words and blows or with both. Because the limits of tyrants are proscribed by the endurance of those whom they oppress. So said Frederick Douglass, so say the people of Milwaukee.'

This same spirit of struggle continued right into the spring and summer as 3,000 activists kicked off the voting rights campaign at Tuskegee Institute and thousands gathered for the annual African Liberation Day celebrations in New York City and in Washington, D.C. Although Mumia Abu Jamal,[2] an activist-journalist from Philadelphia, was found guilty of killing a police officer, Eddie Carthan, the mayor of Tchula, Mississippi and a staunch foe of racism and reaction, was acquitted of charges that he had hired people to murder a former Tchula alderman.

As has also been the case more recently, the Klan and Nazis were highly visible in 1982. When they were not striking furtively on some dark backroad, they were parading boldly up and down the main streets of America. To showcase its developing strength, the Klan planned a large demonstration in Washington, D.C. for November, but it was cancelled when over 2,500 anti-KKK protestors amassed to oppose them. At that rally Anne Braden, a veteran civil rights activist and a spokesperson for the Southern Organizing Committee, told the demonstrators that 'we must expose the Klan's myth that Black people improve their lives at the expense of white people . . . the truth is that only when Blacks and other people of color advance have all people advanced. And when Blacks are pushed back we all suffer.'

Although it was rarely covered by the mainstream media, Black activists, workers, students and other progressives regularly confronted the Klan wherever they surfaced. In Athens, Georgia, over 400 University of Georgia students held a vigil against the Ku Klux Klan. In Detroit, the Klan postponed a rally after hundreds of concerned citizens gathered at downtown Kennedy Square. Through the efforts of the National Anti-Klan Network, a well-coordinated monitoring of Klan activities was devised. It was now possible, on a nationwide basis, to observe and report Klan movements and to alert forces to oppose them.

Along with the concerted resistance against the Klan, there were also numerous protests against the inhumane policies of the Reagan administration. One continuing assault against Reaganism was orchestrated by the Southern Christian Leadership Council. Over a two month period, the SCLC led a nationwide march from Tuskegee to Washington, D.C. in opposition to the Reagan administration's attempt to weaken the 1965 Voting Rights Act. When Reagan visited Nashville, over 1,000 people, led by the NAACP, demonstrated against his budgetary reductions in human services. In Louisville, Kentucky and New York City, thousands marched, voicing their objections to racial discrimination and demanding an increase in jobs and housing. From one end of the nation to the other, disgruntled forces were slowly merging, gathering steam for what would be a massive display of disenchantment with Reagan by 1983.

Victory in Chicago, Disaster in Grenada

In 1983, there were three major events that were either effected by or had an impact on the Black left. First, there was the successful candidacy of Harold Washington, who, with the help of revolutionary nationalists, workers, and several minority groups, became the first Black mayor of Chicago. Secondly, there was the historic March on Washington in which 300,000 people demonstrated their opposition to Reagan's policies at home and abroad. The third event, the invasion of Grenada by U.S. armed forces, was directly and indirectly felt by progressives in America who had sought and found both political hope in and inspiration from Maurice Bishop's socialist government.[3]

Harold Washington's victory in Chicago revealed beyond a doubt that it was possible to weld revolutionary nationalists, Black socialists, workers, Latinos and white liberals into a potent political base. Instrumental to Washington's campaign was the Task Force for Black Political Empowerment. Although the core of this group was composed of Black professionals, one cannot ignore the pivotal role of such organizations as Operation PUSH (People United to Save Humanity), the African Community of Chicago, the National Black United Front (NBUF), the Marxist-oriented People's College and several other grassroots organizations. However, in terms of political support, Washington's strongest constituency was clearly among Black workers.

When Washington won the Democratic primary in February, according to a report of the election by Abdul Akalimat and Don Gills, 84 percent of his support came from Black voters, 10 percent from whites, and 6 percent from Latinos. For the majority of voters, race was the determining factor, and Washington's victory was accomplished because the two white candidates had split the somewhat larger white vote.

In the general election in April, Washington won in a very close race against Republican candidate Bernard Epton. Again, most voters were motivated along racial lines, but the turn-out of Black voters was greater than the white turn-out. In addition, Washington received a significant percentage of votes from white liberals and other progressives. In the end, Washington's political movement had triumphed over Chicago's corrupt political machine and Epton's 'Great White Hope' campaign.

Washington's nationalist-based victory, shored up by a sizable coterie of Black workers, some Latinos, welfare mothers, the unemployed and others beyond the pale of the Daley-Byrne machine, also showed the Black petty bourgeoisie what a galvanized movement—with the right candidate—could accomplish. Of course, winning the mayoral race is but one, however crucial, step in Washington's political odyssey to wrest the city from the traditional machine. Whether his tenure will in any way curtail the rampant political corruption, cronyism, police brutality, and municipal racism is far from clear. Nor is it certain to what extent Washington will reward those key workers and activists who were so resourceful during his mayoral quest, and thus begin to create an alternative political apparatus to the still powerful white patronage system in the city.

Given the vast number of marches and demonstrations that had occurred across the United States since the ascendancy of Reagan and his pernicious policies, it was perhaps inevitable that a massive March on Washington, D.C. would occur. The first public mention of such a march came from within SCLC, which under the leadership of Martin Luther King, Jr. had played such a prominent role in the historic 1963 march. With something more than a mere twenty year anniversary in mind to mark the occasion, Reverend Joseph Lowery, head of SCLC, and Coretta Scott King issued the call for another March on Washington. In their view, the march would resemble the 1963 mobilization and offer the broadest possible national united front.

It was a call that, if not greeted with mass enthusiasm, nonetheless struck a chord in most radical, progressive and Black nationalist circles around the nation. Several Black conservative detractors, however, criticized the plan, charging that not enough money was available to finance such an undertaking and that the march would not attract the numbers needed to make it an overwhelming success. But the voices of dissent were muffled by the unanimous roar from labor, the Black church, and, unlike 1963, from Black nationalists and revolutionary socialists. True, the Black left was at first reluctant to participate, conceding that the mobilization was basically controlled by 'Black bourgeois and petty-bourgeois' leaders, but by mid-summer most had agreed to take part—it was, as one Black nationalist said, 'too large an event to ignore'. Activist-artist Amiri Baraka echoed this sentiment: 'When the Black masses move forward in any shape and forceful manner, the whole society must feel the impact.'

On August 27 the impact began to reverberate as 300,000 people assembled at the hall under the banner of 'Jobs, Peace and

Freedom' and cheered speakers Benjamin Hooks, Dorothy Height, Audre Lorde, Bella Abzug, Andrew Young, Louis Farrakhan, Harry Belafonte and Jesse Jackson. Among the more hopeful signs from the mixture of activists was the easy camaraderie between Black nationalists and integrationists. More than one commentator observed the temporary unity of forces which at another time in history had been as ideologically divided as Malcolm X and Martin Luther King, Jr. (This would prove, regrettably, a short-term relationship, and the political possibilities of this union symbolically came to an end in 1984 when Jesse Jackson distanced himself from Louis Farrakhan.) Of all the speakers that day, none was as compelling as singer-actor Harry Belafonte, who not only made a fervent call for global peace but also let it be known that 'racial injustice is still our crippling burden and America's shame'.

There is no way to assess accurately the overall impact of the march, but it certainly sent an unequivocal message to the White House. Manning Marable has suggested that the mobilization led directly to Jesse Jackson's presidential bid and contributed as well to the successsful candidacy of W. Wilson Goode in Philadelphia. Like the previous march in 1963 and the threatened march of 1941, the impact of this march will have consequences far beyond our time and well beyond our shores.[4]

One obvious extra-territorial ripple of the march was felt among the progressive forces on the small island of Grenada, where the socialist government of Maurice Bishop and the New Jewel Movement stood like a beacon to Black radicals in America. Even during the planning stages of the march, Dessima Williams, the Grenadian Ambassador to the Organization of American States, was on hand to endorse the mobilization and to assert how such actions were inspirational to people in her country and in other parts of the Third World. But it was inspiration that went both ways, for many Black American radicals had visited Grenada and swore by its drive toward developing a multi-racial, socialist society.

Toward the end of October, this promising bubble exploded in a nightmare of blood and carnage. Black revolutionaries the world over were as stunned by the events that shattered Grenada, as they were uninformed about what precipitated the ghastly counter-revolution. Several writers and historians have attempted to analyze what transpired there to create a situation that would give the U.S. armed forces an opportunity to invade the island. Don Rojas, press spokesperson for Grenada under Bishop, has offered what may be the best analysis of the coup and the subsequent invasion: 'What happened . . . was that the New Jewel Party took a leap forward so drastically, so dramatically as a result of rampaging ultra-leftism that it very quickly alienated itself from the broad masses of the Grenadian people . . .' Rojas further noted that what happened in Grenada was part of the rapid militarization of countries in the Eastern Caribbean and the intensification of anti-communist hysteria sweeping the region. This communist witch-hunting, Rojas suggested, 'is going to eventually spill over into a rejuvenated, right-wing orchestrated campaign against progressive people in the United States itself.' And as the remaining months of the year would show, Rojas' prophecy wasn't far off the mark.

The stepped-up campaign of repression aimed at the Black community in general and at Black radicals in particular took two forms. The most obvious, malicious police brutality, was familiar and represented little more than business-as-usual. So rampant was police abuse and misconduct that before the year ended, Congressman John Conyers (D-Michigan), head of the Subcommittee on Criminal Justice, was compelled to initiate a hearing on police brutality in Harlem. This was the first New York hearing to be conducted on police brutality since 1980. Conyers' inquiry grew out of a number of citizen and civic leaders' complaints. According to the National Black United Front, 'deaths of Black citizens at the hands of New York police officers has risen to over a thousand.' Since 1979, NBUF claimed, about 70 Blacks had been killed by police officers; many of those slain were minors. The climate of police abuse enshrouding this period would be unchanged by 1984 and through 1985, with the well-publicized murders of Eleanor Bumpers, Michael Stewart and Edmund Perry by New York police and transit officers indicative of the persistence of state-sponsored violence that is a horrific though familiar fact of Black people's life.

Less obvious to the public is the other form of repression practiced by the police and FBI: surveillance and dirty tricks. None of these tactics, however, come as a surprise to the Black left; such measures were but the natural extension of COINTELPRO, the FBI domestic intelligence program that had been instrumental in the destruction of the developing Black liberation movement of the 60s and the 70s. Singled out for special wiretaps were the RNA and any activist linked to the Black Liberation Army. Although a clear manifestation of all this surveillance would not surface until October 1984, with the arrest of the New York 8+, the bugging operation actually began in 1981, following the Brink's robbery in Nyack. Only the international celebrity of Jesse Jackson and his later presidential candidacy would act as a partial shield to blunt the FBI's full surveillance operation on Black activists.

Jackson and Farrakhan

With the arrival of 1984, Black radicals and the broad Black left were wondering how—if at all—to assess and respond to Jackson's Rainbow Coalition and the presidential campaign. To be sure, very few Black activists harbored any illusions about Jackson's candidacy; they realized, like many others, he had no realistic chance of becoming president. Theirs was a minor dilemma, similar to the one in 1983 when they had to decide whether or not to participate in the March on Washington. And like the March on Washington in 1983, Jackson's campaign offered the Black left an opportunity to do some recruiting and possibly some influencing of the candidate's political platform and direction. Of course, for many Black radicals, merely to participate in electoral politics was in itself problematic.

That a significant proportion of Black radicals rallied behind Jackson's run to glory nonetheless is undeniable. For some, Jackson's campaign offered an opportunity forcefully to attack Reaganism; others were possibly swayed by Jackson's anti-imperialist veneer, his progressive positions on Grenada, South Africa and Central America. Jackson's charisma, the rainbow aspects of his candidacy, and the fact that his bid was a historic occasion that would probably touch millions of people, were inducements that few Black activists could ignore. Unfortunately, save for a few Black activists, and well known political strategists and theoreticians such as Jack O'Dell and Ron Walters, there was little room in Jackson's think tank for Black leftists.

After Walter Mondale's victory in the Democratic primary, many Black activists still held a glimmer of hope that Jackson might be chosen as a vice-presidential running mate. That dream soon vanished in Mondale's choice of Geraldine Ferraro—a strategy that proved totally ineffective in breaking Reagan's hold over white female voters. What remained for Jackson after paying his debts and licking his wounds was to seek ways to keep the Rainbow Coalition alive and functioning. To the degree that Jackson maintains contact with the masses and continues to broaden and brighten the rainbow, aligns himself with progressive leaders and developments in the Black community, and stops feeling the need to be an arbiter to every dispute—as he sharpens his anti-imperialist, anti-capitalist perspective—he will endear himself, not only to the Black left, but to the broad masses of people as well.

No assessment of Jackson's candidacy and eventual defeat would be complete without discussing the crucial role played by Black Muslim leader Louis Farrakhan, or what Maulana Ron Karenga has termed the 'Farrakhan Factor.' Contrary to most media reports, Louis Farrakhan's emergence on the national scene should not be viewed as an 'overnight phenomenon'. He certainly was no stranger to those of the Black left who had been weaned on the politics of Malcolm X and Elijah Muhammad. For it was under the tutelage of these men, especially Elijah Muhammad, that Farrakhan hardened his nascent nationalism and laid the foundation for his present retrogressive Islamic ideology.

What was surprising to the Black left, however, was Farrakhan's sudden appearance alongside Jesse Jackson as a consultant on Middle East affairs and front man cum 'opening act' for Jackson's campaign stumping into urban ghettoes. It was, as they say, a marriage of convenience—Jackson got the spellbinding orator who could attract disparate nationalist elements and then provide an introduction, while Minister Farrakhan found a direct route out of political marginality and onto a national forum. But like most such arrangements, the mutual convenience soon disappeared. When Farrakhan began further to pepper his already strident rhetoric with such phrases as 'Judaism is a gutter religion' and 'Hitler was a great man', the two agreed to go separate ways, and Jackson moved quickly to distance himself from yet another campaign liability.

After the split from Jackson, Farrakhan continued to command the spotlight, and with every utterance that smacked of anti-semitism his coverage from the media increased. Throughout 1984 and 1985, Farrakhan's mass appeal grew astronomically. From a gathering of 5,000 in Los Angeles in 1984, Farrakhan's appearances would pull audiences of 25,000 toward the end of 1985. He had suddenly become a force to contend with in both Black and white America.

Generally, for the Black left, Farrakhan represented an odd convergence of positive and negative possibilities. While they readily applauded his economic proposals, which are partially though not inappropriately captured in the acronymn POWER (People Organized and Working for Economic Rebirth), and his anti-Zionism, the Black left rejected his excessive and even offensive rhetoric that far too often alienated potential friends and allies. Recently, on Gil Noble's TV talk show 'Like It Is,' which originates from New York City, several segments were set aside to discuss the implications of Farrakhan's political views and econo-mic plans. Of the panelists for this series—including Rev. Calvin Butts, assistant pastor of Abyssinian Baptist Church in Harlem, activist-writer Paul Robeson, Jr., Newsday reporter Les Payne and Abdul Wali Muhammad, a spokesperson for Farrakhan's Nation of

Islam—only Robeson has any real ties to the left. His response to Farrakhan centered mostly on anti-semitism and Farrakhan's 'irresponsible and dangerous rhetoric.' Maulana Ron Karenga, in an extensive article for *Black Scholar*, voiced a similar concern and further noted that one of the major problems with Farrakhan is his inability to function within the context of a Black united front. 'Farrakhan lack[s] historical experience in working in a Black united front and therefore appears to lack sufficient appreciation for his allies' goals and the need to compromise at crucial junctures.' As I write this article, the public clamour around Farrakhan is slowly abating. But there's sure to be, in the coming weeks and months, some incident to propel him once again into our living rooms via the media. Until then, the Black left has more pressing responsibilities in the rapidly spreading anti-apartheid struggle.

The Future of the Black Left

Perhaps the most dramatic development for the Black left in 1985 was the intensification and increased mobilization in the USA against South Africa's brutal racist regime. In nearly every major US city there were massive turnouts of people protesting South Africa's draconian measures and demanding the release of the imprisoned African National Congress leader Nelson Mandela. Beginning in September 1984, when a number of noted citizens, following the lead of Trans-Africa (a Washington-based anti-apartheid group headed by Randall Robinson), were arrested for demonstrating outside the South African embassy, the movement gathered steam, but the enthusiasm was not enough to halt the spread of violence and wanton killing, which by winter 1985 would reach a death toll of more than 1,000 Black South Africans. During this period, with a state of emergency in effect in most districts, Winnie Mandela would gradually emerge as a forceful symbol of the resistance, as she courageously defied South Africa's police and repressive laws.

On the national front, by the fall of 1984, the grim realities facing the Black left had by no means vanished. On October 18, 500 agents of the Joint Terrorist Task Force, in coordinated raids from Queens, New York to parts of Massachusetts, rounded up eight Blacks who, according to US Attorney Rudolph Guiliani, were plotting revolution and were linked to the Black Liberation Army. The eight activists, all of them highly skilled professionals, faced a

61-count indictment for conspiring to rob armored cars and assist in prison breaks. During the trial, which began in summer 1985, it was revealed that the defendants had all been under surveillance for nearly two years, ever since the attempted hijacking of a Brinks' truck in Nyack, New York by three white members of the Weather Underground in alliance with the Black Liberation Army. After one of the three copped a plea, the other two, Judy Clark and David Gilbert, announced that they were freedom fighters who had taken the Black liberation movement to a higher level of armed struggle. It had taken almost a year to seat a jury and reach a verdict for the New York 8+. In October they were exonerated on the conspiracy indictments, but they still faced possible sentencing for possession of illegal weapons and carrying false identification.

If the harassment and eventual arrest of the New York 8+ had a chilling effect on the Black left, the barbarous attack by the Philadelphia police on the back-to-nature group MOVE made it unequivocally clear that law enforcement officials were more inclined to use force than to negotiate. In the aftermath of this seige, 11 members of John Africa's family were killed and 61 homes destroyed by fire. The Black left was incensed by this action and the National Committee of Inquiry on the Philadelphia Crisis was hastily formed. Among those involved were such well-known activists as Sonia Sanchez, Dr. Francis Welsing, Molefi Asante, Haki Madhubuti, Ron Walters and William Strickland. More support might have emerged if people had been aware that MOVE had modified much of its inflexibility and had, by 1985, reduced its confrontational approach in the neighborhood.

Through the winter of 1985, racism, police brutality and Reaganism were no less odious and repressive. In one Philadelphia suburb, hundreds of whites demonstrated outside the home of an inter-racial couple who had integrated their neighborhood; in Harlem, college-bound scholarship student Edmund Perry was senselessly gunned down by police officers, and in Washington, Reagan's henchmen, having effectively gutted affirmative action, were busy applying the finishing touches to their punitive workfare program. In Battle Creek, Michigan, all of these social maladies seemed to converge at once as the Black community there struggled vainly to end the ongoing assault of white racism and police abuse. One Battle Creek family in particular, the Guys, has since 1981 when Robert Guy was killed by a bomb explosion, been continually at odds with the police. Theirs is a small fight, in a small city, but in many ways it personifies the battles waged by Black leftists over the last five years—just as it presages the struggle ahead.

This struggle continued as hundreds of Black workers conducted a limited but determined resistance in Waynesboro and Ashburn, Georgia against brutal police terror. In New Orleans, massive rallies occurred in response to the murder of Vernell Foster, who was shot in the back by an admitted white supremacist. In Detroit, an aroused Black community continues to demonstrate against police brutality, which recently claimed the life of Mrs. Alleane Richardson, a 64-year-old grandmother.

Organized resistance also continues to escalate against the devastating social and political policies of the Reagan administration. In cities all across the nation the Black left is actively involved in demonstrations against Reagan's support for apartheid and the ravages of his foreign policy in Central America and the Caribbean Basin. On the home front, the Black left has been unstinting in its commitment to salvage precious gains of the 1960s like the Voting Rights Act and affirmative action. For these activists, there is no difference between the struggle in Soweto and the struggle in Detroit. The issues are linked, said State Senator Julian Bond, and 'the same people who want to erase affirmative action here are the same people who want to erase the Sandinistas.'

There is every reason to believe toward the end of the 1980s, as was the case in the 1960s and in almost every other decade of Black history, that the Black liberation movement will be once again fully mobilized and at the cutting edge of social and political change. All the objective conditions for such a development are present, as well as at least some of the subjective agents necessary to mobilize the mass political will which has galvanized Blacks into a powerful and cohesive force in the past. What distinguishes the present conjuncture in Black history, however, is the historic opportunity to transcend the racial limits of Black political action, to incorporate the growing Hispanic and Asian populations in the United States and on its borders into an ethnically and racially integrated broad class movement. Only with the recognition among the Black left that their political future lies across racial and ethnic boundaries can the level of resistance now evident in the ghettoes hold out any promise for authentic social revolution. Continuing the isolation among different ethnic groups that has characterized the political activism among people of color up to the present will only serve to sustain the hegemony of the rulers whose divide and conquer strategy has effectively isolated Blacks from Hispanics and Asians—and, of course, from those sections of the white underclass with whom their economic interest would otherwise have naturally identified them. The future of the Black left lies in the articulation of race with class, for it can only be through an alliance forged on the basis of the latter that the former will cease to provide foundation for invidious social discrimination and the grounds for continued oppression.

3

Chicano Politics:
The Current Conjuncture

Carlos Muñoz, Jr.

On the eve of the 1980s, *Time, Newsweek,* and other mainstream print media devoted much attention to the 'Hispanic' population in the United States. Early reports of the 1980 Census data reflected that 'Hispanics' numbered 12 million people (with over 7 million Mexican Americans), with an additional estimated 2.5 million 'illegals' or undocumented immigrants from Mexico and other Latin American nations. The discovery of the 'Hispanic' population explosion led to predictions on the part of demographers that Afro-Americans would cease to be the USA's largest minority group by the year 1990. *Time* magazine went on to predict that the present decade would be characterized by an intense quest for 'Hispanic' political power equivalent to the struggle for Black Power in the 1960s. Political scientists, journalists and others began to perceive 'Hispanics' as a major force in American politics.

In preparation for his re-election campaign against Ronald Reagan, President Carter appointed a record number of Chicanos and other 'Hispanics' to important government posts. This gesture did little for Carter's campaign. After the 1980 presidential election, predictions for the rise of 'Hispanics' as prominent actors in the arena of American politics nevertheless continued. The *Washington Post,* for example, in its national weekly edition of April 9, 1984, trumpeted 'HISPANIC POWER' on the front page accompanied by an equally bold full-page sketch of a raised brown arm and clenched fist grasping a white piece of paper with the inscription 'EL VOTO.'

In California, with the largest 'Hispanic' population in the country, predictions were that the state would become the nation's first mainland (Hawaii still qualifying as 'offshore') nonwhite region of the 'third world,' primarily because of the rapidly growing Chicano population. Chicano political activists were quick to predict further that this demographic phenomenon would result in the political control of the state by Chicanos and other people of color. The right wing took another slant on the future development of California politics. Led by former US Senator S.I. Hayakawa, they began a campaign of fear, especially amongst the white population, and predicted California would become another French Quebec, characterized by the emergence of an un-American, separatist, bi-lingual and bi-cultural politics.

What should we make of all this? Have 'Hispanics' indeed become a major national political force? Is California really shaping up as a third-world state? In what direction are 'Hispanic' politics moving? What evidence supports the possibility of a 'Rainbow Coalition' amongst Afro-Americans, Mexican-Americans,, Asian-Americans, and Native-Americans? Before we can meaningfully address any of these questions we must first examine critically the concept of 'Hispanics'.

The 'Hispanic' Problematic

The term 'Hispanic' originated in the corridors of the federal bureaucracy and in the offices of the one Puerto Rican and four Mexican American members of the US Congress during the 1970s, after the decline of the Chicano Power Movement. For bureaucrats it was a convenient term to apply to all Spanish-speaking people in the United States, especially in the context of health, education, and welfare programs. As for the members of Congress, it was a useful label to promote a coalition politics amongst their respective Spanish-speaking constituencies; it aided in their forming a caucus and thus was a means for them to play a more effective role in Congress. The major problem with the term is that it ignores the complexities of a multitude of different cultural groups, each with its own special history, class realities, and experience in the United States. It can be said that all may share the common denominator of the Spanish language, but it cannot be said that all share the same position of racial and class inequality—and relatedly the same prospects for upward class mobility.

Historically speaking, as people of Mexican descent, Chicanos are, after Native-Americans or Indians, the oldest inhabitants of North America. They are products of the imperialist wars waged by the United States against Mexico in 1836 and 1846 which resulted in the loss of half of Mexico's territory to the United States. To complicate matters, Chicanos are also products of contemporary Mexican immigration into the United States. While some can therefore trace their roots to the 15th century when the Spaniards colonized New Mexico, most have families who arrived during Mexico's revolution between 1910 and 1920, while others are children of more recent arrivals. Puerto Ricans, on the other hand, became colonial subjects and citizens after the United States defeated Spain in 1898. Puerto Rico remains a colony of the United states, although officially classified as a commonwealth. Puerto Ricans have 'immigrated' to the US mainland in flight from poverty in Puerto Rico. Anti-Castro Cubans first arrived in the United States in significant numbers after fleeing the Cuban revolution of 1959. Central Americans, notably Salvadoreans, are the more recent immigrants. They are in the United States to escape political repression and civil war in their homeland.

The term 'Hispanic' also complicates the question of identity for each of the groups it covers. The concept is rooted in the old melting pot theory of assimilation first applied to European ethnics. It implicitly underscores the white European culture of Spain at the expense of the nonwhite cultures that have profoundly shaped the experiences of all Latin Americans. According to the dictionary meaning, 'Hispanics' refers to those who 'are lovers of Spain and Spanish culture'. Hispania was the Roman political designation for the Iberian peninsula as a whole. Nothing in the original meaning of the term relates to any of the non-white indigenous cultures of the Americas, Africa, and Asia, which historically have produced multicultural and multiracial peoples in Latin America and the United States. The US Census Bureau does not have a separate racial category to identify 'Hispanic'.

Historically it has been difficult, if not impossible, to mobilize these diverse groups along the lines of a single political conscious- ness founded upon racial identification, as has been the case for Afro-Americans. The prediction of an imminent emergence of an intense quest for political power amongst 'Hispanics' equivalent to the Black Power movement of the 1960s has not therefore borne any fruit. Nor will it bear fruit in the future. What has happened and will continue to happen is that 'Hispanics', or Latinos as one might more accurately term them, have become more visible in American politics as a consequence of their increased participation in electoral politics and the closer attention of the state to their growing numbers in some parts of the country. Visibility, however, ought not to be confused with power. Let us now take a critical look at the case of Chicano politics, which, we will note once again, represents only one sector (albeit a numerically decisive sector) among Latinos.

Chicano Political Activism

To understand the current conjuncture of Chicano politics requires a basic understanding of its historical development. The fact that Chicanos became a minority group as a consequence of the expansion of the North American Empire in the 19th century continues to be a decisive determinant for their current social and political position in the United States. Victims of US imperialist wars, they have never been considered either a constitutional or a moral issue by liberal capitalists or by the society at large. Similar in this regard to Native-Americans, Chicanos underwent a process of classic colonialism which, in addition to virtually eradicating their indigenous culture, relegated the majority to the role of a permanent cheap labor pool for the conquering capitalists. The Mexican-American landed gentry and upper class who welcomed the white colonizer with open arms eventually suffered a process of downward class mobility and loss of social status and political power. This was the case especially in Texas and California.

Resistance to white or 'Anglo' rule has been more or less continuous since the end of the US—Mexico War of 1846, and has taken many forms: from social banditry in the 1800s, to insurrections, cultural survival strategies, and class struggle in more recent history.[1] The Mexican American landed gentry played a direct role in writing state constitutions in Texas, New Mexico, and California, attempting to maintain their power through participation in the early phases of the electoral process in several southwestern states. With the exception of New Mexico, they signally failed. Nevertheless, over time they became the political leaders of the Mexican-American masses recognized by the white ruling classes. Only after World War II did distinct struggles for political equality and representation emerge, led by the small Mexican-American middle class.

The League of United Latin American Citizens (LULAC) is the oldest and best known of the middle-class Mexican-American organizations. They have historically promoted their class interests while trumpeting patriotic Americanism amongst all Mexican-Americans. Formed in Texas in 1929, LULAC did not become involved with issues of political equality until the 1940s, when it intervened directly in anti-discrimination activities. It was not until the 1960 presidential elections, however, that distinct Chicano *political* organizations became visible in the national political arena. Examples of these were the Mexican American Political Association (MAPA), and the Political Alliance of Spanish Speaking Organizations (PASSO). These continued to be dominated by the middle class, and their ideological orientation was basically liberal capitalist. These organizations pursued a politics of assimilation and accommodation within the institutions of the state, primarily in the Democratic Party. They were a significant factor in electing John F. Kennedy in 1960. 'Viva Kennedy Clubs' became the breakthrough for Chicanos at the national political level.

Middle-class Mexican-American political organizations, while attempting to speak for all Chicanos, have historically failed to achieve mass unity. With the exception of the early phase of the 1960's Chicano movement, ethnicity has never been a unifying factor. Chicano workers have been mobilized successfully in the past, but generally around their class interest. The major factor for the failure to mobilize Chicanos under one ethnic or racial political consciousness has been the fact that Chicanos have been a mixed-race people. Chicanos, more so today than in the past, are a multicultural and multiracial group. Their identity was originally rooted in the various indigenous Indian cultures of Mexico and the Southwestern United States, as well as in that of the colonizing Spaniards. Later on, this cultural identity broadened to include the African culture brought by the slaves to parts of Mexico, Asian culture, notably Chinese, and in more recent history, other white European cultures including Irish, English, German, and French. All have been, albeit in various degrees and with differing weights, assimilated into Mexican society. Add on to this historical, cultural, and racial mixture the results of inter-marriage among Chicanos, Afro-Americans, Asian-Americans, and white Americans and one sees how complex and confusing a notion Chicano identity is. The selection of a particular ethnic identity becomes a political choice for most Chicanos. Middle-class Mexican-American political activists have historically chosen to identify with whites in the interest of gaining acceptance by the white ruling class and the larger society. The white identity and the question of assimilation is complicated. Members of LULAC, for example, have not truly rejected their Mexican culture but have promoted a white identity as a political strategy *outside* the Chicano community.

Another equally significant factor in the absence of Chicano political unity has been the fact that Chicano politics has been and continues to be overwhelmingly *regional* in focus. Regionalism derives primarily from the fact that the integration of Chicanos into the capitalist political economy has historically been an uneven process. The result has been different levels of assimilation into both the class structure and mainstream dominant culture of the United States.

In addition to class differences, there are important internal cultural differences. Northern New Mexicans cherish a proud and generally aristocratic Spanish legacy as opposed to a native Mexican tradition, although this has been changing in recent times. They identified themselves as 'Hispanos' long before the term 'Hispanic' became popular (mainly since the 1970s). Colorado Chicanos, in turn, cultivate an identity both similar and subtlely different from their counterparts in New Mexico. California and Texas, on the other hand, constitute a wholly different set of social identifications from the Hispanos while evincing significant differences from each other. The former have been historically 'less' Mexican than their counterparts in Texas where Mexican national identity remains intransigent. The majority Mexican society of South Texas has had little difficulty reinforcing its cultural pride or recalling its status as an 'occupied society'. Chicanos in California, on the other hand, in a different demographic mix have been more readily assimilated and 'Americanized'. (Even when California was part of the Mexican nation, it was divorced from the heartlands of Mexican society by geographical isolation.)

These fundamental differences in state-regional cultural evolution are amplified by important local variations on an intra-state level. Thus Chicanos in South Texas differ from those living in the dissimilar economic and topographical context of the Anglo-dominated urban metropolises in the center and northern parts of the state. This difference is especially reflected in musical cultures. The same holds true for Chicanos in California where the North-South divide is imposed on an urban-rural split. Los Angeles Chicanos tend to be products of a urban Mexican culture whereas those in Fresno and other Central Valley towns come from a rural Mexican environment. Those in San Francisco evince the influences of the city's mixed urban Latino culture, preferring Salsa (the 'cosmopolitan' music of Latinos) to the indigenous North Mexican ranchero music still predominate in the interior valleys.

The Chicano Power Movement

The multicultural, multiracial, regional, generational, and class character of the Chicano people has contributed to the uneven development of political consciousness. Chicano identity has therefore been a central problem in political organizing. The middle-aged leadership of middle-class organizations has promoted a white ethnic identity in the shaping of tactics and strategies for a politics of assimilation, integration, and accommodation. The leadership of working-class organizations, on the other hand, has largely forsaken the question of ethnic identity and promoted the class interests of Chicano workers in organizing strikes and unions. The Chicano Power Movement of the late 1960s and early 1970s was the inaugural attempt to shape a politics of Chicano unification on the basis of nonwhite identity and working-class interests.

In the new Chicano politics of the 1960s youth became, for the first time, a central sector. The civil rights, anti-Vietnam War, and Black Power movements contributed to the shaping of a more critical political consciousness among the younger Chicano leadership, especially those who had gained entry to institutions of higher education. Coupled with the inspiration they received from the farmworkers' struggle led by Cesar Chavez and the land grants struggle led by Reies Lopez Tijerina, student activists in the midst of campus student revolts organized the Chicano student movement. In 1967 the United Mexican American Students (UMAS) and the Mexican American Student Confederation (MASC) were founded in California. In the same year, the Mexican American Youth Organization was organized in San Antonio. By 1969 the various student organizations in California had merged into the El Movimiento Estudiantil Chicano de Aztlan (MECHA). Other MECHAs were subsequently formed at university and college campuses across the United States, wherever Chicano students were enrolled. The student movement became the rank and file and, in some instances, the leadership of the Chicano Power Movement. Jose Angel Gutierrez, a student at St. Mary's College in San Antonio who founded the La Raza Unida Party in Crystal City, Texas, was among the most charismatic figures at this rising generation of Chicano leaders. Non-student youth groups later emerged to become part of the same broad trend, including Brown Berets, who modelled themselves on the Black Panthers, along with other barrio organizations. These latter became the movement's most familiar symbols of militancy.

The Chicano Power Movement directly challenged the politics of the old-guard Mexican-American organizations, rejecting their assimilationist and accommodationist ideologies. The leadership of the movement developed a counter-ideology of 'Chicanismo,' or Chicano cultural nationalism as they termed it, stressing Indian elements in Chicano identity. The tactics and strategy of the movement were characterized by militant, although most often nonviolent, mass protest and confrontation with the dominant political institutions of the state. 'Chicanismo' was an ethnonationalism that called for Chicano self-determination. The Chicano student manifesto made clear the objectives of the new ideology. 'We will move against those forces which have denied us freedom of expression and human dignity . . . the self-determination of our community is now the only acceptable mandate for social and political action.'[2]

The Chicano Power Movement focused on two central objectives: the quest for a non-white identity, and the struggle for political and economic power. The movement attempted to build 'a nation within a nation' through the development of independent Chicano institutions and community control of existing institutions. A multitude of alternative Chicano community institutions emerged, ranging from schools to legal aid and community mental health centers. La Raza Unida, a viable political party, was forged. Barrio theatre flourished at the grass roots in neighborhoods, and art groups were organized. All these institutions assumed the task of remaking a Chicano identity based on the legacy of the ancient Indian indigenous cultures of Mexico and the working-class character of the Mexican-American people. Students and younger Chicano intellectuals succeeded in establishing Chicano Studies programs on college and university campuses to teach about the Chicano experience and to develop the critical scholarship necessary to rewrite American history and refocus the social sciences, hitherto blind to the legacy of Chicano experience. Most importantly, those programs aimed to create organic intellectuals who would return to their communities and lead struggles for social and political change.

The Chicano Power Movement emerged in the late 1960s, but already by 1972 it had begun to decline as a political force. Several factors contributed to this process. State repression and cooptation, internal divisions and conflict, the failure of 'Chicanismo' to take root amongst the Chicano masses, the decline of the broader student movement as a whole, the end of the Vietnam War—all were significant components to this historical trajectory. Nonetheless the movement did accomplish much during its brief heyday. La Raza Unida Party took power in Crystal City, Texas, and for a time became a formidable force elsewhere in the state. It failed, however, to galvanize mass support elsewhere in the South and the Midwest. It did notably contribute to the raising of a more critical Chicano political consciousness, as well as to putting the issue of Chicano politics on the national agenda of the Democratic Party, paving the way, in an ironic twist of historical fate, for the election of Mexican American candidates in the Democratic Party. Prominent politicians like San Antonio Mayor Henry Cisneros and Denver Mayor Federico Peña have notably profited from the issues raised by La Raza Unida Party, as have Congressmen Bustamante (Texas), Torres (California), Martinez (California), de la Garza (Texas), and

Richardson (New Mexico). A more lasting contribution was the creation of Chicano Studies programs in institutions of higher education. Those programs have begun to produce a new progressive intellectual and professional sector among Chicanos, with the result that Chicano artists and writers are beginning to make their mark in American society by producing significant works critical of its structures and its ideology.

Resurgence of the Old Guard

The decline of the 1960s Chicano Power Movement and the political climate of the present historical moment have led to the resuscitation of the old guard pro-assimilationist and liberal reformist Mexican American organizations. LULAC in particular has resurfaced as the leading national Chicano political organization. Together with the Mexican American Legal Defence Fund (MALDEF), it has been the principal Chicano lobby in the corridors of ruling-class power. Neo-liberal politicians like Henry Cisneros, mayor of San Antonio, who was bruited for the 1984 Democratic Party vice-presidential nomination, and Federico Peña have become the national Chicano leaders for the present decade, replacing the more militant leaders of the 1960s Chicano movement. Cisneros and Peña are products of the shift that took place during the 1970s from a politics of militant protest to a politics focused on the electoral process and the two-party system.

The tradition of Chicano electoral politics inaugurated by middle-class elites was never entirely eclipsed by the Chicano Power Movement or the politics of the 1960s. Ironically Chicano militancy and protest actually created more opportunities for the elites to participate in the higher circles of the Democratic Party. Chicano politicians from the old guard (like their counterparts in the Black community) initially spoke out harshly against the tactics and ideology of the militants. Congressman Henry B. Gonzalez, for example, denounced Chicano militants as racists in reverse and tormenters of hatred.[3] More liberal voices were moved by the Chicano movement to become more aggressive in the quest for Chicano equality and representation in the political process. The late U.S. Senator Joseph M. Montoya expressed such progressive sentiments. As keynote speaker at a national conference of 'Hispanic' organizations held in Washington, D.C., in 1971, he echoed many of the central concerns of the Chicano Power Movement:

We have come to belabor the conscience of America . . . to awaken it to injustices . . . Our people are victims of a series of evils . . . We come to remind America of our presence and plight . . . Nor do we come as supplicants, with hats in hand and eyes cast down, as did our forebears. Rather, we are here as equals, unafraid [sic] of no man; determined to settle for full equality and nothing less . . . The Hispano, Chicano, and Boricua now possesses an aggressive identity. He is spiritually armed with La Causa. He wants action, progress, self-determination, true equality . . . We shall do this without giving up our heritage, customs, culture or language . . . We seek our own leaders, our own professionals . . . For too long we have been the 'Silent People', quietly enduring a second class role . . . Ya Basta![4]

His language was noticeably less radical than in the speeches of most Chicano Power leaders, but the message was effectively the same. The key difference in inflection lay in Montoya's continued adherence to the middle-class elite's loyalty to the capitalist ideology of the state. In Montoya's words, 'We assemble because we retain faith in this country, its ideas and institutions . . . in spite of what we have suffered at its hands.'[5] As the militant and radical organizations comprising the Chicano Power Movement began to decline in strength, the Democratic Party politicians and the leadership of liberal reformist organizations picked up the slack, thus benefitting from, while they deflected momentum generated by, the Movement.

By the mid-1970s, many former activists in the Chicano Power Movement had committed themselves to electoral politics. The Southwest and Midwest Voter Registration and Education Projects and the MALDEF organization jointly struggled to open up the electoral process through litigation and the implementation of procedures made possible by the Voting Rights Act. The result was increased Chicano participation in political campaigns at the local, state, and national levels, and a growing Chicano presence in the struggle for reapportionment. In California, for example, former leadership of La Raza Unida Party spearheaded the successful effort to create new state and congressional districts to aid in the election of Chicano politicians.[6]

Mexican American congressional representation increased from four prior to 1980 to nine by 1984. Two Mexican Americans have been elected govenor of New Mexico: Jerry Apodaca from 1975 to 1979, Tonu Anaya currently. In addition, Mexican Americans have played for the first time important roles in both the Democratic and Republican conventions. Democratic Assemblyman Richard Alatorre from California chaired the important Convention Credentials Committee, the first Chicano to serve in that capacity in the history of the Democratic Party. The vice chair of the Democratic

National Committee, Colorado state Senator Polly Baca, proudly proclaimed that the 1984 convention featured the largest number of Chicano and 'Hispanic' delegates in the history of the Party, 271, with 92 alternates. As she put it prior to the convention, 'We will be visible on the floor, in the caucuses, with the candidates, and on the air. It's no longer a question of inclusion, we're there, and we're making the most of it.'[7] At the Republican convention, Katherine Ortega, Treasurer of the United States, was the first 'Hispanic' person to be the convention keynote speaker in the history of the Republican Party—or indeed any major political party's convention.

The Impact of Reaganism

Chicanos have come a long way from their days of invisibility in American politics. In spite of the gains in political representation, however, Chicanos remain under-represented at all levels of government, and therefore far from achieving substantial political power. The visibility of Chicanos in the two major party conventions and the relative upswing in Chicano electoral victories, when measured against the realities of Reaganism and the conservative politics of the 1980s, add up to little in the way of improving the conditions endured by the Chicano masses. Poverty and unemployment are as much on the upswing as political visibility. Chicano workers, like the working class as a whole, have lost much ground since the election of Ronald Reagan. His administration's attack on unions has resulted in the Chicano workers losing ground, with a dismal record of losses in organized strikes. Anti-unionism has contributed to keeping most Chicano workers among the unorganized labor force. In addition, cutbacks in social welfare and educational programs have had a profound negative impact on the Chicano working-class poor.

Reaganomics has also made an impact on the politics of the liberal reformist Chicano political organizations. The lack of federal funding to support their programs and organizations has resulted in the shift to the private sector as a new source of funding. MALDEF, for example, lost $600,000 in federal grants in 1981. The result is that MALDEF has since been compelled to work and form partnerships with the same corporate sector which supports the Reagan Administration. Although the MALDEF ideology remains liberal reformist, as it continues to mount legal struggles for Chicano civil rights in the courts, there is no question that it has become discrete in avoiding any challenges to the class and power status quo lest it lose its new source of funding. Another example of similar cooptation is the National Council of La Raza, founded in 1968 for the explicit purpose of fostering community organization and mobilization. It has in the interim become 'brown capitalism' and works closely with the corporate sector.

The largest Chicano political organization, LULAC, has also undergone a marked shift in political direction, returning to its original conservative roots. Liberal attorney Mario Obledo, its outgoing president, was replaced by insurance executive Oscar Moran, a conservative Democrat and Reagan booster, at the 1985 LULAC election. Under Obledo's leadership the organization had been an outspoken liberal critic of the Reagan Administration, especially over immigration legislation. Obledo had also taken the lead in protesting United States intervention in Central America.

Upon assuming office, Moran made clear what the new LULAC policies would be. First, he signed an agreement with Adolph Coors Co., pledging support to the anti-union brewery's controversial plan for aid to the Latino community. He hailed the agreement as 'another bridge for the Hispanic community with corporate America.'[8] (Previously, LULAC had joined in the national labor boycott of Coors.) Moran has also announced that LULAC will not criticize US policy in Central America until the organization completes a new two year study of the region. He has also made clear that LULAC will not take a militant stand against efforts underway by the Reagan Administration drastically to curtail bilingual education. The new LULAC ideological direction has been pithily summarized by Moran: 'It's time for Hispanics to make the system work for us instead of trying to go against the system.'[9]

The shift in LULAC leadership reflects a nationwide conservative trend amongst Chicanos as a whole. The fact that Reagan received between 33% and 52% of the Latino vote in his bid for re-election speaks directly to the point.[10] The ranks of Chicanos in the Republican Party are growing as a result of the Party's aggressive recruitment of young Chicano middle-class leadership and its all-out effort to get the Chicano vote in 1984. The Democrats spent approximately $120,000 to promote the Mondale-Ferraro ticket amongst Latino voters, whereas the Republicans spent $6 million to promote Reagan and Bush.[11] Aspiring Chicano Democratic politicians are switching their registration to the Republican Party in response to its enticements to future elective or appointive office. Certainly Chicano support for Reagan and the Republicans is not as strong as it is amongst Cuban-Americans, but it is rapidly growing.[12]

Chicano Anti-Communism

Chicanos have not been exempt from the anti-Communist impulse in American society. State hegemony has resulted, as in the society as a whole, in a deeply rooted aversion to radicalism. While it is true that the Communist and Socialist Parties achieved some legitimacy amongst the Chicano working class from the 1920s to the 1940s, this was largely eroded during the era of McCarthyism. Persistent anti-radicalism, partially explained by overcompensating patriotism, has made it difficult for Chicano leftists to gain a foothold in Chicano communities.

The Chicano Power Movement produced two major Marxist currents: the August Twenty-Ninth Movement (ATM), which emerged out of the La Raza Unida Party Labor Committee; and the Centro de Accion Autonoma (Center for Autonomous Social Action, CASA). The ATM was the first Chicano Marxist-Leninist organization to develop independently of the white ideological left. The organization's basic objective, however, was to create a multi-national Communist Party to replace the 'revisionist' Communist Party USA. The ATM suffered through various phases of ideological fragmentation, those members who survived eventually contributing to the creation of the currently active League of Revolutionary Struggle (LRS), a multi-national Communist organization. Its Chicano and Latino members participate directly in Chicano political struggles, but they remain outside of the Chicano political mainstream and isolated from the Chicano working class.

CASA has disappeared altogether in the wake of internal power struggles. Originally founded by former longshoreman and long-time Chicano labor activist Bert Corona to defend the rights of undocumented Mexican workers, it was taken over by more radical elements. The new leadership aimed to give the Chicano Power Movement a new ideological direction in accord with the ideas of a revolutionary nationalism rooted in the concept of 'sin fronteras' ('without borders'), which defined Chicanos as an extension of Mexican working class. The issue of immigration was pushed as the focal point of political activism. Some former CASA members have continued to participate in the struggles to defend immigrant worker rights and to lobby support for the defeat of congressional efforts to restrict immigration from Mexico.

But CASA's objectives of uniting the Chicano working class with its Mexican fountainhead never came close to materializing; nor have the efforts of its former members and other political activists to generate support for the undocumented amongst the majority of Chicanos produced significant gains. Chicanos remain divided over the issue of immigration, and, given the high unemployment rate among them, are vulnerable to the Reagan propaganda that the undocumented take jobs away from American workers. The major reason that Simpson-Mazzoli and other proposed legislation were opposed by the progressive forces in Congress derives from the potential risks, inherent in the legislation, of losses to Chicanos and Latinos of civil rights and job opportunities.

The Reagan Administration has directly profited from the historic anti-Communism among Chicanos. Chicanos have been noticeably scarce in the ranks of those protesting against the war in Central America and against aid to the Contras. The 'Rambo' mentality of Reagan and his foreign policy and military advisors is taking hold, especially amongst Chicano youth. Chicanos and other Latino soldiers have served as advisors in El Salvador and to the Contras in Honduras, and no doubt will continue to play a prominent role as the war escalates in Central America. At one time during the various US maneuvers in Honduras in 1985, most of the US forces were Chicanos of the Texas National Guard. California's Governor Dukmejian approved sending two Chicanos and Latino military police units from the California National Guard to Honduras. A spokesman for the Guard rationalized the act, saying that 'our people will be able to communicate with the locals'.[13]

Elected Chicanos politicians in the Democratic Party also reflect the anti-Communism of their constituencies. The Hispanic Caucus in Congress, for example, has yet to speak out forcefully against the policies of the Reagan Administration. The chair of the Caucus, New Mexico representative Bill Richardson, voted in favor of the $27 million in 'humanitarian aid' to the Contras in 1985, as did two others, Lujan and Bustamante. None of the Hispanic Caucus members who travelled to Nicaragua and met with President Ortega prior to the congressional debates over this aid returned with a positive word for the Sandinistas. The Hispanic Caucus as a whole has aligned itself with the progressive forces in the Congress, but it has not played a comparable role to the Black Carcus in aggressively challenging the Reagan Administration on foreign policy issues. Whereas the Black Caucus has spearheaded the denunciation of apartheid in South Africa and has had members arrested during their participation in protests, none of the Hispanic Caucus has been willing to champion the cause of the Sandinistas. Afro-Americans have historically identified globally with other Black people whereas Chicanos do not have a similar tradition of broad racial identification (for reasons outlined at the outset of the present paper), and this has made it difficult for members of the Hispanic Caucus to follow in the footsteps of the Black Caucus.

The only time the Hispanic Caucus has been outspoken on a foreign policy-related issue against the Reagan Administration and the conservative pro-Reagan forces in a Congress has been over immigration.

The leading Chicano politician in the nation, Mayor Henry Cisneros, has thus far not taken any strong stand against US foreign policy in Central America. As a member of the Reagan-appointed Kissinger Commission on Central America, however, he did challenge the Commission recommendations which supported the Reagan Administration's military policy. Cisneros thus effectively personifies the dominant trends in Chicano politics. He is a centrist in the Democratic Party and could be accurately identified as a neo-liberal. At the same time, he is pragmatic about the necessity to maintain a degree of ethnic identity that will sustain his political base in the Chicano community. Progressive on economic and social issues directly affecting Chicanos, he is unlikely to venture beyond the narrow range of these causes in any political crusade.

The conservative trend in Chicano politics, however, does not necessarily translate into a purely right wing politics. The shift that has occurred amongst the moderate liberal reformist organizations, LULAC and MALDEF, from demands for federal to bargaining for corporate funding does represent a significant modification. It is, at this writing, too early to tell if these organizations will drift further rightward than their current corporation. This would in any event be a more likely scenario for LULAC than for MALDEF. Similarly it is not probable that Chicanos will shift en masse to the Republican Party from the Democratic Party. But there is little doubt that Democratic Chicano politicians will continue to support the Party's traditional centrist leadership.

The Future of the Chicano Left

What are the prospects for the emergence of a progressive force in Chicano politics at present? The fact that there has been no significantly visible Chicano resistance to US foreign policy in Central America does not translate into unequivocal support for the Reagan Administration. In certain parts of the country the sanctuary movement appears to be gathering increasing sympathy amongst Chicanos, particularly as a result of the strong support for the movement from the more progressive sectors of the Catholic Church. For example, on March 28, 1986, Tony Anaya proclaimed the entire state of New Mexico a sanctuary for Central American refugees. Chicano political activists in the Texas and Arizona border towns and in the Bay Area of California have also become more visible in this movement.

The 'Hispanic' pro-white identity label notwithstanding, Chicanos have increasingly been victims of racism. The right wing has fueled racial prejudice against both Mexicans and Chicanos by branding them 'illegal aliens'. The Ku Klux Klan has been engaged in a racial harrassment campaign against Chicanos in the recent past, and white politicians are increasingly willing to echo and thus legitimize them. In Dallas, for example, the deputy mayor pro tem took a strong stand against Mexican immigration, situating his claims in letters to state legislators and congressmen as follows: ' . . . neighborhoods are totally being destroyed by the invasion of undocumented aliens. Envision if you would . . . your mother, grandmother, or elderly aunt, etc., who has worked hard over the years to maintain and upkeep her property . . . all of a sudden her security is threatened because illegals with no moral values have moved next door to her. As a result, daily her health begins to deteriorate because she gets little or no sleep for fear of being robbed, raped, or killed.'[13]

The 1984 senatorial campaign in Texas provided yet another instance of racism directed toward Chicanos. Kent Hance, one of the Democratic Party candidates in the primary, campaigned on the issue that Texas was threatened by the invasion of 'illegal aliens'. Ostensibly the target of the right wing was undocumented Mexican workers, but Chicanos are often readily lumped together with the Mexicans in popular ideology. The darker skinned Chicanos especially are directly affected by the attacks on the undocumented. Hance's campaign played upon the prejudices and fears of this popular ideology, turning supposedly economic arguments in favor of immigration controls into a nakedly racist attack on the entire Chicano population.

But such primitive political tactics are not without their positive (if unintended by the authors themselves) effects. Chicanos did not sit idly by while their civil rights and economic position were being openly attacked. Racism directed against Mexicans and Mexican Americans provoked vehement counterattacks from within the progressive sectors of the Chicano community. In Dallas, for example, in response to the deputy mayor's crude playing on the fears and phobias of whites concerning nonwhites, the chair of the Coalition of Hispanic Organizations and the president of the Mexican American Bar Association both angrily denounced the viciousness and crude racism of the immigration control campaign. White racism is likely to meet with increasing resistance from Chicanos, and it may turn out that the net political effect of the

Simpson-Mazzoli-Rodino immigration bill will be to galvanize Mexican Americans into a cohesive bloc in opposition to the white-dominated capitalist state.

In this conjuncture, the potential for a coalition politics with Afro-Americans and other people of color is therefore quite real. Jesse Jackson received 15% of the Chicano vote in the California Presidential primaries in 1984, although not much support elsewhere. Most Chicanos supported Mondale or Hart during the primaries, but a visible group of Chicano political activists, mostly 1960s radicals, participated in the Jackson campaign and continue to be active in the further development of the Rainbow Coalition. The ultimate success or failure of the Jackson Rainbow lies in how aggressively it is able to recruit Chicano leadership and establish a viable organizational structure at the local and state levels. Hitherto, Chicanos have been conspicuous in their absence from the higher circles of the Rainbow's decision making process. It remains thus far a Black-led organization, headquartered in Chicago and Washington D.C., far from the political centers and realities of the Southwestern United States. Jesse Jackson must follow the lead of Harold Washington in Chicago, where the Chicano and Latino communities were decisive in his mayoral election, and recently provided him with the parliamentary majority he has sought in the City Council. Washington has not aggressively pursued the Latino vote, but recruited top Latino leadership into his campaign and has since integrated them into all levels of the government. The authentic potential of the Rainbow will be realized only if it indeed becomes an effective multiracial and multicultural coalition. Only then will it realize its goal of effectively challenging the power of the capitalist state on behalf of all the downtrodden and oppressed peoples of the Americas—whatever their skin color.

The emergence of a specifically Chicano left politics is more problematic. Like the American left as a whole, it is fragmented and diffuse. The historic anti-communist and the contemporary conservative trends in Chicano politics are not conducive to the building of a strong left sector. The prospect for an ideologically united Chicano left is at present remote. But the possible emergence of a popular left based in nonsectarian organizations or groups is less so. In the San Francisco Bay Area, for example, Chicano progressive political activists are involved in coalitions with labor, the church, gay and lesbian groups, the anti-apartheid movement, the anti-nuclear movement, Central American solidarity groups, and the progressive sector of the Democratic Party, as well as with several traditional socialist and communist parties and groups—all are working together to build a mass movement for

Peace, Jobs, and Justice. Chicano activists directly contributed to the march and rally of 50,000 people in San Francisco in April 1985 to protest US intervention in Central America, apartheid in South Africa, attacks against labor, and racial, gender, and class injustice.

The trend in Chicano politics for the remainder of the decade and beyond will almost certainly continue to focus on electoral politics at the expense of a politics of mass protest. Assuredly, the socialist alternative will continue to be perceived as not viable in the minds of a large majority among the Chicano masses and majority political activists. Chicano leftists must prepare for the time when conditions in U.S. society change in such a way that Chicanos, especially youths, once again clearly see the contradictions of capitalism and its political institutions. In the interim, they must wage intellectual 'guerrilla war' against state hegemony, while participating directly in both electoral and protest coalition struggles to build multiracial popular fronts.

4

The Political Economy of Black Women

Julianne Malveaux

The term 'doubly disadvantaged' has been frequently used to describe the economic status, and especially the labor-market status, of Black women.* The double disadvantage consists of membership both in a minority group and in the gender that has the least economic power. But the term 'double disadvantage' ignores yet another source of deprivation for the Black woman: the labor market disadvantage experienced by her spouse, or by members of her family unit. Indeed, as Black male employment-population ratios have declined to below 60% by 1984 (compared to white male employment-population ratios of more than 72%), and as the number of Black females heading households has risen to more than 42%, the family status of the Black woman may be perceived as a third labor market disadvantage.

For many Black women the term 'doubly disadvantaged' may also mean 'doubly ignored'. While the thrust of some academic research has expanded to include the needs of Blacks and of women separately, Black women too frequently 'fall between the cracks' and are assumed to be addressed 'someplace else'. It is thus ironic for Black women to observe the rise of 'women's scholarship' while noting that their own presence in this research is ignored. The irony is parallel to an irony white women expressed in their criticism of the 'state of the art'. Marianne Ferber (1982), for example, referred to a tendency toward generalization when she noted that studies concerned only with men tended to be 'globally' labelled, while those that referred to women stated so clearly. She buttressed her case by citing articles with 'global' titles (like 'Work Roles and Earnings,' and 'Economics of Affirmative Action') that refer only to men. Similarly, my review of research on women in the workplace uncovered titles like 'Women in Law', 'Women and Work: Issues of the 1980's', and 'Women, Work, and Wages'. These articles or books refer briefly, if at all, to minority women. Hull, Scott, and

Smith (1982) reinforce Ferber's point as it relates to Black women, entitling their book, 'But Some of Us Are Brave: Black Women's Studies'.[1]

The treatment of Black women in the academic literature on women in the workplace assumes that they, and by extension other women of color, are invisible. But the nearly 6 million Black women in the 1984 labor-force represented 12% of the female labor-force; 2.6 million Hispanic women (or women of Spanish origin) represent 5% of the labor-force. Although Bureau of Labor Statistics data do not report on the status of American Indian or Asian women, the recent influx of Vietnamese and Cambodians suggests that the labor market presence of these women is rising as well. And so, though we are invisible in academic writing, women of color represent 20% or more of the labor-force.

The problem is both a research question and a question of politics. From a policy perspective, the notion that 'women' are similar in status strengthens the concept of a women's movement, lobby, or political base. Many researchers have accepted the premise that 'all the women are white' and tend to gather data on that presumption. For example, Catalyst (1980) gathered data on 816 two-career couples, but did not code their data by race. Similarly, Ann Harlan (1982) studied women who received their MBA from Harvard University. She, too, failed to code for race.

Shirley Harkess (1985) has discussed the literature on women's occupational experiences in the 1970's and has uncovered several shortcomings in existing research. She notes that 'very, very few' researchers 'choose as their focus the systematic analysis of minority women's occupational experiences'. Yet, the Harkess review seems to accept the premise that 'all the women are white' when she non-critically reports the results of several studies that use large data sets, but do not report results by race. In particular, Harkess discusses Cynthia Epstein's (1981) book, *Women in Law*, without observing the cursory treatment Epstein gives Black women attorneys. Epstein's treatment of Black women is particularly troubling because some of her earlier work (1973) had focused on the status of Black women professionals. However, the Epstein discussion of women's participation in bar associations glaringly ignores the role of Black women in associations like the National Conference of Black Lawyers and the National Bar Association. Instead, Epstein scrupulously but exclusively discusses white women's participation in women's law groups and in alternative legal associations like the National Lawyer's Guild.

The Harkess review highlights several other flaws in research on women, especially as it ignores the position of minority women. She cites a Langwell (1982) study on physicians that describes 'men' and 'women' physicians, but ignores racial differences. Similarly, Harkess cites several studies in which, although large samples of women were used, the status of minority women is given inadequate attention. These include a study of more than 10,000 Michigan teachers (DeTray and Greenbery, 1977) where race is mentioned, but where the authors choose, for the sake of 'brevity' to concentrate on sex differences. Given the history of Blacks in the teaching profession (elementary and secondary school teaching was one of the few professional occupations in which Blacks were employed before 1960), such further investigation would have been illuminating. Another study mentioned by Harkess deals with the labor supply of nurses (Link and Settle, 1979). Using a sample of nealy 5,000 married registered nurses, Link and Settle find significant differences in the labor supply of whites versus nonwhites. Although these results are reported with others in tabular form, the finding is neither further discussed nor interpreted in the body of the article.

The Missing Variable of Race

Researchers like Harkess aren't the only ones who paint a portrait of the diversity of women in only the broadest strokes, excluding issues of race whenever convenient. Numerous activists have used the 'feminization of poverty' as a rallying cry, without understanding that this phenomenon may have diverse meanings for women depending upon their race. In 1966, one-third of white families in poverty were female headed; so were 42% of Black families in poverty. By 1982, 40% of white families in poverty were female headed, as were two-thirds of Black families (Department of Commerce, 1982). This trend, first observed by sociologist Diana Pearce (1978), has been further substantiated, dissected, and discussed by feminist sociologists, economists and others.

The 'feminization of poverty' has been more than a discussion about trends in poverty data. It has 'generated the beginnings of a political movement to create a public voice for this new and fragile bond' (Sarvesy, 1983). Women organizers have taken the data out of the census reports and into the streets through organizations like New York's Women's Economic Literacy Project or California's Women's Economic Agenda Project. The goal of these organizations has been to disseminate information about the position of women in the economy, as well as to 'call women to action' ('Women's Economic Agenda,' 1984). For example, the cover sheet of the Women's Economic Agenda Project 'call to action' reads: '2 out of 3 adults in poverty are women. What if we were all to go to the polls?'

The 'call to action' assumes a set of common gender interests among women. Wendy Sarvesy describes the women touched by the feminization of poverty as 'seriously ill women who lose medical insurance coverage when their husbands die, single working mothers who use most of their paychecks for childcare, displaced homemakers who have no marketable skills, teenage mothers who must drop out of school, suburban housewives whose husbands leave the state and default on child support payments, mothers who try to combine part-time work with childrearing, women who must quit their jobs to take care of sick children and other family members.' Sarvesy asserts that these women share a condition which 'cuts across class, race, age and sexual preference.' But her acknowledgement that the bond is fragile is important, for while gender may bind women together at some level, there are important differences among women that prevent the development of a 'women's agenda'.

Although the 'feminization of poverty' is a trend, and the germ of a political movement, it is also a poignant reminder that some problems generate attention only when white people are involved. The proportion of Black women heading households in poverty has been, over the past fifteen years, higher than the proportion of white women now heading families in poverty. And organization around the 'feminization of poverty' ignores the persistent poverty that plagues Black, Hispanic and Native-American communities, a poverty that has a disproportionate impact on minority women and children, as well as on minority men.

Are the economic interests of Black and white women similar? All the data show that the economic status of Black and white women is clearly distinct (Malveaux, 1985). A discussion of the political economy of Black women cannot be sustained only by inspecting selected aspects of Black women's lives. Above all, the economic position of Black women cannot be understood in isolation from the general discrimination in employment practices and the overall economic situation of Blacks as a group. Those who have spoken most persistently about the 'feminization of poverty' summarize the position in the following slogan: 'A woman is a husband away from poverty.' But Black women are poor, even with husbands, because of the institutional racism that bars many Black men from employment. Similarly, the projection that by the year 2000 all the poor will be women and children will prove true if genocide (or full employment) is planned for men of color, and other men who are chronically poor and structurally unemployed.

Pamela Sparr (1984) writes: 'By stressing what is uniquely female, proponents of that argument may leave a mistaken impression that sexism is the fundamental problem. They fail to examine thoroughly the nature of the capitalist economy, which requires and maintains an impoverished class of people.' To the extent that this impoverished class is Black, and to the extent that Black women see the survival of their community as important, a set of policy initiatives addressed solely to the 'feminization of poverty' may have limited interest for Black women.

The Economic Decline of the Black Community

During the middle and late 1970's, economists began to examine Black economic progress and to discuss the improvement in their relative economic status (Freeman, 1976; Smith and Welch, 1979). At the root of their analysis lay an improvement in relative income (until 1975), an improvement in the occupational status of Blacks, and an improvement in Black educational access. Critics of these writers (Darity, 1980) argued that the data were focused too heavily on wages and salaries, thus overstating the gains by excluding those with zero wages and salaries.

Today with a decline in Black income as a percentage of white income, an increase in the amount of Black poverty, and a decline in the employment-population ratio of Black men, it is less easy to assert Black economic progress. Shulman (1984) states he would not describe progress as 'dramatic,' and rejects 'reported' convergence because the nonemployed are frequently excluded from the research that reports convergence. Bates (1984) disaggregates the Black experience regionally and notes that Blacks in 'Northeastern and Midwestern states are losing ground rapidly.'

Even as some of the 1960–1975 gains are eroded, Bates notes several significant factors that have improved the Black economic position. These include Black educational gains, an improvement in the occupational status of young Blacks, penetration into jobs from which Blacks had previously been excluded, and a significant change in the occupational status of Black women (largely the result of the declining proportion of Black female private household workers). Bates further notes that a set of 'perceptual factors' have led to the appearance of Black economic progress. These include an increase in the number of Black elected officials, alterations in media stereotypes, and the increased visibility of Black managers and other professionals.

The 'perceptual facts' Bates mentions, while undoubtedly real, must nevertheless be used with caution. One of the most visible changes among Blacks in the past two decades has been their entry into professional, technical, and managerial jobs. When this entry is viewed over time, however, it is clear that the pace of occupational gains was most rapid between 1964 and 1972. The rate of occupational improvement declined somewhat between 1972 and 1977, at the same time that the rate of white female occupational improvement was rising (Malveaux, 1981).

While the improved educational status of Blacks has provided a ticket to upward occupational mobility, and while researchers have reported Black and white college graduates being hired at nearly identical incomes (Bates, 1984), Black college graduates find their educations do not prevent their being slotted differentially in the labor process. For example, while 13% of white male college graduates over age 25 have incomes in excess of $50,000, fewer than 2% of Black male college graduates have similar incomes (Malveaux, 1984). Interviews with Black MBAs indicate that the most advantaged Blacks in the labor market still experience discrimination as they move up the hierarchical ladder in corporations (Wallace, 1984).

Despite occupational advancement, fewer than 20% of Black men and women worked in white-collar occupations; in 1982, fewer than 9% of all Blacks were college graduates. Those Blacks not employed in professional and managerial jobs can be described as either 'those who are not highly educated, yet not below average in skill and years of schooling,' and 'those on the bottom, perhaps representing a semipermanent lumpenproletariat' (Bates, 1984). Those with average skills experience cyclical employment, while those on the bottom face uncertain job prospects. There is some evidence that the size of the group of Blacks on the bottom is growing.

The economic progress of the Black community may have been impeded by lax enforcement of affirmative action policies, by reinterpretation of the Civil Rights Act by the Reagan Supreme Court, and by judicial decisions that have made it more difficult to prove discrimination (see EEOC v. IBM, 34 FEP 766). Given poverty, high unemployment rates, declining Black male participation in the labor-force, and a public policy shift that has reduced social programs, the economic condition of Blacks remains as precarious as ever.

The economic progress of Blacks as a group is central to a

discussion of the political economy of Black women. This progress is troubling, especially when viewed in tandem with the 'feminization of poverty' and a 'women's agenda'. As the economic position of the Black community has steadily worsened, attention to the needs of Blacks has waned in the national public policy arena. Some Blacks view efforts to place the 'feminization of poverty' in the forefront as an attempt to shift attention from the plight of the Black community. Others view with suspicion the attempts by white women to become spokespersons for the poor. And, while Black women may benefit from programs designed to fight the 'feminization of poverty,' a program for the Black community must do more than focus on its women.

Although few have formally articulated a 'women's agenda', one of the efforts of mainstream women's organizations has been to improve the representation of women in the professions, in managerial jobs, and in highly visible jobs in the public sector. Too frequently, an effort to secure a position for an individual generates little more than symbolic gain for a group. We need to know more about the benefits of having women or Blacks on corporate boards of directors, in visible jobs, and in power. Do Blacks or women tend to hire more Blacks or women? Are women who gain jobs as a result of public pressure more likely to open doors for Blacks? If they are, it may be in the interest of Blacks to support a 'women's agenda'. If not, Blacks have little to gain by casting their lot with a progressive group whose values are color-blind.

Blacks have experienced both discrimination and economic disadvantage, while women have, in general, experienced discrimination but no more economic disadvantage than the men of their race and class. Since white middle-class women are the mothers, daughters, sisters and wives of white middle-class men, Blacks need to know whether these women will support their class interests or a broader set of interests as they enter public life and seek highly visible policy jobs. The answer becomes more critical as the position of the Black community in the national economy manifestly deteriorates.

Black Women in the Labor Market

Those who have attempted to use the 'feminization of poverty' trend as a tool for political organizing have tended to blur differences between women of color and white women as they organize. They find support for their work from research that speaks about the 'convergence' in the status of Black and white women.

Income data give some credence to the 'convergence' argument. In 1984, the median wage for full time women workers was $259 per week; it was $264 (or $13,700 annually) for full-time white women and $242 ($12,600 annually) for full time Black women. Full time Black women's earnings were 92% of full time white women's earnings. Given the comparatively small disparity, does it make sense to talk about the labor-market status of Black women as distinct from the status of other women? Some researchers think not, especially since Black women left private household work in large numbers between 1960 and 1970, to clerical jobs that had been dominated by white women. According to Bates (1984), Black female income rose from 62% of white women's income in 1960 to 96% of white women's income in 1980.

But raw income data only partially reveal the labor-market status of Black women. Black women participate in the labor-force slightly more than do white women, with the December 1985 labor-force participation rate of adult Black women at 59.2%, while white female labor-force participation was 54.4%.

The labor-force participation of young Black women has been dropping for some time, with participation rates for those in the 16−24 year old group below 30% in 1984. Barbara Jones (1985) cites the declining employment opportunities and increased competition for unskilled jobs as part of the reason labor-force participation rates for young women are so low. The paucity of affordable childcare and job training may be other factors in producing these participation rates.

Further, Black women are more likely to work full time than are white women; when they work part time, it is more likely to be for economic reasons than is the case in white women's working part time (Malveaux, 1984). At every educational level, Black women more often work full time than white women. Thus the 'parity' in income levels that has been reported misrepresents the economic condition of Black women, since they reached this level only by working more than white women.

Black women have consistently experienced more unemployment than have white or Hispanic women, with Black women's unemployment levels tending to be twice those of white women. In December 1985, for example, the unemployment rate for adult white women was 5.4%, while for adult Black women it was 12.6%. Black women also lose their jobs more quickly than do white women during recessions. They also find jobs more slowly than Black men, white men, and white women in periods of economic recovery. Black women's unemployment rates have shown less cyclical sensitivity than the rates of Black and white men, while improvement during recoveries is more highly correlated with the length of the recovery than is true of other race-sex groups (Malveaux, 1985a).

Perhaps the greatest difference in the status of Black and white women is in occupational status. At first glance, Black and white women seem to be distributed similarly in occupations.[2] A third of all white women are clerical workers, as are 30% of all Black women workers. Twenty-three percent of all Black women work in service jobs, as do 16% of white women. Fifteen percent of Black women workers, and 17% of white women workers are employed in professional jobs.

However Black women's occupational similarity to white women is less indicative of economic parity than of the impact of sex stratification on occupational attainment. While the gap between Black and white women's occupational status at the two digit level is narrower than that between Black men and white men, there are clear parallels between Black male and Black female occupational status. Black men are far less heavily represented in white-collar and skilled blue-collar jobs than are white men (e.g. Black male professional, managerial, sales, and crafts workers represent 38% of all Black male workers, compared to almost 60% of all white male workers). Similarly, a greater number of Black women work in non-white-collar (though mostly traditionally female) jobs than do white women. About half of all Black women work as operatives, private household workers, and service workers, while just 27% of all white women work in those occupations. Black women also experience occupational segregation distinct from the occupational segregation white women experience. In addition to being employed in jobs that are 'typically female', Black women are also employed in jobs that are 'typically' or disproportionately *Black* female. If Black women are either deliberately or traditionally 'crowded' into a few low-paying jobs, they lower average wages in those jobs where they cluster, and reduce competition (or increase wages) in the jobs where they are excluded. This concept of Black women's crowding explains, in part, why Black women receive lower pay than white women in similar occupations.

'Typical Black female' occupations are defined as those where Black women's representation is more than twice their representation in the labor-force. In service jobs, for example, Black women are overrepresented by a factor of three or four as chambermaids, welfare service aides, cleaners and nurse's aides. Forty-one percent of the Black women who work in service occupations are employed in these four jobs (Malveaux, 1985).

Black women are also overrepresented among child-care workers, whose full-time wage places them below the poverty line; food-counter workers, who earn similarly low wages; cooks, whose wages are also below the poverty line; and hairdressers. In fact, 83.3% of the Black women in service occupations, work in jobs defined as being crowded by Black women (Malveaux, 1982). Sixty-nine percent of all Black women in service jobs both experienced crowding and were employed in jobs where women's full-time, full-year pay, at less then $180 per week, was below the poverty level. (By comparison, 54.2% of white women service workers, a proportionally lower number, held 'typically Black female' service jobs and had low pay.) Another 8.2% of Black women service workers employed in 'traditionally Black female' jobs earned weekly pay that, on a full-time, full-year basis, placed them at less than 125% of the poverty line. (For white women, the comparable number was 1.7%.)

An examination of the data reveals further differences between Black and white women's occupational patterns. While white women are overrepresented as dental assistants, Black women are just proportionately represented in this occupation. Full-time pay for dental assistants is higher than that of nursing aides, a job where Black women are heavily overrepresented. Similarly, Black women are just proportionately represented as waiters, while white women are heavily overrepresented in this occupation. While pay in the food service industry is low, there are reasons this job may be attractive to Black women. Here, discrimination and entry barriers must be considered.

A similar analysis can be done for Black women in 3-digit clerical occupations. Clerical work employs both the largest number and the largest proportion of Black and white women. The 1981 median clerical wage of $219 places the average clerical worker out of poverty, but in the 'near poor' category. Yet, the range of clerical pay is broad: postal clerks have median earnings of $382 per week, or almost $20,000 per year, while cashiers have median weekly pay of $133 per week, or less than $7000 per year. Interestingly, both of these occupations are considered 'typical Black female' jobs.

As with service work, an examination of detailed clerical occupations reveals those enclaves that have become 'typical Black female'. Nearly a quarter of all Black women are concentrated in just six of forty-eight clerical occupations. They are overrepresented by a factor of four as file clerks, typists, keypunch operators, teaching assistants, calculating machine operators, and social welfare clerical assistants. Except for the median wage of social welfare clerical assistants, all of these occupations have median wages associated with the near poor. Those occupations in which Black women are most heavily represented have pay levels at 125% of the poverty level or lower.

Nearly sixty percent of Black women clericals work in 'typical Black female' occupations, as do 40% of female white clericals. Most of these Black women had wages at or below the near poor level. Nearly one in seven (13.7%) of Black female clericals work in 'typical Black female' jobs that pay at the poverty line or lower. Another 31% of Black women clericals are both crowded into Black female occupational enclaves and among the working poor. A lower, but sizeable number of white women share the characteristic of working in 'typical Black female' jobs with low earnings.

It is important to note that nearly a third of Black women clericals were employed by government (Malveaux, 1984). For many Black women, the fiscal health of federal, state and local governments affects wage levels. Further, layoffs of government workers may have a greater impact on Black women clericals than on others, both because of their heavy representation among government employees and because of the fact that many of them are recently hired municipal employees.

Aspects of Black women's crowding and concentrations of low wage workers in other occupations have been reviewed in earlier work by this researcher (Malveaux, 1984). At the two digit level, Black women are more concentrated in 'blue collar' typically female jobs than are white women; at the three digit level, Black women are segregated into 'typical Black female' enclaves where wages are lower than those for white women.

One must also give weight to an important historical dimension of the status of Black women in the labor market. Prior to 1940, the majority (60%) of Black women worked as private household workers. A third of all Black women were still so employed in 1960, but just 6% of all Black women worked in private households jobs in 1980. Partly because of this labor-market legacy, Black women have experienced as much, or more, occupational segregation as white women, but in a different set of jobs. Even as Black women's occupational patterns shifted between 1960 and 1980, Black women continued to be more heavily represented in 'traditionally female' jobs than white women, and were more likely to work in service than in clerical jobs until quite recently.

Since 1970, all women have reduced their representation in 'typically female' jobs. The reduction in the representation of Black women in these jobs reversed itself after 1977, while the representation of white women in such jobs has continued to decline. White women experienced less stratification from the outset, and have left segregated jobs more rapidly than have Black women. While the quality of work among Black women changed, it did so largely because they moved from one set of stratified jobs to another, not because they left 'typically female' jobs.

There is also an age dimension to women's occupational segregation. While white women (especially those under 35) are reducing their representation in 'typically female' jobs, Black women in the same age group are increasing their representation in these jobs. The increase in Black women's representation in white-collar, 'typically female' jobs among 25−34 year olds means that Black women in that age group tend proportionally to be more heavily represented as clerical workers than white women in the same age group.

Occupational differences between Black and white women may mean these women have different labor-market interests and may choose different strategies for improving their status. Because of their high concentration in clerical jobs, white women may target these jobs for their organizing efforts. Although there is also a high concentration of Black women in clerical jobs, the second largest concentration is in service jobs; these jobs may be the target of Black women's organizing efforts. Trends in service work like the privatization of public services will also impact differently on Black women than on white.

The occupational differences between Black and white women can also produce open conflicts of interests. For example, some hospitals have begun to phase out nurse's aides to 'professionalize' nursing services. Registered nurses have supported, and in some cases initiated, these changes. Black women are disproportionately represented as nurse's aides. A purely 'women's agenda' offers few guidelines for balancing the job security of nurse's aides with the demand for 'professionalization' by registered nurses.

'Feminization of Poverty'? Facts and Fiction

Earlier discussion in this paper referred to the 'feminization of poverty' movement. It is helpful, given the discussion of the labor-market status of Black women, to review poverty trends to see whether the sweeping 'feminization of poverty' to which activists refer has actually taken place. Between 1966 and 1973, poverty declined among individuals and families. The Black poverty rate reached its lowest point in 1974, when it was 30.3%. This represented a decline of 27% from its 1966 rate of 41.8%. Among whites, poverty rates reached a low point in 1973, when 8.4% of white families were at or below the poverty line.

Although poverty declined during the late 1960's and early 1970's there has been an increase in poverty in the past decade. The number of Black families in poverty has risen by 35% since Black poverty rates reached their low point in 1974, an increase of 17%. The rate of increase was highest from 1979–1982, when the number of Blacks in poverty rose by about half a million each year.

Trends in poverty among whites were similar to trends among Blacks. The number of whites in poverty has increased by 55% since white poverty rates reached their low point in 1973. The white poverty rate fluctuated in the 1974–79 period, then increased. In each year between 1979 and 1982, roughly two million whites entered poverty.

The 'feminization of poverty' was indeed an important part of these increases. Since 1966, the number of Black female-headed families has increased by more than 78%, while the number of white female-headed families increased by about 44%. The poverty rate for both Black and white female-headed families dropped between 1966 and 1982, but while rates fell between 1966 and 1979, they rose by 10% for Black women between 1979 and 1982, and by 17% for white women.

However the increase in the poverty rate of female-headed families in the 1979–1982 period has been accompanied by a decline in the percentage of poor families that are headed by women. Families headed by women accounted for more than seventy percent of the Black families in poverty in 1978. This number had dropped to 67% by 1982. Similarly, although white women headed almost 45% of the white families in poverty in 1978, they headed 40% of the white families in poverty in 1982.

While the 'feminization of poverty' is important, there are other trends in the poverty status of Blacks and whites that must be considered. For instance, more men have fallen into poverty in recent years. While some male poverty is the short-term result of the 1981–1983 recession, others have suffered the long-term consequences of shifts in the structure of the US economy. During the past 15 years, Black male labor-force participation rates have dropped dramatically. They are now ten percentage points lower than the rates of whites. (Bureau of Labor Statistics, 1984a). Timothy Bates (1984) has shown the substantial deterioration in the labor-market status of young (20–24) Black men, noting that their low labor-force participation rates may negatively affect their chances for future employment.

While all blue-collar workers, especially those in the auto, steel, and other manufacturing industries, will experience negative effects from the deindustrialization of the American economy, there is evidence that Black workers, especially male, will have a longer recovery period than whites. A report on the status of workers who lost or left a job between 1979 and 1984 because of plant closures, slack work, or the abolition of their positions notes that 63% of white workers have been reemployed, compared to 42% of Blacks. More Black than white workers left the labor-force after they had lost their jobs (Bureau of Labor Statistics, 1984b). Although there may be differences in the characteristics of Black and white workers that explain their different rates of reemployment, job tenure was not one of them. Black male workers who are displaced had longer job tenure than did their white male counterparts.

Data about the reemployment of displaced workers merely reinforces the notion that Blacks fare disproportionately worse in the economy and are disproportionately affected by recession. A 1982 comparison of the effects of recession and recovery on Black workers (Malveaux, 1984b) noted that they had begun to experience larger increases in unemployment rates during recessions, but smaller decreases during recovery. Between September 1983 and September 1984, a period of 'recovery', the ratio of Black-white male unemployment rates grew from 2.2 to 2.4 (Bureau of Labor Statistics, 1984c). The Black-white female unemployment ratio dropped from 2.4 to 2.2 during the same period, indicating a short term improvement in the Black woman's employment position, but also indicating a long term erosion in the relative unemployment rate of Black women, since the ratio before 1980 had never reached 2.

The causes of Black poverty are several. Too many Black women receive low pay and suffer uncertain employment while heading families. Young Black men and women have historically had a difficult time entering the labor market, while the labor market position of Black men has eroded in the past several years. The latter condition is illustrated by the increase in the Black-white male unemployment ratio, in the decline in Black male labor-force participation, and in the increase in Black poverty that is less marked in female-headed households.

None of the facts about male poverty reduce the importance of poverty among women and children. However, an agenda that focuses solely on the 'feminization of poverty' may not remedy the real causes of poverty in the Black community. Nor does it consider that the paths to poverty are several. Some people are poor because they are divorced; others are poor because they lack marketable skills; still others are poor because they face systematic institutional racism in labor markets. It is not clear that simplifying slogans like 'the feminization of poverty' (which implies that gender is the only determinant of poverty) are effective. For Black women who experience discrimination because of both race and gender, the 'feminization of poverty' may be an alienating way of referring to problems that are only partly, and probably not primarily, gender-based.

Defining the Interests of Black Women

Black women's special status has been frequently ignored both by researchers and by activists whose goal seems to be to project an image of a unified, homogeneous 'women's movement'. Their assumption that all women have similar or even identical interests has roots in the political need to represent more women, and, understandably, to advance the position of women as a distinct social group.

It is appropriate, indeed, to question the strength of women's 'coalitions' and to test the gossamer threads that frequently hold such coalitions together. Although the left or progressives may have identified a common agenda, the importance of certain items may still be a matter for some disagreement. It is tempting to confuse goals of political moderates with those of the political left, but the symbolism of 'women's equality' in political arenas may have little meaning for Black communities and for Black women in particular.

This is particularly important when we note that the way we have measured gains and improvements in both the status of Blacks and the status of women has been by pointing to the attainment of power or employment in political, corporate, and other elite arenas. But even as these measurable gains (for example, in the number of women elected officials) are achieved, it is appropriate to question their underlying significance. Are powerful women feminists? Are they concerned with the advancement of women? Are they progressives, concerned with a more just society? Do they share our vision of economic power: decent work at decent pay? Lyndon Johnson's almost all-white Women's Commission decided in the mid-sixties that women's greatest problem was their lack of household help. The federal government then spent millions of dollars training women, mostly those of color, to be maids.

Empowerment is a simultaneously political and an economic process. While we may be pleased as women move into influential jobs, we may wonder if these women can share the benefits of their position with the still vast majority of women who occupy the lower strata of the nation's economy.

If women were to write the rules to help women attain economic power, what kind of rules might they write? Possibly, rules to implement comparable worth, or equal pay for jobs of equal value. We might do this because we understand that comparable worth bridges the intentional gap between the Equal Pay Law and the Civil Rights Act. But would women write rules to help overcome the limitations of comparable worth? Comparable worth helps employed women, not the unemployed, who are disproportionately women of color. Would women write rules to ensure full employment? Would women write rules to protect women from the 'contracting out' process which restricts women in service occupations, especially women of color, to low-paying jobs.

If women were to write the rules, they would only be able to write them because they walk into the political arena in significant numbers. When women sit down at the bargaining table, they have access to power by virtue of being able to say: 'I represent several thousand women'. But to mobilize those numbers and wield real power, some women have played games with others. Some have become 'women pimps', or 'feminization of poverty pimps'. Are women together in their quest for power? A careful review of the politics that have surrounded the 'feminization of poverty' suggests a rather different assessment.

The 1984 presidential and vice-presidential nomination process illustrated some of the differences between Black and white women and some of the limitations in political symbolism. While women's organizations like NOW and the National Women's Political Caucus pressured Walter Mondale to put a woman on the ticket, the women of Jesse Jackson's Rainbow Coalition worked for the passage of four minority planks in the Democratic platform. The Jackson positions included a reduction in the defence budget, a position repudiating first use of nuclear weapons, a commitment to affirmative action, and the elimination of run-off primaries. Although the Rainbow Coalition and groups of white women had hoped to cooperate at the convention on the passage of the minority planks, these efforts collapsed when Mondale announced, several days before the convention opened, that Geraldine Ferraro was his choice for a running mate. In an open letter to the National Women's Political Caucus, women of the Rainbow expressed their outrage that minority women's interests had been ignored. White women's organizations, unsurprisingly, celebrated the placing of a woman on the ticket. Women of color could reasonably demand: did Geraldine Ferraro's candidacy make it more likely that the hungry would be fed? That the homeless would be housed? That institutional racism would come to a screeching halt? That nuclear weapons were less likely to be used? That defense spending would be cut? That the budget would balance? Those women of the Rainbow Coalition who circulated the open letter thought not, and they justifiably resented Ferraro's candidacy (and Mondale's selection process, which blatantly ignored them and those whom they represented).

The broad claims that feminization of poverty theorists have made concerning women's poverty age grossly inadequate where women of color are concerned. The political coalitions some white women hope to build will be weak and narrow, not strong and empowering, because these women cannot sit down at the negotiating table and say 'I represent women,' since they manifestly do not speak for women of color.

What some women may see as important are issues other women see as low priorities. The 1984 Women's Economic Equity Act and its impact illustrate this point. The act had five provisions, proposing: reform in tax and retirement matters; dependent care; insurance payments; regulatory reform; and child support enforcement. Of the five, the provisions to provide dependent care are of most interest to a broad cross-section of women. Child care legislation is important to women of color and to poor women because it would make the dependant care credit refundable, thus aiding those women whose incomes are too low to make use of tax credits. The legislation is also important because it would provide communities with funds to make childcare referral information available. But the child care provisions of the Economic Equity Act did not pass.

Women of color and poor women recognize little of interest in the other four provisions of the Economic Equity Act. The tax and retirement reforms would affect few Black women, since so many of them head families, and since so many of their spouses do not participate in the primary labor market where high taxes and pension benefits prevail. The treatment of pensions as a property right, while important for some women, may mean little to many minority women.

Provisions to enforce child support judgments were also part of the Economic Equity Act. Because the earnings of many Black men are so low, Black women will gain little from 'mandatory wage assignment' for child support benefits. Where Black men earn marginal wages, the mandatory reduction of wages to pay child support may make it less advantageous for these men to participate in the legal labor-force. While no one would argue that Black men should be exempt from paying child support, high poverty rates in the Black community suggest that job creation would save more Black children from poverty than will mandatory enforcement of child-support awards.

The provisions of the Economic Equity Act that would reform insurance policies and gender bias in regulations seem to have a race-neutral effect on women. However, because more Black women earn low wages than do white women, fewer Black women have access to insurance, medical, and other wage insurance policies. Thus, these items may have a higher priority in a 'women's agenda' than in a 'Black women's agenda'. Why should women of color use their political capital to support a legislative package that has nothing in it for them? Why help white middle-class women gain insurance rights, when these women have not helped women of color gain child-care benefits?

This discussion suggests that the issue of class is important in determining how women define power, and how Black and white women differ in the policy arena. Some women see economic power as securing raises and promotions. But one woman's raise might represent another woman's salary. Women who hire household help sometimes perpetuate women's lack of economic power by hiring female employees at less than decent wages.

While symbolism may differ for Black and white women, there does exist a set of issues important for all women. Child-care is a critical issue to working mothers regardless of race, income, or occupation. As the number of women in the labor-force has risen, affordable child-care has not grown proportionately. Despite the potential unity among women that could be developed by working on this issue, no national organization as emerged to place child-care availability at the top of the 'women's agenda'. Instead, many national women's groups have focused on comparable worth, an issue clearly important for both Black and white women, especially those employed in government. The problem with using comparable worth as a unifying issue, however, is that many Black women are not measurably helped by comparable worth. Unskilled and semi-skilled workers, unemployed workers, and those whose jobs are contracted out gain very little from this sort of pay equalization.

Still it may be possible for a broadly based political movement to address the needs of all women, especially of women in poverty. But such a movement would need to frankly acknowledge the conflicts between the gender interests and the class interests of women.

Moreover, as it developed a legislative agenda it would need to highlight those programs, like child-care (rather than pension reform), which have maximum benefit for *all* women, regardless of race or class.

Those who write about the 'feminization of poverty' note that 'two out of three adults in poverty are women'. And they then ask: 'What if we were all to go to the polls?' Black women represent more than a third of these female adults in poverty. If they reject white women's leadership in a political movement that has the economic status of women at its foundation, and if they choose not to join white women at the polls, then a 'women's coalition' based on economic status will be narrow in scope and politically weak. This is especially true if white women's commitment to a 'poor women's' agenda is as temporary as their conditions of poverty may be. Without the support of Black women, a political movement around women's issues will necessarily remain limited and fragile, destined ultimately to fail.

A discussion of women, power and politics is, of necessity, a discussion that raises more questions than it answers. But by exposing the underlying contradictions in the slogan 'feminization of poverty' it becomes clear that the political economy of Black women as a distinct group is indispensable to the development of a 'women's agenda. No political movement can be galvanized around gender until the differential status of women of color is recognized in the programs of the women's movement. Both Black and white women are demonstrably disadvantaged in the economic structures of the contemporary United States, but the weight of poverty falls more heavily and for different reasons upon the former than the latter. Acknowledging this fact is the first preliminary step to forging a truly powerful coalition of all women who suffer the effects of an inhumane capitalist marketplace. To the 'politics of gender', we must perforce add a politics of race and class.

Bibliography

Bates, Timothy. 'Black Economic Well-Being Since the 1960's' *Review of Black Political Economy*. 12, 4 (Spring 1984).

Bureau of Labor Statistics, 'Employment and Earnings.' January 1985.

Bureau of Labor Statistics, 1984a. 'The Employment Situation: September 1984.'

Bureau of Labor Statistics, 1984b. 'BLS Reports on Displaced Workers,' November 1984.

Catalyst Career and Family Center, *Corporations and Two Career Families*, 1980.

Darity, William, 'Illusions of Black Progress,' *Review of Black Political Economy* 10 (Winter 1980), p. 153–68.

DeTray, Dennis N. and David H. Greenberg, 'On Estimating Sex Differences in Earnings,' *Southern Economic Journal* 44 (October 1977), pp. 348–53.

Epstein, Cynthia Fuchs, *Women in Law*, New York 1981.

Epstein, Cynthia Fuchs, 'Positive Effects of the Multiple Negative: Explaining the Success of Black Professional Women,' *American Journal of Sociology* 78, 4 (January 1973).

Ferber, Marianne, 'Women and Work: Issues of the 1980s,' *Signs* 8, 2 (Winter 1982). pp. 273–95.

Freeman, Richard, *Black Elite*, New York 1976.

Harkness, Shirley, 'Women's Occupational Experiences in the 1970s: Sociology and Economics,' *Signs* 10, 3 (Spring, 1985).

Harlan, Ann and Carol L. Weiss, 'Sex Differences in Factors Affecting Managerial Career Advancement,' in Phyllis A. Wallace ed. *Women in the Workplace: Management of Human Resources*, Auburn House. 1982.

Hull, Gloria, Patricia Bell Scott, and Barbara Smith eds, *But Some of Us Are Brave: Black Women's Studies*. Old Wesebury 1982.

Jones, Barbara, 'Black Women and Labor Force Participation: An Analysis of Sluggish Growth Rates,' *Review of Black Political Economy* (Winter 1986).

Langwell, Kathryn M., 'Factors Affecting the Incomes of Men and Women Physicians: Further Explorations,' *Journal of Human Resources* 17, 2 (Spring 1982) pp. 261–75.

Link, Charles R. and Russell F. Settle, 'Labor Supply Responses of Married Professional Nurses: New Evidence,' *Journal of Human Resources* 14, 2 (Spring 1979), pp 235–276.

Malveaux, Julianne, 1985a. 'Black Women's Employment in Recession and Recovery,' AEA meetings, December 1985.

Malveaux, Julianne, 1985b. 'Similarities and Differences in the Economic Interests of Black and White Women.' *Review of Black Policital Economy* (Summer 1985).

Malveaux, Julianne, 1984a. 'Low Wages Black Women: Occupational Descriptions, Strategies for Change,' NAACP Legal Defense and Education Fund.

Maleaux, Julianne, 1984b. 'Theoretical Explanations of the Persistence of Racial Unemployment Differentials,' in William Darity, ed. *Labor Economics: Modern Views*, Boston 1984.

Malveaux, Julianne, 'Recent Trends in Occupational Segregation by Race and Sex,' Paper presented May 1982, to the Committee on Women's Employment and Related Social Issues, National Academy of Sciences.

Malveaux, Julianne, 'Shifts in the Occupational and Employment Status of Black Women: Current Trends and Future Implications,' in *Black Working Women: Debunking the Myths, A Multidisciplinary Approach*, Berkeley: UC Berkeley Women's Center, 1981.

Pearce, Diana, 'The Feminization of Poverty: Women, Work and Welfare', *Urban and Social Change Review*. (February 1978).

Rytina, Nancy, 'Occupational Segregation and Earnings Differences by Sex,' *Monthly Labor Review* 104, 6 (June 1981).

Shulman, Steven, 'The Measurement and Interpretation of Black Wage and Occupational Gains: A Reevaluation.' *Review of Black Political Economy* 12, 4 (Spring 1984).

Smith, James P. and Finis Welch, 'Race Differences in Earnings: A Survey and New Evidence,' Santa Monica, Ca.: The Rand Corporation. March, 1978.

Sparr, Pamela, 1984, 'Re-evaluating Feminist Economics,' *Dollars and Sense* (September 1984).

U.S. Department of Commerce, 'Money Income and Poverty Status of Families and Persons in the United States: 1982,' Series P–60, No. 140 (1983).

U.S. Bureau of the Census, Current Population Reports, Series P–60, No. 140, Money Income and Poverty Status of Families and Persons in the United States: 1982. (Washington, DC.: Government Printing Office, 1983)

U.S. Department of Labor, Bureau of Labor Statistics. 1976–1984, Unpublished data on Black Women.

Wallace, Phyllis, *Black Women in the Labor Force*, Cambridge: 1980.

Women's Economic Agenda Project, 'Women's Economic Agenda: A Call to Action By and For California Women,' Oakland, Ca., 1984.

5

Race and Social Theory: Towards a Genealogical Materialist Analysis

Cornel West

In this field of inquiry, 'sociological theory' has still to find its way, by a difficult effort of theoretical clarification, through the Scylla of a reductionism which must deny almost everything in order to explain something, and the Charybdis of a pluralism which is so mesmerized by 'everything' that it cannot explain anything. To those willing to labour on, the vocation remains an open one.
Stuart Hall

We live in the midst of a pervasive and profound crisis of North Atlantic civilization whose symptoms include the threat of nuclear annihilation, extensive class inequality, brutal state repression, subtle bureaucratic surveillance, widespread homophobia, techno-logical abuse of nature and rampant racism and patriarchy. In this essay, I shall focus on a small yet significant aspect of this crisis: the specific forms of Afro-American oppression. It is important to stress that one can more fully understand this part only in light of the whole crisis, and that one's conception of the whole crisis should be shaped by one's grasp of this part. In other words, the time has passed when the so-called 'race question' can be relegated to secondary or tertiary theoretical significance. In fact, to take seriously the multi-leveled oppression of peoples of color is to raise fundamental questions regarding the very conditions for the possibility of the modern West, the diverse forms and styles of European rationality and the character of the prevailing modern secular mythologies of nationalism, professionalism, scientism, consumerism and sexual hedonism that guide everyday practices around the world.

My strategy in this essay will be as follows. First, I will examine briefly the major conservative, liberal and left-liberal conceptions of Afro-American oppression. Second, I shall point out the distinctive strengths of adopting a refined Marxist methodology and analytical perspective. I then will sketch four influential Marxist attempts to understand Afro-American oppression. Last, I shall argue that if we are to arrive at a more adequate conception of Afro-American oppression, we must build upon and go beyond the Marxist tradition with the help of neo-Freudian investigations (especially those of Otto Ranke, Ernest Becker and Joel Kovel) into the modern Western forms of isolation and separation, as well as through poststructuralist reflections (by Jacques Derrida, Paul de Man, Michel Foucault and Edward Said) on the role and function of indifference, otherness and marginality in contemporary philosophical discourse. I will sketch such a genealogical materialist position.

Conservative Views of Afro-American Oppression

We begin with conservative conceptions of Afro-American oppression primarily because we live in a country governed by those who accept many of these conceptions. Conservative perspectives focus on two terrains: *discrimination in the marketplace* and *judgments made in the minds of people*. It is no accident that conservatives tend to valorize neo-classical economics and utilitarian psychology. The basic claim is that differential treatment of Black people is motivated by the 'tastes' of white employers and/or white workers. Such 'tastes', e.g. aversion to Black people, may indeed be bad and undesirable; that is, if it can be shown that such 'tastes' are based on faulty evidence, unconvincing arguments or irrational impulse. Yet it is possible that such 'tastes' may be rational choices made by white people owing to commitments to high levels of productivity and efficiency in the economy or due to evidence regarding the inferior capacities and/or performances of Blacks.

There are three basic versions of conservative views of Afro-American oppression: the *market* version, the *sociobiologist* version and the *culturalist* version. The market version—best represented by Milton Friedman's classic *Capitalism and Freedom* (1962) and his student Gary Becker's renowned *The Economics of Discrimination* (1957)—holds that it is not in the economic interests of white employers and workers to oppose Black employment opportunities. Friedman and Becker claim that such racist behavior or 'bad taste' flies in the face of or is an extraneous factor mitigating against market rationality, i.e. the maximizing of profits. In this way, both understand 'racist tastes' as the irrational choice of white employers and workers that sidetracks market rationality in determining the best economic outcomes. The practical policy that results from this market perspective is to educate and persuade white employers and workers to be more rational or attuned to their own self-interests. The underlying assumption here is that 'pure' market mechanisms (as opposed to government intervention) will undermine 'racist tastes'. Another basic presupposition here is that market rationality, along with undermining 'racist tastes', is in the interest of white employers *and* white workers *and* Black people.

The sociobiologist version—put forward by Arthur Jensen (*Harvard Educational Review*, Winter 1969) and Richard Hernstein (*Atlantic Monthly*, September 1971)—suggests that prevailing evidence leads to the conclusion that Blacks are, in some sense, genetically inferior. Blacks' I.Q. performance, which allegedly 'measures' intelligence i.e. the capacity for acquiring knowledge and solving problems, is such that the 'racist tastes' of white employers and workers may be justified—not on the basis of aversion to Blacks but due to group performance attainment. Unlike Friedman and Becker, Jensen and Hernstein consider the 'racist tastes' of white employers and workers as rational choices made on 'scientific' grounds. In this way, Afro-American oppression is not a changeable and eradicable phenomenon, but rather part of 'the natural order of things'.

Last, the culturalist version—as seen in Edward Banfield's *The Unheavenly City* (1965) and Thomas Sowell's *Race and Economics* (1975)—hold that the 'racist tastes' of white employers and workers can be justified on cultural rather than biological grounds. They argue that the character and content of Afro-American culture inhibits Black people from competing with other people in American society, be it in education, the labor-force or business. For Banfield and Sowell, the necessary cultural requisites for success—habits of hard work, patience, deferred gratification and persistence—are underdeveloped among Afro-Americans. Therefore Afro-American oppression will be overcome only when these habits become more widely adopted by Black people.

Although these three versions of conservative views of Afro-American oppression differ among themselves, they all share certain common assumptions. First, they view market rationality (or marginal productivity calculations) as the sole standard for understanding the actions of white employers and workers. Second, this market rationality presupposes an unarticulated Benthamite felicific calculus or Hobbesian psychological egoistic model that holds self-interest to be the dominant motivation of human action. Third, this calculus or model is linked to a neo-classical economic perspective that focuses principally upon individuals and market mechanisms with little concern about the institutional structure and power-relations of the market and limited attention to social and historical structures, e.g. slavery, state repression and second-class citizenship. Last, all agree that government intervention into the marketplace to enhance the opportunities of Afro-Americans does more harm than good.

Liberal Views of Afro-American Oppression

Liberal conceptions of Afro-American oppression are under severe intellectual and political assault, yet they remain inscribed within our laws and are still, in some ways, observed. It is crucial to acknowledge that liberal viewpoints adopt the same neo-classical economic perspective and egoistic model as that of conservatives. Yet unlike conservatives, liberals highlight racist institutional barriers which result from the 'racist tastes' of white employers and workers. Liberals reject mere persuasion to change these 'tastes' and attack genetic inferiority-claims as unwarranted and arbitrary. Liberals focus on two domains: *racist institutional barriers in the marketplace* and *inhibiting impediments in Afro-American culture.* Those liberals who stress the former can be dubbed 'market liberals'; and those who emphasize the latter, 'culturalist liberals'. Market liberals, such as Gunnar Myrdal and Paul Samuelson, claim that Afro-American oppression can be alleviated if the state intervenes into racist structures of employment practices and thereby ensures, coercively if necessary, that fair criteria are utilized in hiring and firing Black people. Of course, what constitutes 'fair criteria' can range from race-free standards to race-conscious ones. Furthermore, culturalist liberals like Thomas Pettigrew hold that government programs should be established to prepare people, especially Blacks, for jobs. These programs can range from educational efforts such as Head Start to direct training and hiring to the now defunct Job Corps projects. School integration efforts going back to the gallant struggles of the NAACP decades ago are part of this culturalist liberal position. In fact, it is fair to say that the vast majority of Black public officials are culturalist and/or market liberals.

As I noted earlier, both conservatives and liberals subscribe to market rationality as the primary standard for understanding and alleviating Afro-American oppression. Both groups assume that 'rough justice' between Blacks and white Americans can be achieved if Black productivity is given its rightful due, namely, if there is close parity in Black and White incomes. At the level of public policy, the important difference is that liberals believe this 'rough justice' cannot be achieved without state intervention to erase racist institutional barriers, especially in employment and education.

Left-Liberal Views of Afro-American Oppression

It is important that we do not confuse left-liberals with liberals—just as we should not confuse conservatives with neo-conservatives (which latter tend to be market liberals and culturalist conservatives). This is so because left-liberals have what most liberals and conservatives lack: *a sense of history*. This historical consciousness of left-liberals makes them suspicious of abstract neo-classical economic perspectives and sensitive to the role of complex political struggles in determining the predominant economic perspective of the day. In other words, left-liberals recognize that classical economic views shifted to neo-classical ones (from Adam Smith and David Ricardo to Alfred Marshall and Stanley Jevons), not only because better arguments emerged but also because those arguments were about changing realities of 19th-century industrial capitalism and inseparable from clashing political groups in the midst of these changing realities. Similarly the versions of market liberalism associated with Franklin Roosevelt in regard to state/economy relations and John Kennedy in regard to state/economy/race relations were transformations of neo-classicism in the face of the Depression, the rise of organized labor and the struggles of the Southern Blacks under evolving capitalist conditions. Left-liberals understand Afro-American oppression as an ever-changing historical phenomenon and a present reality. They locate the 'racist tastes' of white employers and workers and the racist institutional barriers of American society within the historical contexts of over two hundred years of slavery and subsequent decades of Jim Crow laws, peonage, tenancy, lynchings and second-class citizenship. It is no surprise that left-liberals remain in dialogue with Marxist thinkers and, in many cases, are deeply influenced by sophisticated forms of Marxist historical and social analysis.

Left-liberals such as William Julius Wilson (*The Declining Significance of Race*, 1978) and Martin Kilson (*Neither Insiders Nor Outsiders*, forthcoming), who think seriously about Afro-American oppression, are usually Weberians or followers of contemporary

Weberians like Talcott Parsons and Robert Merton. The major theoretical models they adopt and apply are not those of neo-classical economics but rather structural-functionalist sociology. This difference is not as broad as it may seem, but the historical orientation of left-liberals radically separates them from most liberals and conservatives. In fact, this sense of history constitutes a kind of 'crossing the Rubicon' by left-liberals. After such a crossing there can be no return to ahistorical conceptions of Afro-American oppression.

Left-liberals tend to be a rather eclectic lot who borrow insights from conservatives (e.g., a stress on Black self-reliance and the need to acquire efficacious habits for Black upward social mobility) and from liberals (e.g., the necessity for government action to regulate employment practices and enhance Afro-American cultural deprivation). They acknowledge the crucial structural social constraints upon Afro-Americans and, like Weber, conceptualize these constraints in terms of groups competing for prestige, status, and power over scarce economic resources. For left-liberals, strata and social position supercede class location and financial remunerations at the workplace, i.e., income, serves as the basic measure of societal well-being. The major index of Afro-American oppression for left-liberals is that Black incomes remain slightly less than 60% of white incomes in the USA. The public policies they support to alleviate Afro-American oppression focus upon full employment, public works programs and certain forms of affirmative action.

Marxist Views of Afro-American Oppression

We come now to Marxist conceptions of Afro-American oppression. And one may ask, given the conservative tenor of the times, why Marxist theory at all? Is not Marxism an outdated and antiquated tradition that: 1) has tragically produced widespread unfreedom in the communist East; 2) utterly failed to attract the working classes in the capitalist West; 3) primarily served the purposes of anti-colonial mythologies in the Third World that mask the butchery of present-day national bourgeoisies in parts of Africa, Asia and Latin America; and 4) is presently overwhelmed by information, communication and technological revolutions as well as non-class-based movements like feminism, gay and lesbian rights, ecology, and the various movement among people of color in the First World? These questions are serious indeed, and must be confronted by anyone who wishes to defend the continuing vitality and utility of the Marxist tradition.

I shall begin by making some basic distinction between *Marxist thought* as a monocausal, unilinear philosophy of history which accurately predicts historical outcomes; *Marxism* as it is exemplified in diverse 'actually existing' communist regimes in the Soviet Union, China, Cuba, Poland, et. al.; and *Marxist theory* as a methodological orientation toward the understanding of social and historical realities. Needless to say, I readily reject Marxist thought as a monocausal unilinear predictive science of history or a homogeneous, teleological narrative of past and present events. Such infantile Marxism has been subjected to persuasive criticism by Karl Popper, John Plamenatz, John Dewey and Raymond Aron from outside the Marxist tradition and by members of the Frankfurt School (Adorno, Horkheimer, Marcuse), Raymond Williams and Antonio Gramsci from within. I also reject, although not without sympathy for, the undemocratic regimes which regiment and dominate their peoples in the name of Marxism. As a democratic and libertarian socialist, I find these regimes morally repugnant, yet I wish to stress the detailed historical analysis of why they evolved as they have is required if we are to grasp their tragic predicament. Such analysis does not excuse the atrocities committed, yet it does give us a realistic sense of what these regimes have been up against.

Despite rejecting Marxist thought as a philosophy of history, and Marxism as it has appeared in diverse 'actually existing' communist regimes, I hold that Marxist theory as a methodological orientation remains indispensable—although ultimately inadequate—in grasping distinctive features of Afro-American oppression. As a methodological orientation, Marxist theory requires that we begin from two starting points.

First, the *principle of historical specificity* impels us to examine the various conditions under which Afro-American oppression emerged, the ever-changing structural constraints under which Afro-Americans have accommodated and resisted multiple forms of oppression and the crucial conjunctural opportunities (e.g., those in the 1870s, 1920s and 1960s) which Afro-Americans have either missed or seized. This historicizing approach entails that we highlight economic, political, cultural and psychosexual conflict over resources, power, images, language and identities between Black and other people as among Black people themselves.

The second starting point for Marxist theory is the *principle of the materiality of structured social practices over time and space*. This principle maintains that extra-discursive formations such as modes of production, state apparatuses and bureacracies and discursive operations such as religions, philosophies, art-objects and laws not only shape social actions of individuals and groups but possess historical potency and effectivity in relation to but not reducible to each other. Marxist theory is materialist *and* historical to the degree that it attempts to understand and explain forms of oppression in terms of the complex relation of extra-discursive formations to discursive operations. Classical Marxists view this relation in terms of a more or less determining base and a more or less determined superstructure, whereas neo-Marxists understand this relation as (in Raymond Williams' famous phrase) 'the mutual setting of limits and exerting of pressures'. The explanatory power of Marxist theory resides precisely in the specifying of the complex relation of base and superstructure, limits and pressures, extra-discursive formations and discursive operations, that is, in establishing with precision the nature of determination. This problem remains unresolved in the Marxist tradition, while the most impressive efforts remain those enacted in the best of Marx's own textual practices.

Marx's own effort to account for determination highlights the multi-leveled interplay between historically situated subjects who act and materially grounded structures that circumscribe, i.e., enable and constrain, such action. This human action constitutes structured social practices which are reducible neither to context-free discrete acts of individuals nor to objective structures unaffected by human agency. The dialectical character of Marxist theory resides precisely in the methodological effort to view the interplay of subject and structure in terms of dynamic social practices during a paricular time and in a specific space. The aim of Marxist theory is to view each historical moment as a multi-dimensional transaction between subjects shaped by antecedent structures and traditions and prevailing structures and traditions transformed by struggling subjects. As Perry Anderson has recently put it, Marxism is 'the search for subjective agencies capable of effective strategies for the dislodgement of objective structures'.

Each evolving society then becomes—as an object of investigation—a 'complex articulated totality' produced by social practices (including those that constitute the investigation itself) shot through with relations of domination and conflict in an overdetermined economic sphere and relatively autonomous political, cultural, ideological and psychic spheres. By 'complex articulated totality' I mean that the specific conflicts on the various levels of society are linked to one another, while the specificity of one level is neither identical with nor reducible to a mirror-image of the specificity of another level. Yet the articulation of these specific conflicts within and across the various spheres constitute a 'totality' because the relations of these conflicts are not arbitrary or capricious. They are shown not to be arbitrary in Marxist theorists' accounts of them, nor in explanations useful for effectively resisting prevailing forms of domination. These accounts or explanations privilege the economic sphere without viewing the other spheres as mere expressions of the economic. In other words, Marxist theory claims that social and historical explanation must view, in some discernible manner, the economic sphere as the major determining factor in accounting for the internal dynamics (or synchronicity) and historical change (or diachronicity) of human (and especially capitalist) societies. It should be apparent that Marxist conceptions of Afro-American oppression reject the 'bad tastes' starting point of conservatives, the 'racist institutional barriers' starting point of liberals, and the Weberian views about the economic sphere of left-liberals, i.e. the stress on strata and status. Nonetheless, there remains considerable controversy among Marxist theorists about how to construe the economic sphere, whether as a mode of production, as merely the forces of production, or as primarily a mode of surplus-extraction or form of appropriation of surplus-value. Consensus has been reached only insofar as all hold that the economic sphere is constituted by conflict-ridden classes characterized by their relation (ownership, effective control or lack thereof) to the means of production.

Unfortunately—and largely due to the European character of Marxist scholarship on race—there exists a paucity of sophisticated Marxist treatments of racially-structured societies. Outside of the historical work of W.E.B. DuBois, the grand efforts of Oliver Cox and C.L.R. James, and the pioneering recent writings of Eugene Genovese, Stuart Hall and Orlando Patterson, the richness of the Marxist methodological orientation and analytical perspective in relation to race remains untapped. Instead, Marxist theorists of Afro-American oppression have put forward rather bland and glib views. For example, *class reductionists* have simply subsumed Afro-American oppression under class exploitation and viewed complex racist practices as merely conscious profiteering—or a divide-and-conquer strategy—on behalf of capitalists. Although this view captures a practical truth about racist employers' practices during a particular period in racially fractured capitalist societies, it inhibits more thorough theoretical investigation into other crucial aspects, features and functions of racist practices. Furthermore, it tacitly assumes that racism is rooted in the rise of modern capitalism. Yet, it can be easily shown that although racist practices were appropriated and promoted in various ways by modern capitalist processes, racism predates capitalism. Racism seems to have its roots in the early encounter between civilizations of Europe, Africa and Asia, encounters which occurred long before the rise of modern capitalism. The very category of 'race'—denoting primarily skin color—was first employed as a means of classifying human bodies by François Bernier, a French physician, in 1684. The first substantial racial division of humankind is found in the influential *Natural System* (1735) of the pre-eminent naturalist of the 18th century, Carolus Linnaeus. Yet both instances reveal racist practices—in that both degrade and devalue non-Europeans—at the level of intellectual codification. Xenophonic folktales and mythologies, racist legends and stories—such as authoritative Church Fathers' commentaries on the Song of Solomon and the Ywain narratives in medieval Brittany—operate in the everyday lives of ordinary folk long before the 17th and 18th century. In fact, Christian anti-Semitism and European anti-Blackism are rampant throughout the Middle Ages. In short, the class reductionist viewpoint rests upon shaky theoretical and historical grounds.

The other simplistic Marxist conceptions of Afro-American oppression are those of the *class super-exploitationist* perspective and the *class nationalist* view. The former holds that Afro-Americans are subjected to general working-class exploitation and specific class exploitation owing to racially differential wages received and/or to the relegation of Black people to the secondary sector of the labor-force. Again the claim is that this is a conscious divide-and-conquer strategy of employers to fan and fuel racial antagonisms between Black and white workers and to 'bribe' white workers at the expense of lower wages for Black workers. Again, this perspective contains a practical truth about the aims of white employers during a particular period of particular capitalist societies, yet the 'bribe' thesis is a weak reed upon which to hang an account of the many levels on which racism works. More importantly, this position still views race solely in economic and class terms.

The class nationalist viewpoint is the most influential, widely accepted and hence unquestioned among practicing Black Marxists. It understands Afro-American oppression in terms of class exploitation and national domination. The basic claim is that Afro-Americans constitute or once constituted an oppressed nation in the Southern Black Belt and, much like Puerto Ricans, form an oppressed national minority within American society. There are numerous versions of this so-called Black Nation thesis. Its classical version was put forward in the Sixth Congress of the Third International in 1928, slightly modified in its 1930 resolution and codified in Harry Haywood's *Negro Liberation* (1948). Subsequent versions abound on the sectarian Black Left—from Nelson Peery's *The Negro National Colonial Question* (1978), James Forman's *Self-Determination and the African-American People* (1981) to Amiri Baraka's formulations in his journal, *The Black Nation*. More refined conceptions of the class nationalist view were put forward in the form of an internal colony thesis by Harold Cruse in *The Crisis of the Negro Intellectual* (1967) and Robert Allen in *Black Awakening in Capitalist America* (1969); yet even in these two seminal texts of the sixties the notion of Afro-America as an internal colony remains a mere metaphor without serious analytical content. Ironically, the most provocative and persistent proponent of a class nationalist perspective is Maulana Karenga, who arrived at his own self-styled position that infuses a socialist analytical component within his cultural nationalism. His *Essays in Struggle* (1978) and *Kawaida Theory* (1981) stand shoulders above much of the theoretical reflections on Afro-Americans oppression proposed by the Black Marxist Left.

On the practical level, the class nationalist perspective has promoted and encouraged impressive struggles against racism in the USA. But with its ahistorical racial definition of a nation, its flaccid statistical determination of national boundaries and its illusory distinct Black economy, the Black Nation thesis serves as a misguided attempt by Marxist-Leninists to repudiate the class reductionist and class super-exploitationist views of Afro-American oppression. In short, it functions as a poor excuse for the absence of a viable Marxist theory of the specificity of Afro-American oppression.

Such a theory is, however, in the making. The recent efforts of Howard Winant and Michael Omi to develop a *class racialist* position contribute to such a theory. As I noted earlier, the pioneering work of Eugene Genovese, Stuart Hall and Orlando Patterson is also quite promising in this regard. The Marxist conception of racially-structured capitalist societies as 'complex articulated totalities', buttressed by flexible historical materialist analysis, looms large in their work. Genovese is deeply influenced by Gramsci's nuanced conception of hegemony; Hall, by Althusser and Gramsci's notion of articulation; and Patterson by Marx's own concept of domination, by a homespun existentialism, and by recent studies of Rytina and Morgan in demography. A distinctive feature of these class racialist (or class ethnic) views is that they eschew any form of reductionism, economism and a priorism in Marxist theory. Furthermore, they attempt to give historically-concrete and socio-logically-specific Marxist accounts of the racial aspects of particular societies. This means that they accent the different forms of racial domination and reject racism as a universal and unitary trans-historical phenomenon, e.g., as a prejudicial proclivity of individual psychology or race instinct.

In this way, recent forms of Marxist theory demystify the *conservative* idea of 'bad tastes' by historically situating the emergence of these 'tastes' as socially pertinent, functional and potent; they structurally circumscribe the *liberal* notion of 'racist institutional barriers' by viewing such mechanisms within the operations of racially fractured and fractioned capitalist modes of production; and they contest the Weberian assumptions of *left-liberals* by linking struggles for prestige and status to changing class conflicts and by stressing peoples' empowerment (participation in decision-making processes), rather than mere increased financial remuneration at the workplace (higher incomes). In stark contrast to vulgar Marxist views, this body of Marxist theory holds racism to be neither a mere conspiracy or ideological trick from above, nor a divide-and-conquer strategy of capitalists, but rather a complex cluster of structured social practices that shape class relations and create a crucial dimension in the lives of individuals throughout capitalist societies. The linchpin in this refined Marxist view is that the economic sphere is the ultimate determining explanatory factor for grasping the role and function of racism in modern societies. My own somewhat hesitant rejection of this linchpin leads me to build upon, yet go beyond, this last incarnation of Marxist theory.

Toward a Genealogical Materialist Analysis

In this last section, I shall set forth a schematic outline of a new conception of Afro-American oppression that tries to bring together the best of recent Marxist theory and the invaluable insights of neo-Freudians (Ranke, Becker, Kovel) about the changing forms of immortality-quests and perceptions of dirt and death in the modern West, along with the formulations of the poststructuralists (Derrida, de Man, Foucault, Said) on the role of difference, otherness and marginality in discursive operations and extra-discursive form-ations.

My perspective can be characterized as a genealogical materialist analysis: that is, an analysis which replaces Marxist conceptions of history with Nietzschean notions of genealogy, yet preserves the materiality of multi-faceted structured social practices. My under-standing of genealogy derives neither from mere deconstructions of the duplicitous and deceptive character of rhetorical strategies of logocentric discourses, nor from simple investigations into the operations of power of such discourses. Unlike Derrida and de Man, genealogical materialism does not rest content with a horizon of language. In contrast to Foucault and Said, I take the challenge of historical materialism with great seriousness. The aspects of Nietzsche that interest me are neither his perennial playfulness nor his vague notions of power. What I find seductive and persuasive about Nietzsche is his deep historical consciousness, a consciousness so deep that he must reject prevailing ideas of history in the name of genealogy. It seems to me that in these postmodern times, the principles of historical specificity and the materiality of structured social practices—the very founding principles of Marx's own discourse—now require us to be genealogical materialists. We must become more radically historical than is envisioned by the Marxist tradition. By becoming more 'radically historical' I mean confronting more candidly the myriad of effects and consequences (intended and unintended, conscious and unconscious) of power-laden and conflict-ridden social practices—e.g., the complex confluence of human bodies, traditions and institutions. This candor takes the form of a more theoretical open-endedness and analytical dexterity than Marxist notions of history permit—without ruling out Marxist explanations *a priori*.

Furthermore, a genealogical materialist conception of social practices should be more materialist than that of the Marxist tradition to the extent that the privileged material mode of production is not necessarily located in the economic sphere. Instead, decisive material modes of production at a given moment may be located in the cultural, political or even the psychic sphere. Since these spheres are interlocked and interlinked, each always has some weight in an adequate social and historical explanation. My view neither promotes a post-Marxist idealism (for it locates acceptable genealogical accounts in material social practices), nor supports an explanatory nihilism (in that it posits some contingent yet weighted set of material social practices as decisive factors to explain a given genealogical configuration, i.e. set of events). More pointedly, my position appropriates the implicit pragmatism of Nietzsche for the purposes of a deeper, and less dogmatic, historical materialist analysis. In this regard, the genealogical materialist view is both continuous and discontinuous with the Marxist tradition. One cannot be a genealogical materialist without (taking seriously) the Marxist tradition, yet allegiance to the methodological principles of the Marxist tradition forces one to be a genealogical materialist. Marxist theory still may provide the best explanatory account for certain phenomena, but it also may remain inadequate to account for other phenomena—notably here, the complex phenomenon of racism in the modern West.

My basic disagreement with Marxist theory is twofold. First, I hold that many social practices, such as racism, are best understood and explained not only or primarily by locating them within modes of production, but also by situating them within cultural traditions of civilizations. This permits us to highlight the specificity of those practices which traverse or cut across different modes of production, e.g., racism, religion, patriarchy, homophobia. Focusing on racist practices or white supremacist logics operative in premodern, modern and postmodern Western civilization yields both radical continuity and discontinuity. Even Marxist theory can be shown to be both critical of and captive to a Eurocentrism which can justify racist practices. And though Marxist theory remains indispensable, it also obscures and makes the ways in which secular ideologies— especially modern ideologies of scientism, racism and sexual hedonism (Marxist theory does much better with nationalism, professionalism and consumerism)—are linked to larger civilizational ways of life and struggle.

Second, I claim that the Marxist obsession with the economic sphere as the major explanatory factor is itself a reflection of the emergence of Marxist discourse in the midst of an industrial capitalism preoccupied with economic production; and, more importantly, this Marxist obsession is itself a symptom of a particular Western version of the will to truth and style of rationality which valorizes control, mastery and domination of nature and history. I neither fully reject this will to truth, nor downplay the crucial role of the economic sphere in social and historical explanation. But one is constrained to acknowledge the methodological point about the degree to which Marxist theory remains inscribed within the very problematic of the unfreedom and domination it attempts to overcome.

Genealogical materialist analysis of racism consists of three methodological moments that serve as guides for detailed historical and social analyses.

1) A *genealogical* inquiry into the discursive and extra-discursive conditions for the possibility of racist practices, that is, a radically historical investigation into the emergence, development and sustenance of white supremacist logics operative in various epochs in the modern Occidental (Orient, African, Indian) civilization.

2) A *micro-institutional* (or localized) analysis of the mechanisms that promote and contest these logics in the everyday lives of people, including the ways in which self-images and self-identities are shaped and the impact of alien, degrading cultural styles, aesthetic ideals, psychosexual sensibilities and linguistic gestures upon peoples of color.

3) A *macro-structural* approach which accents modes of over-determined class exploitation, state repression and bureaucratic domination, including resistance against these modes, in the lives of peoples of color.

The first moment would, for example, attempt to locate racist discourses within the larger Western conceptions of death and dirt, that is, in the predominant ways in which Western peoples have come to terms with their fears of 'extinction with insignificance', of existential alienation, isolation and separation in the face of the inevitable end of which they are conscious. This moment would examine how these peoples have conceptualized and mythologized their sentiments of impurity at the visual, tactile, audial and, most importantly, olfactory levels of experience and social practice.

Three white supremacist logics—the battery of concepts, tropes and metaphors which constitute discourses that degrade and devalue people of color—operative in the modern West may shed some light on these issues: the *Judeo-Christian racist logic* that emanates from the Biblical account of Ham looking upon and failing to cover his father Noah's nakedness, thereby provoking divine punishment in the form of blackening his progeny. This logic links racist practices to notions of disrespect for and rejection of authority, to ideas of unruly behavior and chaotic rebellion. The *'scientific' racist logic* which promotes the observing, measuring, ordering and comparing of visible physical characteristics of human bodies in light of Greco-Roman aesthetic standards associates racist practices with bodily ugliness, cultural deficiency and intellectual inferiority. And the *psychosexual racist logic* endows Black people with sexual prowess, views them as either cruel, revengeful fathers, frivolous, carefree children or passive, long-suffering mothers. This logic—rooted in Western sexual discourses about feces and odious smells—relates racist practices to bodily defecation, violation and subordination, thereby relegating Black people to walking abstractions, lustful creatures or invisible objects. All three white supremacist logics view Black people, like death and dirt, as Other and Alien.

An important task of genealogical inquiry is to disclose in

historically-concrete and sociologically-specific ways the discursive operations that view Africans as Excluded, Marginal, Other, and to reveal how racist logics are guided (or contested) by various hegemonic Western philosophies of identity and universality which suppress difference, heterogeneity and diversity. Otto Ranke and Ernest Becker would play an interesting role here, since their conception of societies as codified hero-systems or as symbolic action systems which produce, distribute and circulate statuses and customs in order to cope with human fears of death or extreme otherness may cast light on modern Western racist practices. For example, with the lessening of religious influence in the modern West, human immortality quests were channeled into secular ideologies of Science, Art, Nation, Profession, Race, Sexuality and Consumption. The deep human desire for existential belonging, and for self-esteem—of what I call the need for and consumption of *existential capital*—results in a profound, even gut-level, commitment to some of the illusions of the present epoch. None of us escapes. And many Western peoples get much existential capital from racist illusions, from ideologies of Race. The growing presence of Caribbean and Indian peoples in Britain, Africans in the USSR, Arabs in France, and Black soldiers in West Germany is producing escalating Black/white hatred, sexual jealousy and intra-class antagonisms. This suggests that the means of acquiring existential capital from ideologies of Race is in no way peculiar to the two exemplary racist Western countries, the USA and South Africa. It also reminds us that racist perceptions and practices are deeply rooted in Western cultures and become readily potent in periods of crisis, be that crisis cultural, political or economic.

The second moment, the micro-institutional or localized analysis, examines the elaboration of white supremacist logics within the everyday lives of people. Noteworthy here is the conflict-ridden process of identity-formation and self-image-production by peoples of color. The work of Goffman and Garfinckel on role-playing and self-masking, the insights of Althusser, Kristeva and Foucault on the contradictions shot through the process of turning individual bodies into ideological subjects (e.g., 'colored', 'Negro', 'Black' subjects), and the painful struggle of accepting and rejecting internalized negative and disenabling self-conceptions (e.g. pervasive lack of self-confidence in certain activities, deep insecurities regarding one's capacities) among people of color as highlighted in Memmi and Fanon are quite useful to this analysis.

The third (and last) moment, the macro-structural analysis, deepens the historical materialist analyses of Genovese, Hall and Patterson, with the proviso that the economic sphere may, in certain cases, not be the ultimate factor in explaining racist practices. As I noted earlier, there is little doubt that it remains a crucial factor in every case.

6

Historical Subjects and Interests: Race, Class and Conflict

Leonard Harris

Philip Foner's *American Socialism and Black Americans: From the Age of Jackson to World War II* (1977) is a pathbreaking narrative of the evolution of the 'race question' within the American Left and of Black responses to socialist policies.[1] Unlike some of the more uncritical celebrations of Left historiography, Foner declares at the outset that 'no book which seeks to present the views of a movement dedicated to the principle of solidarity of all workers can refrain from voicing criticism of ideas, concepts, and practices which flagrantly violated those principles.'[2] Foner, with characteristic mastery of archival sources, recovers important and moving portraits of dedicated white radicals promoting racial equality among all workers, often at great personal risk; of Black socialists engaged in struggle long before it was believed that there were any Black socialists; and of the united fronts that Blacks and whites have often formed in struggle with national and international capital. Yet while offering us this rich picture of a little-known past, Foner also inadvertently opens a Pandora's Box. In particular he provokes us to ask searching questions about the interrelationship of race, class and the socialist project: (1) Are political policies based on the belief that the working class as an historical subject will act almost exclusively on behalf of its own class interest likely to misguide socialist strategy? (2) Are historically shaped commitments to racial and ethnic solidarities motive-forces in ways that Marx's model of capitalist development fails to capture? (3) Which evil—racial oppression or class exploitation—is the more 'primary'? (4) Should practical efforts and policies focus primarily on racial or class oppression when material resources are insuffient to combat both simultaneously? (5) Is eradication of class oppression the necessary precondition for the abolition of racism, or vice versa?

Foner does not claim to answer all these questions. Nevertheless they emerge from any careful consideration of his account of the consistently misguided policies and attitudes of white socialists towards Blacks. Conflicting answers by Black and white socialists to the last three questions, in particular, have been repeated causes of discord. The first two questions moreover have been points of departure for some of the more important attempts to generate a Marxist analysis that is inclusive of the historical experience of people of color. (I'm thinking especially of Cedric Robinson's *Black Marxism: The Making of the Black Radical Tradition* [1983]. Robinson surveys Black responses to a broad spectrum of socialist currents, with the aim not just of criticizing actually existing Marxism but of offering the outline of a reformed historical materialism that invests African people with the status of historical subjects.)

In light of Foner's account of failed socialist policies and theories, I think the unavoidable starting point for any new attempt to reconcile race analysis with class analysis must be the deployment of a concept of 'differentiated interest'. By this I mean the existence of fundamentally distinct benefits, goods and advantages which accrue, or can accrue, to different groups of people from the same programs and policies. Men and women, for example, share a common interest in the success of cancer research, but women have a special, 'differentiated' interest in successful research on breast cancer. Further, by a 'differentiated interest' I mean an interest people have which should not be construed as less compelling or important than a correlative general interest. An undifferentiated or general interest is one that all members of a group share but each member need not share equally. For any given undifferentiated interest of the working class, for example, it does not necessarily follow that there is a correlative immediate interest held by any particular sector. Moreover a group or class can possess an interest even if no members individually possess it. Neither Foner nor Robinson argues for perceiving the interests of working class as differentiated, but I believe this concept gains an inevitable warrant from their analyses. In what follows I suggest that the development of a notion of differentiated interests may provide a sounder basis for socialist thought and praxis, deriving much of my empirical support from Foner and Robinson who do not explicitly embrace this conceptual scheme.

Early Socialist Views

The historical articulations of race and class in different social formations in different epochs have been too complex and overdetermined to submit to any single theoretical adjudication. If, for instance, racial oppression is the most 'primary' and morally reprehensible injustice in a given society, it still does not logically follow that the alleviation of racial oppression must precede the alleviation of class exploitation, or vice versa. American slavery, however, was a concrete case—exceptional or not—where racial oppression determined the whole field of class relations in society. White Americans were not inclined to work with Blacks to overthrow capitalism whether the Blacks were slaves, waged workers, or successful entrepeneurs. The enlightened long term material interest of Black and white workers was arguably identical, but the immediate perceived material interests remained radically distinct. Persons concerned with human liberation did not ignore the plight of workers, but focused their efforts on the eradication of chattel slavery. Ontological commitments to ethnic and racial identities skewed class relations under chattel slavery because society legitimized the belief that existing identities were natural or ordained by God. The most morally reprehensible condition, and the most materially debilitating existence, was suffered by slaves. Marx, Engels, and early American Marxists held that the eradication of slavery was a precondition for the liberation of the working class.

Orlando Paterson has argued that slavery is a system that denies the slave the possibility of honor.[4] Regardless of whether the slaves were accomplished craftsmen or wealthy entrepreneurs, their bodies could be mangled by the poorest white person, who would go unpunished for the crime; the only offense punishable was the damage done to the master's property. American slavery denied all African people their humanity. Slavery thereby denied them the possibility of honor. On Paterson's account, the fact that slaves were held as the immediate private property of an owner in America was not unique in world history.[5] But being held as property, coupled with race as objective insignia of slave status, made the African-American slaves' existence significantly different from that of white wage earners. The questions of moral priority and whose condition was worse nonetheless plagued early utopian socialists and abolitionists.

Foner captures the tension between utopian communitarians, whom he considers the forerunners of formal Marxist socialist groups, and abolitionists. Utopian communitarians like Robert Owen, Charles Fourier, George Henry Evans and their followers believed that the need to abolish slavery was but one aspect of a larger, and more important, problem: the need to abolish wage slavery: 'The view that conditions of white wage slaves under capitalism were either as bad as or worse than those of Black chattel slaves was already commonly shared by all utopianists—Owenites, associationists, and National Reformers.[6] Owenites criticized abolitionists for focusing exclusively on chattel slavery while ignoring wage slavery. The freedom of Blacks would be achieved in the communes as envisioned by the utopianists. French and American followers of Fourier argued that 'chattel slavery could not be destroyed, or the condition of Negroes improved, without prior elimination of wage slavery'.[7] George Henry Evans, leader of National Reformers, believed that the abolition of wage slavery was the essential problem facing workers. Concern with the abolition of slavery was for him a distraction. He preferred either colonization or settling Blacks in separate Western communities. If chattel slavery was as morally repugnant as wage slavery, priority was normally accorded by utopianists to the abolition of wage slavery.[8] Frederick Douglass was among Black abolitionists who distinguished between the utopian reformers who condemned equally chattel and wage slavery, and those who only attacked wage slavery. He praised the first but condemned the second. Nonetheless, hostility continued between abolitionists and utopian reformers over the issue of moral stature and the difference in degradation between chattel and wage slaves.

Early American Marxists took a different view from the utopian reformers. They were primarily German-American immigrants and less inclined to establish utopian communes. Among them, Joseph Weydemeyer and a little recognized but powerful advocate, Adolph Douai, receive special attention from Foner. Following Marx, 'Weydemeyer believed that the free labor movement could not develop as long as slavery existed and hampered the growth of industrial capitalism.'[9] Weydemeyer and Douai encouraged German immigrant workers to stand against slavery. Of particular note is Douai's view that 'the Negro was demoralized by slavery, but the white slaveowner [and those who condoned slavery] was himself reduced to a state of demoralization . . .'[10] This view was common among abolitionists. Douai consistently condemned slavery as an absolute evil and not just an obstacle to the organization of wage-labor.

But if the moral and political priority of abolitionism was firmly established by the personal practice of early Marxists like Weydemeyer and Douai, it was far from resolved at the level of larger working-class organizations. The vanguard Communist Clubs to which they belonged exerted an influence only as wide as the radius of German-language immigrant culture (and only in its most progressive sectors).

The next generation of Marxism in the United States was also dominated by German immigrants. As Foner explains, the Socialist Labor Party—the dominant radical organization of the 1880s—was founded in 1877 as the *Sozialvstiche Arbeiter-Partei*, and throughout the next decade ninety percent of its membership remained foreign-born, predominantly German. Engels criticized these early American Marxists on several occasions for their refusal to learn English and to expand the party's recruitment into the native-born working class, Black and white. (Foner, in turn, chides Engels for not emphasizing any specific demands for Blacks other than full suffrage.)[11]

The SLP, on paper, supported the 'universal and equal rights of suffrage without regard to color, creed, or sex'. 'But', as Foner notes, 'deeds rarely followed words when it came to socialism and Black Americans . . .'[12] The failure of socialists to promote Black equality, in the North as well as the South, led to the early exodus of its few Black members. Thus pioneer Black socialist Peter H. Clark of Cincinnati resigned from the SLP in 1879 not long after being elected to its National Executive Committee. Clark, dismissed from his hardwon position as principal of Gaines High School, discovered that he could expect no support in the battle to regain his job from white party members, and was forced, instead, to rely solely on his supporters in the Black community. This incident, amongst others, revealed the largely indifferent attitude of the SLP towards its Black membership, much less to any serious commitment to fight Black oppression.

Foner rightly insists on this discrepancy between party programs and the lackadaisical, even sometimes hostile, attitude of white socialists to racial oppression.[13] Yet it is important to recall that their class position and ethnic background scarcely put them into significant contact with Blacks, nor were they likely to recognize the particular forms of oppression under which Blacks, above all poor Southern Blacks, suffered. In accounting for the distance between the principles and the practice of the SLP towards Blacks, no simple condemnation of bad faith can be sufficient. Rather, an analysis of the complex articulation between race and class is required to understand the color blindness of these early socialists.

Twentieth-Century Socialism

The twentieth century saw a significant transformation of the terms of the debate on race and class. Whereas abolitionists and utopian reformers had differed over the *moral* status of chattel versus wage slavery, twentieth-century radicals focused primarily on the *strategic* question of whether the battle against racism was as crucial to the overthrow of capitalism as the class struggle in the workplace—and, therefore, whether resources should be expended to fight racism if to do so might cost signifiant support amongst white workers. These issues divided socialists everywhere, but the debate was particularly keen in Harlem.

Early twentieth-century Harlem, with its composite neighbor-hoods of Finns, Germans, Jews, and, of course, the increasing Afro-American community, was a privileged site for Black radical-ism. Already by 1911 New York locals 5 and 7 of the Socialist Party, including the Harlem membership, were calling for the party to address the urgent needs of Blacks. The racial and ethnic mixture of the Harlem Socialist milieux, moreover, attracted leading Black militants like Du Bois and, especially, Hubert Henry Harrison.

In 1911 Harrison, Socialist Party member for several years, lost his job in the New York Post Office because of two letters he had published in the *New York Sun* criticizing Booker T. Washington. Charles W. Anderson, a leading Black Republican and ally of Washington, was instrumental in firing and blacklisting Harrison. Harrison subsequently offered his magnificent oratorical ability, together with his self-taught knowledge of Afro-American and African history, to the SP, who hired him as the first paid Black organizer and Socialist campaigner. In his speeches Harrison stressed that racism was 'essentially an economic problem. Race prejudice was the fruit of economic subjection and a fixed economic status'.[14]

Harrison joined with Isaac Max Rubinow (who had first encouraged Du Bois to join the party) to organize Colored Socialist Clubs. The rationale for their establishment was in one sense inoffensive: the best organizers of Blacks were Blacks. 'One must know the people, their history, their manner of life, and modes of thinking and feeling . . . It stands to reason that this work can be better done by men who are themselves Negroes to whom these considerations come by second nature.'[15] But the Clubs soon produced controversy. Both Du Bois and Rev. George F. Miller, for example, criticized this approach for giving the impression that socialists supported segregation. Integrated clubs, they argued, were more valuable than separate clubs because they were vehicles for Black and white socialists to come to know one another as human beings.

The national and Local New York branches concurred with this position and in February 1912, it was recommended that the Clubs be terminated, Harrison's objections notwithstanding. This was the first of a series of conflicts between Harrison and the party prior to his dismissal in May 1914. Harrison had, among other things, supported the IWW and criticized the party's close affiliation with the AFL. The IWW's focus on shopfloor organization, its emphasis on the unskilled, and its more open involvement with Black workers appealed to Harrison. Du Bois had left the party for similar reasons. The Black exclusion from, or subordination within, white unions was well documented. White socialists who condoned Black exclusion or subordination along with those who condemned it but believed it would change in the future were perceived by Harrison as fellow travellers.

Foner again places the onus for conflict between Black and white socialists on Socialist Party policies and attitudes. He contends that 'by its neglect of the Negro question and its antagonistic attitudes toward militant black socialist spokesman, Local NY also succeeded in alienating precisely those Negroes whom it needed most if blacks were to be recruited.'[16] It is certainly true that socialist policies towards Blacks caused splits, and that prejudicial attitudes on the part of party members did not endear the party to Black militants. However, Marxist parties of various kinds have had similar shifts in their approaches to the recruitment of Blacks and their analyses of the historical role of Black workers while continuing to attract Black militants to their ranks.

The Socialist Party in the summer of 1919 split between old guard and proto-Leninist factions (the latter, in turn, giving birth to two Communist Parties). Numerous issues were involved, among them the party's policies toward various foreign countries (53% of the party's membership in 1919 were foreign-language speakers), support for the AFL or the IWW, and the applicability of Bolshevik methods for winning state power in the United States. Socialists and Communists alike continued to see the working-class struggle as a transnational one and the oppression of Blacks as a 'phase of the social problem' facing all workers under capitalism.[17] All this despite the lynch terror of 1919 as 120 Blacks were tortured and killed by American mobs. Although all factions of the disintegrating Socialist movement condemned the lynchings, none took up the question of why one section of the working class was singled out for such barbarous treatment—often only for the offence of 'insolence'.

It finally took an impetus from abroad to force white radicals to focus on some aspects of the differential character of Black oppression. The importance attached to the self-determination of nations in the writings of Lenin and in the policies of the October Revolution ensured that American Communists, albeit reluctantly, had to reconsider the status of Blacks from the standpoint of the 'national question'. Moreover by the middle 1920s the Communists were approaching the practical questions of Black representation and leadership with some energy. In contrast to the traditional practice of the Socialist and Socialist Labor parties, the CP seriously sponsored the organization of Black workers, ensured the representation of Blacks on leading bodies and fielded Black candidates on the Party's electoral ticket.

Initially Communist agitation amongst Blacks was confined to the North, but by the late 1920s, with the emergence of 'red unions' like the National Miners Union, the CP became bolder in its appeal to Southern Blacks—organizing miners, iron workers, even share-croppers. Later in the 1930s, after memorable feuds with the NAACP during the Scotsboro defense, the Communists broadened their network of Black sympathizers and allies to include many well-known community leaders, unionists and writers. The National Negro Congress served as a rallying point for much of the Popular Front in the Black community.

The energy of the Communists roused the Socialists to new efforts. The Socialist Party became the prime-mover behind the Southern Tenant Farmers Union which experimented with inter-racial organizing. Meanwhile the Negro Work Subcommittee of the SP gained new authority and coordinated union agitation in support of A. Phillip Randolph's campaign to end the color bar in the AFL. By 1937, again through the Subcommittee's efforts, the SP was also giving support to the National Negro Congress. Unfortunately this was shortlived as the Socialists, led by Frank Crosswaith, broke with the Congress in face of growing Communist success. The Communists had the inestimable advantage of mass support from Blacks in the CIO, while the Socialists had little involvement with Black workers in heavy industries. Finally at the SP's last convention before the war, it adopted a line of support for the NAACP: this, as Foner notes, was 'indeed a classic example of the mountain laboring and producing a mouse.'[18]

Despite a greater attention to the Black working class and intelligentsia in this period (largely as a result of the impact of self-organized Black struggles and initiatives), the Socialists had not broken in any fundamental way with their age-old conception of the subordination of race to class. The Communists, much more energetic and audacious in practical matters, achieved a partial breakthrough with their recognition that the Black 'community' as a whole, and not just Blacks as workers, was specially oppressed. But even the Communists by the late 1930s had lapsed back into a more traditional politics, asserting that Black and white workers had the same material interests and should simply 'unite and fight'.

If Blacks failed to support Socialists or Communists in significant numbers, or if their involvement with the Left was often shortlived and conflictual, it was not simply a failure of leadership. Underlying the difficult relationship between Blacks and the Left (certainly the most sympathetic sector of American society) was the real material factor that any serious, frontal struggle against racism, capable of mobilizing the Black masses on a sustained basis, risked the loss of significant support in the white working class.

Ontological Identity and False Universality

It has been argued that we cannot account for revolutionary activism by seeing the working class as only motivated by material self interest.[19] No individual or class would sacrifice themselves if they were moved by material interests alone. They would wait, like 'free-riders', for the inevitable collapse of capitalism, or, like the capitalist, send someone else to do their dying for them. Moreover any calculation of interests involves a distinction between short-term and long-term (or 'historical') interests.

It can be argued that the white working class *vis a vis* Blacks has pursued classically short-term and free-rider strategies. On one hand, whites have accepted interim wages, credits or powers gained from differential advantages in the production process or political system which, in turn, rested on the super-exploitation of Black labor. On the other hand, white workers—female as well as male— have repeatedly been free-riders to the social reforms or benefits won by the struggles of Black people.

What, then, are we to do with the category of 'general, enlightened' class interest? Does racism preclude the unification of working-class interests that is key to a socialist strategy? In answering these questions, Robinson's *Black Marxism* is an invaluable guide. True, Robinson does not use the free-rider argument to criticize Marx, nor does he argue that racism is a motive force greater than material interests. What he does do is to map 'the historical and intellectual contours of the encounter of Marxism and Black radicalism...'[20] It is not just what Marx and Engels didn't say that troubles Robinson, but also what they did say. Robinson argues for a reconstruction of historical materialism through an exegesis of classical works by W.E.B. Du Bois, C.L.R. James, and Richard Wright. Robinson also surveys the history of slave revolts, maroon communities, and Black worker protests against capitalism and colonialism. The import of Black radical

theories and struggles for Robinson is that: 1) ontological commitments to race and ethnic identities play a far greater role in shaping
historical struggles than Marx, Engels, and white Marxists have
tended to recognize; 2) that racism is not a pre-capitalist ideology
and historical fetter but an integral feature of capitalism; and 3)
Marx's model of the working class, to the extent that the working
class is pictured as a historical subject compelled to pursue
unerringly its own enlightened undifferentiated material interest, is
misguided.

Although Robinson does not define exactly what he means by
'ontological commitment' or 'ontological identity',[21] I think we
should interpret these terms as pointing to how an individual's or
group's self-perception is structured in terms of its practical
historical being. An ontological commitment to being an American,
for example, would be structured in terms of one's family ties,
language, and norms of behavior for obeying civil laws or for
supporting imagined or real threats to America's sovereignty.
Ontological commitments are not features of consciousness existing
in a nether world of ideas, juxtaposed to the real world of
materiality. Ontological commitments are the stuff informing day-
to-day norms and perceptions of what it is to belong to a
community, nation, or race. An ontological commitment shapes
what, it seems to me, Benedict Anderson considers as an 'imagined
Community.'[22] Other than in small villages or communes, few
people actually know, or ever meet, the people they consider
members of their community. Members of imagined communities
may not know one another face-to-face, 'yet in the minds of each
lives the image of their communion.'[23] Communities are real
subjects—vendors, bankers, peasants, industrial workers, cadres,
commissars—personally unknown to one another yet bound
together in their nationness. Robinson similarly contends: 'What
the Marxists did not understand about the political and ideological
phenomenon of nationalism is that it was not (and is not) an
historical aberration (of proletarian internationalism). Nor is it
necessarily the contrary: a developmental stage of internationalism.'[24] Anderson's analysis of nationalism in Asia, and Robinson's
analysis of nationalism within Marx's works, and among European
and Black Marxists, hold one salient feature in common: that a
myriad of communal commitments enlivens the praxes of various
peoples. Such commitments do not disappear, nor do they wither
away, if the state is communist, socialist, or capitalist. Rather, new
forms of identity and collectivity arise.[25]

The radical nationalism of African people, from this perspective,
is a historical form of subjectivity; it is a form of collective being-in-

the-world, shaped and re-shaped by struggles against capitalism. 'Harboured in the African Diaspora [and Africa] there is a single historical identity which is in opposition to the systemic privations of racial capitalism. Ideologically, it cements pain to purpose, experience to expectation, consciousness to collective action . . . Moulded by a long and brutal experience and rooted in a specifically African development, the tradition of radical nationalism will provide for no compromise between liberation and annihilation'.[26] An ontological commitment enlivens the reified identities of African people, shaped and reshaped by an African cultural past, and standing in conflict with both Western civilization and capitalism.

The significance of ontological commitments manifest in radical nationalist sentiments is evidenced for Robinson in the works of Richard Wright. Wright was a member of the Communist Party in the 1930s. Michale Farbre's *The Unfinished Quest of Richard Wright* interprets Wright as having come to terms with his nationalism and revolutionary Marxism. Others, for example Harold Cruse in *The Crisis of the Negro Intellectual*, interpret Wright as having been blinded by the smog of Jewish-Marxist internationalism, which prevented him from coming to terms with his own Black nationalism.[28] Robinson finds in the various tensions within Wright's novels and essays a consistent 'struggle towards a synthesis of Marxism and Black Nationalism'. That struggle entailed Wright's recognition that 'at the moment when a people begin to realize a meaning in their suffering, the civilization that engenders that suffering is doomed'.[29] The importance Wright places on the psychological dynamics of oppression, the way the symbols of oppression in the form of white skin, white walls, white codes of civility conjoin with the laboring activity of the oppressed to form the everyday life-world of oppression makes any reduction of the causality of Black radicalism to the blind dialectical wisdom of material forces and pursuits of material interests seem implausible. It is not that material interests do not figure into Wright's understanding of why Bigger Thomas in *Native Son* slays a white woman, but that an understanding of the phenomenon of racist capitalism requires a different over-arching matrix of explanation. Wright, like W.E.B. Du Bois and C.L.R. James, when accounting for racism within capitalism and for the roots of Black radicalism found himself engaged in new theoretical beginnings. The occasions when all three deviate from classical Marxian accounts are the moments of their producing classical texts on Black life: Du Bois' *Black Reconstruction*, and James's *Black Jacobins*. Marxism formed for them what Wright called a 'beginning point', but not Archimedean point.

Marx's works, even as a beginning point, are for Robinson filled with non-universalizable, contextually shaped conceptions. In Robinson's account, Marx and '... European Marxists have presumed more frequently than not that their project is identical with world-historical development ... they have mistaken for universal verities the structures and social dynamics retrieved from their own distant and more immediate pasts. Even more significantly, the deepest structures of "historical materialism," the fore-knowledge for its comprehension of historical movement, have tended to relieve European Marxists from the obligation of investigating the profound effects of cultural and historical experience on their science.'[30] The verity which Marx in particular mistook as universal is the character of the working class as historical subject compelled to pursue its material self-interest, and this as a function of how the laws of the dialectic operate in capitalist systems. The global working class is not motivated to pursue its material interest in the same way as the capitalist class is so motivated. If the European and white American working classes are motivated by material self-interest, that historical motive force is not universalizable in the way Marx and Engels took it to be. Rather, the ontological commitments people have, as evidenced by their dedication to their nations, geographical regions, and races are equally important for an understanding of what people are and thereby what motivates them.

Marxists, Robinson claims, have acted as if the political policies of their particular local parties are, *pari passa*, the requisite policies for all peoples everywhere. The vagaries and relative neglect by white radicals to fight slavery and racism, for example, are not explained by Robinson in terms of the failure of white radicals to follow socialist principles, prejudicial attitudes, or willful neglect. Rather, he takes into account operative concepts legitimizing policies and actions among socialists. The conception of racism as a by-product of capitalism is given significant attention.[31] In Robinson's view, racism does not stand on the periphery of the capitalist system as simply an ideological and historical fetter. Racism is not just functional for capitalism, not just a convenient means to divide workers, a means for assuring an industrial reserve army of labor, or an instrument for expropriating greater amounts of surplus-value from a despised sector of the working class. Racism has these features, but it is also part of the very matrix of capitalism. As Robinson points out, much of the conflict between white and Black radicals has stemmed from the former's refusal to see racism as integral to capitalism. For those 'who believed that through the movement of capitalism they had discovered the nature, that is, the basis for historical change',[32] the unanticipated roles of nationalism and race have been frustrating. A simple 'class interest' analysis is incapable of understanding the actual motivations of African and Afro-American peoples, including their desires to assert or recover their identity, to delimit the impact of Western civilization and to engage in their own, autonomous meaning-giving and symbolization. The nature of historial change cannot be fully encompassed by Eurocentric pictures of materially-grounded class conflicts.

In emphasizing that the self-interested, materialistic character of the working class is a Eurocentric concept Robinson offers an interpretation of Marx is uncomfortable to many Marxists. Yet quoting 'better' samples of Marx's views, including his statements in support of anti-colonial struggles or in opposition to racism in the labor movement, does not overcome the problem.[33] Rather than defending a spurious 'orthodoxy', it seems better to adopt the perspective of Black radicals like Du Bois or C. L. R. James who utilized Marx as a 'beginning' rather than a mode of legitimizing blind loyalty to a political organization.

At this point, it is relevant to draw attention to contemporary work within the Marxist tradition itself which has affinities with the critique of universalism mounted against the theories of Marx and Engels in *Black Marxism*. Adorno, Habermas, and André Gorz come immediately to mind as Marxist theorists who have in their different ways challenged the exclusivity of class as an analytic category for the understanding of history generally and revolutionary struggles in particular.[34] Their revisions (along with some others) of the classical Marxist conceptions of class and social identity suggest that it is possible to arrive at a critical perspective on the relationship between race and class from other than a strict adherence to the tradition and heritage of Black struggle.[35] The specificity of Black radicals' rejection of certain features of historical materialism does not lie in the simple act of repudiation (which it shares with these other tendencies within Marxism itself), but in the particularity of its form: to wit, in the importance attached to ontological commitments toward racial identity and to the ways in which these impact on social relations in a given historical formation. Robinson's voice can thus be added to this tradition of critical examination within historical materialism, at the same time that his work can be seen, paradoxically, to continue on a different terrain some of the universalizing tendencies in Marxist theory which Robinson himself begins by taking to task. Let me elaborate on this last point.

Conceiving of Black interests as undifferentiated and enlightened presents the same problem that conceiving the interests of the working class as undifferentiated and enlightened entails: it requires the negation of substantive historical, cultural, and experiential distinctions. Ignoring substantive distinctions between the actual agents of history and their immediate interests is one way of reifying and deifying social categories. That is, it is one way of treating 'African people' or 'the working class' as actual subject-entities. Why believe, nonetheless, that the struggles of African people against racism, colonialism, and capitalism invests them with an undifferentiated interest?

It is one thing to argue that Africans constitute a 'people' and another to argue that, as a people, they constitute an historical subject, i.e., that they are invested with ontological commitment, historically contiguous experience, *and* a definite historical situation such that their immediate interest is identical with an enlightened undifferentiated interest. Africans constitute a people not because they are members of the same race[36]—there are racial conflicts among Blacks—but because as Robinson aptly suggests they possess common cultural roots, suffer similar distinctive types of oppression and have engaged in comparable forms of revolt. But do the ontological commitments and historically contiguous experience of Africans imply that their immediate interests are identical with an enlightened undifferentiated interest? If a major reason for the failure of Marx's account of the working class as a historical subject is its inability to encompass the differentiated interests and motive forces germane to non-Europeans, then why believe that the need to recognize differences is captured by the immediate interests of African people?

If Robinson's account does help establish the existence of differentiated interests, we still need an account of why historical subjects—whether conceived as a working class or as a people—should be treated as real subject-entities with real undifferentiated interests neatly fitting immediate interests. Since there are significant differences between the individual social collectives said to represent broad social categories—for example, differences between Black and white workers who make up the working class, or differences between African people in the Caribbean and those in South Africa who seem in various ways to share a (single historical identity) of African civilization—in what ways are these differences more or less definitive of their historical subjectivity? I raise these issues as a way of suggesting future directions for research and as an indication of some theoretical problem in the re-formation of an historical materialism that has not shed the conceptual categories of the very form of historical materialism Robinson and others have found inadequate.

Towards a Differentiated Analysis

The policies of various socialist and communist parties have, to some extent, relied on a conception of the working class as an historical subject, a real ontological being, pursuing an enlightened undifferentiated material interest. Foner's account of the actual history of the interaction between Blacks and the socialist movement, however, dispels the illusion of any such 'undifferentiated' interest. Indeed, far too often in the name of pursuing such general interests socialists have, in fact, only espoused ethnocentric, if not racist, goals. Their ethnocentricity has been masked by a facile reduction of race to class, and class to a single sector of white workers.[37] Black oppression has been submerged in a bogus universality. In effect the historical contextuality, the unavowed ontological commitments, and the specificity of worker interests are abdicated in favor of prioritizing an undifferentiated interest. But so doing only negates, or at least limits, the possibility of cooperation against a common enemy.

Conversely if we recognize that African people have a historical identity and 'ontological commitment', it does not follow that they are an historical subject with an undifferentiated material/ontological interest. To believe that one social category brings into reality an undifferentiated interest by progressively achieving its immediate interest is no less problematic if the social category is Africans than if it is white workers. The problmatic involves identifying, reducing, or subordinating the immediate interests of peoples to a given undifferentiated one. Shading the real differences between what is required for the liberation of peoples, as manifest in their day-to-day interests, legitimates the types of party policies that historically have prevented working-class unity.

A scientific analysis, as Marx and Engels conceived it, requires moving conceptually from particular cases and the specificity of objective conditions to generalizations. Moving conceptually the other-way-around is characteristically Hegelian. Moving from how a working class should behave over time according to Marx's model of class conflict, moving from the standpoint of the world-historical system of capitalism to how a particular working class does behave, is to see world historical development as *ipso facto* the development of a pre-given model disjoint from actual human affairs. A basic feature of historical materialism, however, requires that we should begin from the standpoint of what people are by virtue of how in fact they live, produce, and reproduce themselves; how they in fact shape and reshape their world in actual praxis; how they manifest, shape, and reshape their species being as active agents from within their own history. If we begin from this standpoint, the interest of the working class is differentiated because its interest includes ontological commitments in praxes. The working class can be conceived as having an undifferentiated interest, but that should not be confused with the immediate interests of its sectors. Ignoring or treating Blacks functionally in relation to a socialist party's perception of what appears to be in their interest, for example, is to proceed as if the interest of Blacks to be liberated from the domination of white Western civilization will be satisfied by white workers' ascendancy to power. If not racist, such an approach is at least ethnocentric. The contrary notion of differentiated interest gains support from Foner's account of failed socialist policies and it is the missing link in Robinson's critical account of Marxism and race. It is only by incorporating this conceptual innovation in analyses of the articulation between race and class that the actual social praxis of present and past struggles by Black and white workers alike can be properly comprehended. This, in turn, is the pre-condition for any useful integration of political struggles now in the ascendant in the First and Third Worlds, thus for the realization of what has been the goal of Marxism from the beginning: authentic proletarian internationalism.

7

On Race and Class,
Or, On the Prospects of
'Rainbow Socialism'

Lucius Outlaw

To raise the issue, within the context of Marxian discourse, whether 'race' and/or 'class' are/is the most appropriate notion(s) for understanding and guiding the transformation of the historical situation of people of African descent in the USA is of course to return to a very old debate. However, the longevity of the debate, certainly its constant recurrence, signifies a complex of problems, including that of how to deal with racism in Marxist theoretical, organizational, and transformative practices.

The obvious ambiguity here is deliberate: the plurality of possible ways of reading the last statement opens onto the real, complex, and related histories of Marxist theory's attempts to account for racism in capitalist social formations, the United States in particular; onto the history of racism *in* the theorizings, on the part of the theorists; onto the history of organizational and transformative efforts to confront racism; and onto the history of racism *within* Marxist organizations and practices. These issues make clear in a particular way the relation of theory to practice and make equally evident the extent to which theorizing is a particular kind of *practice* which has to be viewed and critiqued as such.

This need is made clear whenever Marxian theoretical and organizational efforts become interracial or multi-ethnic—in terms of objectives, participants, or both—and, depending on the commitments and agendas of the theorizing and organizing, run up against limits posed by the particularities (historical, cultural, etc.) of different racial/ethnic (or gender, sexual preference, age) groups. This has often been the case in the United States, especially in recent history, since a great deal of the effort devoted to comprehending and transforming America has involved (as participants and as objects), been inspired by, and been led by people of African descent. Since the 1960s in particular, much attention has once again been devoted to trying to work through, theoretically and organizationally, the matters of race and/or class.

For many, these efforts were recently given new impetus by Jesse Jackson's Presidential campaign, which was consciously bent upon organizing a 'Rainbow Coalition', i.e., a multiracial, multi-ethnic transformative social movement within bourgeois-dominated politics.[1] I have borrowed the 'rainbow' metaphor from this campaign to use as a frame for this essay and to draw from its suggestiveness objectives for present and future emancipatory theoretical and organizational endeavours.

While the focus of this essay is the 'race and/or class' debate, the objective is to contribute to what has been termed 'Analytical Marxism': 'the systematic interrogation and clarification of basic concepts and their reconstruction into a more coherent theoretical structure'.[2] But more is involved. I offer this contribution from the context of a set of commitments that have been characterized in part as 'Left Black Nationalism'. In short, my concerns and commitments include identifying myself with the articulation (theoretical work) and realization (organizational and transformative work) of a democratic, socialist society within which peoples of African descent, along with all citizens, will enjoy viable, flourishing lives and will be able to live them *distinctively and self-consciously as people of African descent*.

These concerns and commitments are shared by other Black folk, and by many non-Black persons as well. But they are not shared universally, either by Blacks or non-Blacks, nor, certainly, by many who work from and within Marxian traditions. As Manning Marable has noted: 'Nothing has perplexed Marxists more than the issue of Black Nationalism'.[3] As the Jackson Presidential campaign became something of a rallying point for left nationalists, Marxists, and liberals of numerous racial and ethnic groups, and as it made the theory and practice of multi-racial, multi-ethnic organization for social transformation a burning issue, the enormous theoretical and organizational tasks to be accomplished in realizing the promises suggested by the rainbow metaphor (i.e., *unified* groupings of diverse peoples) had to be faced once again.

The Impasse of Classical Marxism

Are those of us who continue to work from within Marxist traditions any better prepared to resolve 'the race-class question' now than a few decades ago, or better than theorists and organizers of previous generations? Why is it that this question continues to haunt leftists' and nationalists' endeavours, and continues to impede the building of viable and lasting multiracial/multi-ethnic, Marxist leftist, and nationalist organizations?

Certainly a part of the answer is to be found in the racism and paternalism toward Blacks practiced by some persons on the left and in the racism of some Blacks as well. Equally serious, however, is the degree to which Left theory itself has been without consensus about 'the race-class question'.[4] It is this absence which blocks many Black thinkers nurturing nationalist commitments from recognizing in Marxism the instruments for sustained social struggle. Black nationalists understandably find it difficult or impossible to accept the loss of racial identity in the reductionist constructions of some class analyses. But when one reviews the histories of Marxist organizational and theoretical efforts as they relate to the situations and struggles of African-Americans and notes the consistency with which this phenomenon appears, one is led to reconstruct its theoretical and practical sources. Only then will it be possible to get on with emancipatory social reconstruction in ways that will satisfy the best interests of all peoples by preserving their racial and ethnic integrity.[5]

To the extent that there was a position on 'the Negro question' in Marxist circles, particularly after 1917, the official stand seems to have been that classes, in traditional Marxist terms, are the locus of primary contradictions in capitalist social formations; 'race' is a factor in capitalist America and becomes a device used by capitalists to manipulate and divide the working class for exploitation; however, racism will disappear with the achievement of socialism.[6] This position was to remain dominant until 1928–29, when the Communist International, influenced by Black communists and directed by Stalin's strategic imperatives, adopted the view that Blacks in America constituted a 'submerged' or 'Black belt' nation.[7] (At the time most American Blacks were concentrated in the contiguous states of the old southern Confederacy, thus the 'Black belt' designation.) The official program for Black liberation, then, mediated by the Communist Party, was support for national independence and self-determination—i.e., a separate Black nation-state (at least for the *right* to a separate nation). This was to remain the official position until 1944, when it was replaced by the 'revisionism' of Earl Browder that lasted until 1946 and his ouster and replacement by William Z. Foster. Under the latter's leadership, Black political independence was still a part of the long-range program of the Party, but separation was de-emphasized.[8] That de-emphasis has continued for the most part until the present, not only in communist organizations but in Marxist organizations generally. With the resurgence of Black nationalism during the 1960s and '70s, the debate over 'race or class' was reopened.

From this brief overview we can identify persistent strands in the debate. From the orientation of 'class-centered' Marxist groups, the nature of, and the struggle against, capitalism should be theorized, organized, and conducted without regard to race as an essential (whether historical or cultural) factor or personal identity or social life. Or at best, perhaps, the organization of distinct racial groups might be attempted or required for (temporary) tactical or strategic reasons having to do with particular situations.[8] A socialist society will have no need for the preservation of racially or ethnically distinct groups and institutions; undue regard (i.e., beyond tactical or strategic considerations) for race and/or ethnicity is chauvinistic and counter-productive in attempts to organize an international workers' struggle against capitalism.

This 'classical' position has been challenged repeatedly from a number of different vantage points. The Comintern itself, and the CPUSA in its train, promoted national independence off and on for nearly thirty years (1928–1957). Others have argued that the emphasis on organizing workers overlooks the fact that white workers and their unions are or have been racist on their own, i.e., without the provocations of capitalists. To make matters worse, there are many instances of racism on the part of communists and other socialists themselves.[10] Further, some argue that racism is a trans-class ideological and social-psychological phenomenon, or that in the context of a labor market split along racial and ethnic lines, it is the capitalists' commitment to economic expediency—not their racism—which leads to the differential treatment of blacks.[11]

Of course, the strongest critiques have come from Black nationalists who have made clear their refusal, minimally, to expose the race to the risks of white racism by joining forces with whites in organizations in which they (whites) comprise the numerical majority, or, maximally, to submerge Black racial identity in the universalism of proletarian internationalism.[12] This position was well expressed by Aimé Césaire upon his resignation from the Communist Party in 1956:

> What I demand of Marxism and Communism is that they serve the black peoples, not that the black peoples serve Marxism and Communism. Philosophies and movements must serve the people, not the people the doctrine and the movement . . . A doctrine is of value only if it is conceived by us and for us, and revised through us. . . . We consider it , our duty to make common cause with all who cherish truth and justice,

in order to form organizations able to support effectively the black peoples in their present and future struggle—their struggle for justice, for culture, for dignity, for liberty.[13]

And in the words of Robinson:

> Black radicalism is a negation of Western civilization, but not in the direct sense of a simple dialectical negation . . . Black radicalism . . . cannot be understood within the particular context of its genesis. It is not a variant of Western radicalism whose proponents happen to be Black. Rather, it is a specifically African response to an oppression emergent from the immediate determinants of European development in the modern era and framed by orders of human exploitation woven into the interstices of European social life from the inception of Western civilization . . .[14]

Why has Black nationalism in particular, and the problematic of race in general, been so difficult for Marxism? Why is it that in each generation of Marxists there are those who are convinced that a 'class analysis' of America is both necessary and sufficient to account for its racism? The answers are to be found, in large part, in the works of Marx and Engels, which provide much of the textual base for the debate. Of course, there is the much discussed problem of the underdevelopment of the notion of 'class' in the works. But more is involved, having to do with what Robinson refers to as the 'naivete of the theoretical grammar' of Marx, Engels, Lenin, and other Marxists when brought to the American context:

> It was naive because of its ahistoricity and its tendency towards the use of aggregative concepts to the point of superfluousness. Ultimately, its naivete was contradictory: at the historical point of massive immigration, the application of race and class, the grammar's two most fundamental categories, presumed the existence among the majority of American workers of a white working class; thus the eventual appearance of a Black nation suggested an opposite historical momentum.[15]

But why the 'ahistoricity' in a project of thought and praxis that sought to be historical in ways that radicalized in practice Hegel's already revolutionary view of history? The reasons, I think, are to be found elsewhere, in a form of bi-polar thinking (e.g., 'race or class?') which traces its lineage to Marx and, ultimately, in the gounding concepts of the theoretical grammar: in Marx's 'philosophical anthropology.'[16]

The locus of this bi-polar reasoning among Marxists, on my reading, is to be found in part in the dogmatic fixation on the terms of Marxian dialectical logic presented, among other places, in the conceptual schemes of *classes* and *class struggle* as definitive of social-historical conditions in capitalist social formations. Further, the focus on classes is grounded on (or at least is rationalized by) the construction of a definitive picture of human *essence* (thus a *philosophical anthropology*), articulated on the level of the *species*, as 'free, conscious, creative activity'.[17] Man, says Marx, is an animal distinguished as a species by the fact that he produces the means for his own existence, hence reproduces his life, beyond the satisfaction of immediate needs, to the satisfaction of needs he himself has created, possibly in tune to a sense of beauty, out of his own free (because, universal, as a *species being*), conscious, creative activity, within the natural environment (which is man's *inorganic* body). Even more, all of man's activity, is constitutively *social*.

It is in this development of the notion of *species being* in the early writings (1844 *Manuscripts*) that we find the philosophical-anthropological platform and moral yard-stick for the critique of capitalism. Within this ensemble of features constitutive of human existence, the reproduction of the means of existence is, for Marx, the *determining* aspect. It then follows that the means of production (the means of reproducing life) are determinative of social life, so much so that *all* of social life is conditioned by that sector of society wherein this reproductive process is structured and becomes operative. Social *classes* arise when we get the historical situation in which the social means of production come under the control of private individuals who act in concert to secure a dominant position from which they extract surplus value from those who labor to produce what is exchanged for profits; and when, on the other side, those who labor have only their labor-power to sell for wages and have only an alienated relation to the process of production, to the product, to other persons in the process, to the society as a whole, and to him/herself, i.e., to their own species being. This situation will be corrected only with the achievement of a classless society, when, that is, the working class as the embodiment and mediator of the interests of the whole of society successfully frees itself by abolishing private ownership of the means of social production and the state and organizes a society of free producers/owners who first and foremost produce and consume according to genuine need, and, beyond that, according to the dictates of creative freedom and beauty.[18]

Powerful as an instrument for the critique of capitalism, this model is nevertheless inadequate on several grounds: the deficiencies of key components of the conceptual apparatus, and the epistemological, ontological, and philosophical-anthropological strategies governing its deployment which serve as building blocks of the 'foundations' of Marxism. The difficulties bequeathed by these deficiencies are manifested in the now apparent *universalism* which infected Marx's theorizing in its unstinting commitment to a rationalist project with roots in Greek-*cum*-Western European philosophy and intellectual history generally. This tradition has continued to infect various incarnations of the legacy (albeit with less philosophical pretensions), particularly in the United States. This *universalism* is mediated throughout the analytical-theoretical corpus and 'grammar', particularly in its structuralist features: e.g., the specification of those features termed definitive of all capitalist social formations (classes, class struggles, certain relations of production, a characteristic circulatory scheme of money and its expansion, labor as the foundation of value and the nature of its exploitation, the place and role of consciousness and ideology, etc.), and the claim that with the spread of such features into other lands—the development of capitalism into a *world* system—these features would be sufficiently definitive to render relatively inconsequential the cultural and historical particularities of the peoples or nations affected. Out of this came that most problematic of matters: the proletariat as a 'universal class.'[19]

But it is not enough to know that persons are 'objectively' members of one or the other class, with all that follows from the analytical deployment of the theory to the exclusion of the positive significance of other factors of racial/ethnic identity and cultural history. The assumption is that, combined with more information about the 'laws' of capitalist society and insight into the development logic that fixes these laws (à *la* Hegel), one is then able to script a society's development and cast the various members and groups. Such presumptions have led to persons and groups appointing themselves the 'vanguard' of history, and thus the producers and directors of grand historical transformations. The arrogance derived from myopic commitments to the grammar of a binary logic, to the complementary, grounding conceptual/evaluative scheme of species being, and to the strategies of deployment of both in later works analyzing capitalism proper, have contributed more to obfuscation and misdirection than to enlightenment and successful political praxis in matters of race, ethnicity, gender, and nationalism. The continuing debate over race and class is rooted in this impasse.

New Perspectives on Race and Class

Is there a way out of this apparent dilemma? Can Marxist theory be 'improved' by bringing it into line with the lived realities of groups—Black people, in this case—hitherto not adequately dealt with when brought under its coverage? A number of persons have offered various proposals for either revising Marxian class theory or substituting for it, and others have attempted to sort through the proposals on the way to a more adequate theory. It might be well to review briefly some of these discussions.

There is no shortage of authorities prepared to condemn (or, in milder efforts, critique) Marxist theory, in whole or part, for various inadequacies when it is brought to bear on modern conditions and situations. Among the more insightful voices is that of Stanley Aronowitz who, in his *The Crisis in Historical Materialism*,[20] identifies Marxism's 'will to uniformity' as one of its major weaknesses. Aronowitz means by this Marxism's overcommitment to abstraction and the reductionism of its key categories (e.g., 'class' as a definitive category). One consequence is the inability of Marxism to theorize properly oppressed groups like Blacks and women. In his words: 'There is no theoretical space for . . . the moral economy of different groups within the reductionist assumptions of class theory. Moral and normative structures that cannot be explained by means of the categories of political economy are either ignored or denounced as diversions from "real" struggles.'[21]

Aronowitz has identified a major difficulty. To the extent that Marx and Engels (and the later inheritors of the tradition) constructed their theory in the context of a critique of capitalism and did so in service to the problems and revolutionary prospects of 'the working class', it is a serious question whether this theory can be refined without loss of identity, that is, while still remaining a critique of capitalism servicing one side of the class struggle. Two recent efforts along these lines are both interesting and promising, even in their explicit disagreements: the work of Nicos Poulantzas and Eric Olin Wright.[22] While I find their work promising, it is nevertheless instructive that *neither* deals extensively (if at all) with the problems of race and ethnicity. Wright in particular is explicit about this lacuna: 'While I do believe that the question of race is of great importance, particularly in the political context of the United States, and that it deserves sustained treatment, I have not engaged the debates over race and class sufficiently to discuss the relevance of the class framework proposed here for the problem of race.[23] The 'promise' of the work of both Wright and Poulantzas lies in their reconstruction of the Marxist theory of class within an explicitly meta-theoretical project that opens space for what Aronowitz terms the 'moral economy' of racial/ethnic (and other) oppressed groups.

For Poulantzas, classes are constituted by a *structural* (position in the process of production; relations of production) and *relational* (that is, ideological and political) ensemble, and thus are grounded in a historically specific conjuncture of a social formation and a dominant mode of production. This constitutes the 'objective' nature of classes, their 'structural determination'. But this structual determination is different from the *position* of a class, i.e., its concrete situation in class struggle in the historicity of a particular social formation. Here political and ideological relations are constitutive and, along with differentiations within the relations of production, define the subgroupings of classes into different 'factions', 'strata', and 'social categories' although the relations of production continue to play the dominate role in all of this.[24] Further, within the social division of labor there are other 'specific articulations' such as the sexual division and, we might add, racial/ethnic divisions.[25]

What is the promise in the brief sketch? It lies, I think, in the opening provided by Poulantzas towards understanding racial/ethnic oppression as a set of invidious practices and relations that have their foundation in ideological and political commitments and relations. These play a principal role in the constitution of class fractions or strata that determine the ensemble of value and interest orientations and concrete practices that we call *racism*. The latter is thus well accommodated *within* class theory in a way that is neither *ad hoc* nor reductionist.[26] To that important extent, adequate space is made available in (reconstructed) class theory for recognizing and preserving the integrity of Black nationalists' commitments relative to racial/ethnic identity in particular and to Black life-worlds in general. Erik Olin Wright's work is promising for similar reasons. He is involved in a sustained effort to reconstruct Marxian class theory in part through concept transformation stimulated by what he terms 'empirical' conditions: that is, the identification of problems that are 'not adequately mapped' by prevailing concept specifications.[27] (For Wright the problem derives from the inadequacy of the concept of 'class structure' for mapping 'middle classes' in contemporary America.)

At the heart of Marxian class theory, Wright identifies two 'clusters of explanatory claims' for the concept of class: 'one revolving around the inter-connections among class structure, class formation, class consciousness and class struggle, and a second revolving around the relationship between class and the epochal transformation of societies.'[28] Of particular relevance to this discussion is the first of several 'conceptual constraints' identified by Wright which help to shape the explanatory agenda of much of Marxian class theory: 'Class structure imposes limits on class formation, class consciousness and class struggle.' Class structure is therefore the 'basic determinant' of the other three.[29] Wright's promising opening in his critical reconstruction culminates in the following:

> The claim that class structure limits class consciousness and class formation is not equivalent to the claim that it alone determines them. Other mechanisms (race, ethnicity, gender, legal institutions, etc.) operate within the limits established by the class structure, and it could well be the case that the *politically* significant explanations for variations in class formation or consciousness are embedded in these non-class mechanisms rather than in the class structure itself... What is argued... is that these non-class mechanisms operate with limits imposed by the class structure itself.[30]

The critical question, of course, is whether this opening is sufficient to contribute to a reconstructed *Marxist* theory of exploitation and oppression in particular social formations that are striated by class *and* racial/ethnic (gender, etc.) divisions—a theory, however, that does not presuppose or require that racial/ethnic identity, its socially constructed reality, be forever transcended with the realization of a *classless* society.

Other thinkers on the left have offered extensions and/or refinements to Marxian theory that involve explicit discussions of the race/ethnic-class problematic. Edna Bonacich, in 'Class Approaches to Ethnicity and Race', discusses a number of models (nation building, super-exploitation, split labor-market, middleman minorities), critically examining the explanatory force of each.[31] Of interest are her discussions of notions of *people*-class, *eth*-class, and *nation*-class proposed by various thinkers. One of these is James A. Geschwender, who has contributed significantly to the race-class debate, particularly in his *Racial Stratification in America*.[32] Of particular note in this work is the discussion of the 'internal colonial/submerged nation' perspective. The latter (submerged nation), as noted, was promoted by the Comintern/CPUSA. The 'internal colony' model emerged during the 1950s and 1960s and shares with the classical model the view of Black exploitation as a feature of capitalism, but stresses white domination and the need for independance as a key feature of Black liberation and views *indirect rule* (i.e., neo-colonialism) as a key feature of the contemporary oppression of Blacks.[33] Of signal theoretical importance here is Geschwender's proposed 'internal colonial-class' model, one that seeks to build on what he terms the 'valuable features' of both the class (or capitalist exploitation) and internal colonial models:

> Each describes a portion of reality and provides valuable insights regarding the American system of racial stratification. Neither is sufficiently general to subsume the other. Therefore it is necessary to select elements from each of the two models to develop a comprehensive model with utility for the analysis of racial stratification in America. Black Americans are a people who have been proletarianized and who, for the most part, are currently members of the proletariat. They experience exploitation as blacks. The black community is differentiated by class. The two dimensions interact. Most blacks comprise a marginal or subproletariat. The differential position of blacks within the proletariat may be more compatible with the internal colonial than with the class model.[34]

Going further, Geschwender notes that 'all Blacks experience oppression as Blacks', a fact which makes for common interests that unite us in opposition to whites, whatever their class. Thus, relative to Blacks, the two dimensions of class and nation 'intersect' to make the *nation class*, 'a social collectivity comprised of persons who are simultaneously members of the same class and the same race', a grouping that has 'the maximum combination of shared interests'. This, and not economic class alone, is the 'natural unit' for both social analysis and political action.[35]

Geschwender's contribution involves yet another theoretical advance: to wit, his understanding of the *limits* of theory *vis a vis* the lived experiences of real people. Elaborating upon the notion of nation-class, he notes: 'this merely provides the starting point for a structural analysis . . . participation in any change-oriented move-ment is not strictly determined by objective analysis. Subjective states such as class or national consciousness are extremely important. Objective reality does not entirely determine the manner in which consciousness is formed.'[36] This openness to the 'subjective side' of human existence is crucial, for as he notes, ethnicity (and race, we should add) is still important to the formation and maintenance of personal and group identity, in addition to serving others as markers for invidious discrimination and oppression. The nation-class concept preserves space within Marxist theorizing for respectful recognition of racial/ethnic identity in its integrity as a key feature of a people's life-world.

Finally, yet another valuable contribution to the race-class discussion by Geschwender is the insight that the application of a particular model in the effort to understand Black existence in America *must* take proper note of historical conditions. Viewing African-Americans as a 'submerged nation' is most accurate for the periods of enslavement (from the initiation of enslavement to 'emancipation' in 1865) and the creation of a nominally free peasantry (1865–1910, when Blacks were transformed from slaves into agricultural workers under the system of share-tenancy, a period that also involved an increased number of whites in a similar position and led to the development of an interracial class movement which was subsequently destroyed by the exploitation of racial differences).[37] The 'nation-class' model, by contrast, is most appropriate for the period extending from the beginning of Black proletarianization (1910–1940)—when World War I halted massive European immigration, stimulated industry, and created opportunities for Blacks that became the pull for migration to Northern (and Southern) cities[38]—to the completion of the transformation of Blacks into an urban proletariat (World War II to the present).

The Black Nationalist Tradition

What have we gained from the preceding recapitulations and discussions of the promises of theoretical reconstructions? What is the relevance of these theoretical programs to the 'rainbow' project? The chances of our realizing the promises of 'rainbow socialism' are heavily conditioned by our being able to resolve the theoretical—and thus practical—difficulties bequeathed us by Marxian traditions. Marxism has historically failed to comprehend the realities of the *Africanity* of African-Americans as a constitutive, indeed *irreducible* dimension of the reality of our lives under capitalism, a dimension rooted in our forced relocations and thus the constitution of the African diaspora. Black nationalist traditions have been the keepers of this Africanity. And the continuing contributions of a long line of Black left-nationalists (including, for example, C.L.R. James, Eric Williams, James Boggs, Amilca Cabral, Julius Nyerere, Angela Davis, Cornel West, Manning Marable, Adolph Reed, Jr., and Robert Allen) to the effort to transform Marxist theory are crucial. This discussion has been aimed at identifying possible spaces opened by the theoretical work of a number of *non-Black* thinkers whose work might in turn open the way to revisions of Marxist theory that will make it more accommodating to properly tempered Black nationalist agendas in the context of democratic, multi-racial, multi-ethnic socialist theoretical practices.

In my view, race and ethnicity (and gender as well) are constitutive of the personal and social being of persons, and are not secondary, inessential matters. These factors have both absolute and relative (i.e., in relation to other racial, ethnic, gender groups) value to the extent that, and for as long as, persons take them to be constitutive of who they are. A theory of society that sets itself the task of understanding, scripting, and producing (that is, guiding the realization of) revolutionary social transformation while disregarding these basic 'social facts' is, in my judgment, seriously deficient and would be guilty, if it focused only on 'classes', of at best *ad hoc*, tactical, and often condescending and paternalistic sops to race, ethnicity, and gender.[39]

What I wish and work for is the preservation of the diversity of human social practices in a democratic socialist society. African peoples have *always* been a sticking point in the Marxian legacy. Neither the full nature and extent of our oppression, nor our historical-cultural being as Africans has been adequately comprehended by the concepts and logic involved in the Marxist analysis of capitalist social formations. In part this has been a function of the subtle but pervasive racism mediated in the Marx(ist) voice(s) that narrated periods of the histories of particular European peoples as though, on one hand, they were the histories of *all* peoples, and, on the other, as though Hegel had in fact provided the definitive word on Africans: a people without history because a people not yet sufficiently developed to be makers of history. In part this deficit was a function of the failure to deal with the heterogeneity of the populations of European centers of the rise of capitalism,[40] in part a failure to deal with racism as an indigenous element of European history and culture.[41] These failures were both institutionalized and compounded in the construction of the false universality that infected key concepts and strategies of the analysis.

In the United States, the practical manifestations of these deficiencies were seen in the ways in which Marxist organizations tried to deal—or elected not to deal—with Black people as a particular oppressed group, and with Black organizations devoted to ameliorating or eliminating the conditions of our oppression.[42] Where they elected to deal with people of African descent, the general posture was to regard us as simply a component of the working class, its 'super-exploited' segment.

For many years, however, socialist and communist organizations actively disregarded Black people. These shortcomings have their source in the racism and paternalism of many of the socialists and communists involved at the time,[43] and in the failures of Marxist theory, except for a brief moment, to appreciate the *national* integrity of Black peoples (or of any people, for that matter).[44] Our racial, historical, multi-cultural particularity is our *Africanity*. And it is out of this *Africanity* that those traditions of Black radicalism which have been most sensitive to—and explicit mediators of—our national character have emerged.

The history of Black nationalism is not without its failures and shortcomings, nor, in some of its manifestations, its racism and chauvinism. What I continue to contend, however, is that it is the better, more critically determined 'progressive' moments and forms of this tradition that mediate our best interests as *African* people and that *should* be at the center of concerns articulated during any systematic efforts to fashion organizations and programs, strategies and tactics, for the transformation of the American social order into something we would find more emancipatory and life-enhancing.

Rainbow Socialism?

But can this articulation, organizational formation, and strategic implementation all take place in a context conditioned by the exploration of difference, by an explicit valorization of differences, as part of an agenda to fashion and realize the 'rainbow' project? There is the danger, of course, that we could well flounder on our differences and thus recapitulate the situation of the Democratic Party: i.e., become a confusion of particularistic 'interest groups' without any unifying principles that bind us into a real, living community. Pernicious racism, paternalism, and theoretical limit-ations were not the only factors conditioning early socialism's orientation to the particularities of various groups.[45] We might well become another Tower of Babel.[46]

This danger is real enough, but it cannot be removed by a theoretical fiat. It is a danger concomitant with existential realities that should not be bleached out by ahistorical, universalist categories intended to secure us against possible fragmentation. The new society must be won in the struggle to realize it. The excursion through a 'rainbow' of differences involves, potentially, more than a concern on the part of people of African descent (and women, Ameri-Indians, Hispanics, Asians, gays, etc.) to tell our own stories and, in doing so, to re-affirm ourselves. The important point is *why* the histories and cultures—the modalities of being the life-worlds—are meaningful and important, *why* they have an integrity worth preserving and struggling for while subjecting them to progressive refinement. The challenge they pose is to the Marxian legacy we have inherited, and to socialism as its ideal. This challenge is to take on *democratic* socialism as an ideal and as a concrete, real possibility that can be made actual through praxes, shared in by all of us 'different' folks, involving commitments to a possible future in which we maintain our own integrity without encroaching on the integrity and well-being of others.

The issue, in its theoretical, practical, and *existential* reality, is whether there is sufficient commonality in our sufferings and our hopes, in the modes and sources of our oppressions and in the requirements for a social order that would eliminate them, to allow our coming together and forging a concrete universal, a unity in diversity. If so, then we must move from theory to praxis by moving from univeral conceptual strategies to universality in the form of democratically-based existential projects *in our theorizing and in our practical action*. The stress is on 'project', that is, on constant practical efforts constantly reconciled by the renewed recognition that no amount of 'knowing' or 'critical thought' secures the laws, meaningfulness, and trajectory of human history. Rather, it is a constant 'doing' that is constituted in the very micro-cells of daily existence and is structured by the powerfully binding forces of race, ethnicity, nationality, gender, and sexuality as mediated and mediating elements of cultural historicity. It is my sense, my hope, that this is the genuine promise of 'rainbow socialism', and that the motivation for struggling to realize it comes in part from a recognition and acceptance of the tasks we left-leaning keepers of sometimes conflicting racial, ethnic, gender, sexual, and national legacies have been bequeathed by our shared and different histories, as well as by our commitments to a truly revolutionary, if as yet incomplete, Marxist legacy.

SECTION TWO
The Culture of Color

8

Chained to Devilpictures: Cinema and Black Liberation in the Sixties

David E. James

> *... mourn for us soldout and chained to devilpictures.*
> (Amiri Baraka)

The integral role of Black arts in the cultural and national identity that nourished the civil rights and Black Power movements can hardly be overestimated. Although in instances like post-Coltrane jazz, the popular and indeed revolutionary aspirations of the most avant-garde artists may have outstripped their social base,[1] Black dance, theater, writing and music combined aesthetic and political vanguardism in cultural practices whose origins in popular traditions were reciprocated by their availability for popular use. Distinguishing Black art from that of other groups, the similarities and frequent interdependencies between achievements in these different mediums made possible the definition of a specifically Black aesthetic, even as the clarification of the African origins of Afro-American culture made available pragmatic conceptions of art of the kind that have been suppressed by idealist aesthetics in the West since culture became commodified.

The Black aesthetics of the late sixties transcend the split within the Black movement between cultural nationalism and the material-ist understanding of the situation of racial minorities within capitalist social formations. They were radical, not because they invoked ironic inversions, stylistic switches indetectable from the outside, subversive adaptations of hegemonic forms or other formal qualities that reflected ghetto life (although they certainly pre-supposed these), but because they stressed a populist functionalism:

> Tradition teaches us, Leopold Senghor tells us, that all African art has at least three characteristics: that is, it is functional, collective and committing or committed. . . . And by no mere coincidence we find that the criteria is not only valid, but inspiring. That is why we say that all Black art, irregardless of any technical requirements, must have three basic characteristics which make it revolutionary. In brief, it must be functional, collective and committing . . . Black art must expose the enemy, praise the people and support the revolution. (Karenga, 1972:32)

Given the privileged position the cinema has occupied in pragmatic aesthetics since Lenin, a large investment in the cinema by Black artists during the sixties and the development of film as a Black art, one capable of participating in the creation of a revolutionary Black subject committed to political struggle, would not have been illogical. But apart from one or two notable exceptions, film played a marginal role in the Black movement, and if anything the sixties marked the culmination of a decline in the Black cinema, whether it be defined rigorously in terms of Black control over all stages in production, or more generally as any measurable degree of Black participation or responsiveness to Black needs.[2] The failure of Black people to develop a film practice responsive to their political needs directly reflects the intrinsic conditions of the medium and its hegemonic use, and does so in a way that makes that failure exemplary for a materialist understanding of film and of minority cultural interventions generally.

On the one hand, the double integration of the dominant film industry summarized as 'Hollywood' into the institutions of the capitalist state—the contribution of its narrative and formal codes to bourgeois ideological reproduction and its own economic determination as itself a capitalist enterprise—allowed only one role for the proletariat, that of consumer. Defining and setting the limits to film's ideological work, the industrial function ensured that the lack of representation of Blacks in the film industry would be reciprocated by their absence from the screen itself; the imprisonment of Black people as consumers of commodity film culture reproduced their imprisonment in the proletariat.

On the other hand, traditional Black cultural practices were both outside the institutions of cinema and also, characteristically, antipathetic to the conditions of film. As Amiri Baraka pointed out, only those non-material aspects of African culture, 'music, dance, religion [that] do not have *artifacts* as their end product' (1963: 16),[3] survived the diaspora and slavery. When, as with popular song, these performing arts entered into industrial production, Blacks did not successfully engage technology, and their general unfamiliarity of film technology and its inimicality to their cultural traditions[4] reinforced the general difficulty the proletariat as a whole has had in obtaining access to the means of industrial commodity production. For Blacks, it is especially difficult to break through that fetishization of advanced technology by which Hollywood maintains its domination over film production and distribution. While it would not have been impossible for Black filmmakers to inflect an avant garde practice of their own with Black motifs or qualities, and so to inscribe blackness as a filmic function (as indeed the underground so often had done, and as Bill Gunn did to some extent with the anomalous *Ganja and Hess* in 1970), to make such an endeavor the focus or vehicle of popular resistance would have meant retreading the Beats' attempts to wrest a community practice out of industrial functions, but at a time of great political urgency and without the resources of a subculture in which film was the privileged medium or in which independent distribution was feasible.

Reformism and Cinematic Realism

Increased Black enrollment in higher education in the seventies did, however, give rise to an ongoing independent Black cinema in university and semi-academic milieux. The work of Haille Gerima (*Bush Mama*, 1975), Larry Clark (*Passing Through*, 1977), Charles Burnett (*Killer of Sheep*, 1977), Ben Caldwell (*I and I: An African Allegory*, 1977) and Julie Dash (*Four Women*), produced by graduates of the UCLA film school, typifies the independent momentum and social responsibility attained by what was initially an artifically-nursed practice. Ironically, the increased enrollment of Black students in film schools that generated this alternative film culture itself followed from the same liberal thrust that had destroyed the only previous instance of a genuinely Black cinema. The liberal commitment to integration that continued the anti-racist rhetoric of the World War II era produced an increase in the visibility and participation of Black people in the industry; and an industrial genre of Black problem pictures from *A Raisin in the Sun* and *To Kill A Mockingbird* (both 1963) to *Guess Who's Coming to Dinner* (1967) preached a reform of race relations on a personal, if not a systemic, basis. But the gains made by the NAACP and through government pressure in bringing Blacks into the mainstream destroyed what before the war had been a sizeable Black feature industry which, although invariably white-financed, was still Black-controlled and in some cases entirely Black-operated for the exclusive patronage of Black people.[5] With the failure of independent Black production companies after the thirties, subsequent Black cinema was white-funded and almost entirely white-written and white-directed. In this latter cinema two groups, corresponding to the liberal integrationist and the radical separatist phases of the Black movement, may be distinguished.

The first, developing from the social intersections between Beat subcultures and Black bohemianism, from attempts by the underground to model film practices on jazz,[6] and from the reformist intellectual milieu of the New American Cinema Group, is best illustrated by Shirley Clarke's *The Cool World* and Robert Young's and Michael Roemer's *Nothing But A Man*, both of 1964. The sensitivity and courage of these new-realist dramatizations of Black life, in the urban north and the rural south respectively, exhibit the best of the liberal hope to change social conditions through knowledge and good will. Clarke's use of *cinéma vérité* strategies— hand held camera, cut-away shots to details of the environment, rapid and unpredictable editing—for what is mostly a staged drama, allows her to texture her story of a Harlem teenager's fall into crime with both the energy and the aimlessness of slum life. Young and Roemer's more extended narrative, detailing the attempt of a Black laborer to maintain his young bride and their household in the face of opposition from her middle-class parents, the pull of a rootless and irresponsible bachelorhood, and especially a racist society which will allow him financial stability only at the cost of his self-respect, is similarly unsentimental and largely free from studio stereotypes. Both films represent the claustrophobic restrictions that hem in the Black community, the lack of social opportunity for people trapped in the ghetto, as well as the psychic damage these conditions inflict. In this, they do create a sense of the Black world; and appropriately in both, although especially in *Nothing But A Man*, the dominant social forms appear as a suffocating horizon peopled by gargoyle caricatures.

Yet despite their real achievements, both films remain refinements, however subtle and courageous, of the problem films of the late fifties,[7] their formal limits marking the limits of their liberal ideology. They strain industrial representational and narrative codes, but they cannot pass beyond them any more than they can conceive of alternatives to humanist appeals to the social plight of the Black people they present as sensitive and courageous but essentially impotent and condemned. They cannot envisage structural social change any more than they can envisage the transcendence of the illusionist narrative film. The importance for the civil rights legislation of the mid-sixties (the Civil Rights Bill of 1964 and the Voting Rights Act of 1965) of the liberal social currents from which these films emerged cannot be overestimated; but the year after their appearance, riots in Los Angeles, New York and Newark, combined with the assassination of Malcolm X, revealed a social urgency to which they could not speak.

Documentary Radicalism

With the failure of reform to keep pace with the explosion of desire after 1964, integrationist demands and non-violence gave way to the nationalist aspirations of SNCC and Stokely Carmichael and the anti-racialist, revolutionary program of the Black Panther Party. As liberal reformism was left behind, films like *The Cool World* or *Nothing But A Man* were no longer ideologically or formally possible. Increasingly militant action demanded the speedy circulation and mass accessibility of the newsreel documentary. But like the Black community at large, the Black Power leaders had neither experience in filmmaking nor access to means of production and distribution. So, continuing a tradition that began with *Troublemakers* (1966), Robert Machover's film about community organizing in the Newark ghetto, radical Black films in the era of the assassination of Martin Luther King, the publication of *Soul on Ice* and riots throughout the country were made by radical white filmmakers.

Exemplary was the collaboration of San Fransisco Newsreel with the Oakland Black Panther Party on three films (*Black Power*, 1968; *MayDay*, 1969; and *Interview With Bobby Seale*, 1969); the Los Angeles Newsreel's (finally aborted) project, *Breakfast For Children*; Third World Newsreel's early seventies films about Black prisoners (*Teach Our Children*, 1973; and *In the Event Anyone Disappears*, 1974); and various ad hoc productions of a similar documentary/agitational nature, like Leonard Henney's *Black Power, We're Goin' Survive America* and the collaboration of Stewart Bird and Peter Gessner with the League of Black Revolutionary Workers that produced *Finally Got the News*. Making such films typically proved educational for white filmmakers. The first instance radicalized San Francisco Newsreel and turned them away from the counter-culture towards Marxist-Leninism, while the integration of Third World Newsreel within the proletariat approached the conditions of a truly popular practice. Of the films made by white radicals in co-operation with the Panthers, at this time, the most substantial were *The Black Panthers: A Report* (1968), Agnes Varda's documentary of Black Protest during the imprisonment and trial of Huey Newton on a charge of murdering an

Oakland policeman, and *The Murder of Fred Hampton* (1971), Mike Gray Associates' documentary on the Chicago Panthers, focused on the infamous murders committed by the Cook County Sheriff and his deputies.

Both films attempt to explain and vindicate the Panthers and, apart from a single voice-over by Varda noting that the Panthers want Newton freed 'without even raising the question of his possible guilt', both are entirely devoid of qualification or assessment of the justice of the Panthers' cause, of the correctness of their methods, or of the police program to eradicate them. This is not to say that either film emerges directly from the processes of Panther political activity or that either allows an absolutely unmediated transmission of the Panthers' own discourse. Despite Varda's sympathy, locutions like her claim that Stokely Carmichael is 'the leader of all Afro-Americans', in addition to its patent inaccuracy, ring with a cultural unfamiliarity that elsewhere—in an awkward interviewing technique, a touristic lingering on an item of dress or mannerism—tends to reify Black people, imaging them as the exotic natives of an ethnographic documentary. While the makers of *Fred Hampton* are socially and ideologically closer to the Panthers, the film's poor sound quality, its grainy images and its generally low production values interpose a scrim between the Panthers and their audience—although this impediment can translate into a suggestion of financial exigency that reciprocates the Panthers' own economic marginality. But these interventions are minor. By and large both films are successful attempts by white radicals to make themselves, their skills and their access to the apparatus the vehicle for a discourse that is essentially the Panthers' own; they are the means by which the Panthers can be mediated into alternative cinema or allowed that voice in the media at large which by themselves they were unable to secure. Since the audiences for these films were comprised of immediately adjacent groups in the Black community, white American radicals and third world sympathizers generally, and were therefore predisposed to be sympathetic, the filmmakers' task was as far as possible to allow the Panthers to speak for themselves. Thus their speeches—at rallies, in conversation amongst themselves and also in direct address to the camera— make up the bulk of the films, supplying both their ideological stance and their formal organization.

In *The Black Panthers*, an interview with Newton in jail supplies a center of authority from which radiate the other ratifying discourses of Eldridge Cleaver and Stokely Carmichael at a rally in Newton's support, of lesser known figures from the Oakland community, of more or less casual presences at the rally, and finally of Varda herself. In support of these mutually corroborating speeches, the film produces illustrative images. For example, the recitation of the 10 Point Plan, almost a generic convention of Panther films which, as in Newsreel's *Black Panther*, is usually simply inserted while the camera tours the ghetto streets, is here formally integrated. At the 'Free Huey' rally on which the film concentrates, Bill Brent, a captain in the party from Oakland, introduces himself. This provides the motive for a survey of Oakland with voice-over information about its size and population, the nature of its police force, and the formation of the Panthers up to the time of Newton's arrest. Then, returning to the rally, the camera allows Brent to give the details of Newton's incarceration before a cutaway to a jail interview with Newton himself. Among his remarks is a list of the reading material which the prison officials have intercepted, and when he mentions Mao's writings, a series of cutaways reveals young people at the rally reading the Little Red Book. Back in the cell Newton describes some of the features of the Party: that it follows a Marxist-Leninist program, and that its members are practical revolutionaries who identify with the armed struggle of colonized people throughout the world. Next, the film returns again to the rally for a speech by Stokely Carmichael about the war being waged upon Blacks in the USA. The camera picks out Brent in the crowd and, at appropriate points as he recites the 10 Point Plan, community people extend his references: a young woman discusses the demand for education; several young men talk about draft resistance when Brent mentions exemption for Blacks; and when he demands the release of all Blacks in jails, the camera returns to Newton's cell. In addition to providing the editorial logic for a densely textured and thematically coherent film, this constant interweaving of many voices, each explaining the Panther position with illustrative and corroborative material from their constituency, produces an effect of ideological consistency. The Panther spokes-people are seen to speak with the voice of the community, accurately representing their interests. Conversely, the community is seen as deriving its own self-consciousness from the Panthers' analysis.

With almost no voice-over narration, *Fred Hampton* is constructed from inter-Panther dialogue and direct address by Panthers, and admits non-Panther discourse only to discredit it. The first part is built up around situations inside the Black community—speeches at rallies, meetings between Panthers and representatives of other groups, visits to a Panther breakfast program and a community medical centre—but after this community is violated by the murders of Hampton and Clark, the diegesis is similarly penetrated by the mendacious discourse of the establishment. The press conferences held by State's Attorney Edward B. Hanrahan, the accounts of the shootout in the *Chicago Tribune* and the inconsistent accounts of the police officers involved are all as much in conflict with themselves as with the evidence the Panthers produce. The ease with which the Panthers prove their propositions about the state's intentions verifies their argument about the State's attitude towards Black people in general, demonstrates the accuracy of their social analysis and so justifies Hampton's own exhortations that his audience 'live for the people . . . struggle for the people . . . die for the people'.

While one liberates Huey Newton's discourse from incarceration, and the other redeems Fred Hampton's from the murderers' guns, neither film can be faulted for infidelity to the Panther position. By making that position their own, they gave it a public dissemination wider than the limited circulation of the Panthers' public speeches and the *Black Panther* newspaper, and more honest and sympathetic than the sensationalistic, exploitative version of the Panthers cooked up by the establishment media. Where these films nonetheless become problematic—providing the ground for their unpopularity on the left and within sectors of the Black community[8]—is in their failure to confront the contradictions of the Panthers' position, especially as they were duplicated and exaggerated in the volatilized and reified Panther image constructed by the mass media.

While the Panthers' class analysis of the situation of Blacks and their identification of the Black struggle with third world liberation was superior to rival analyses by cultural nationalists and liberal integrationists, their assumption of a Leninist vanguard role and their decision to militarize resistance to the state finally destroyed them. Whether or not American Blacks were (and are) a colonized society, they manifestly lacked the resources of the Vietnamese or the Algerians, and thus they could scarcely expect to throw off the *colon* with Vietnamese or Algerian methods. Similarly, media promulgation of the image of the Panther and urban guerrilla, quite eclipsing any notice of the breakfast and education programs, only ensured that the Panthers' most adventurist gestures were brought to public attention with no accompanying sense of their legitimate grievances and demands. So while the various African revivals, the leather jackets and the dark glasses and all the other accoutrements of the outlaw uniform distinguished Panther militancy from the intergrationist programs of the civil rights period and stimulated recruitment by providing an alternative role model to the self-deprecation that Fanon and Freire diagnosed as the essential mechanism of oppression, the audacity of the imagery was not backed up by any means for achieving political power. The Panthers' para-military posture simply polarized public response to the point where the white community's fear, the media's demonizing, and the knee-jerk paranoia of the state permitted a systematic, extra-legal police offensive against them.

As with Fred Hampton's prediction that he wouldn't die by slipping on a piece of ice but in the service of the people, the aggression and paranoia of the Panthers' rhetoric could only be justified by the destruction of its speakers. Both films appropriately emphasize the fury that the police reserved for *images* of the Panthers. Varda's for example, ends with a shot of the Panthers' devastated Oakland headquarters, dwelling on posters of Newton riddled by police bullets. But neither film is capable of critical attention to the deleterious social and political effects of those images, nor of self-critical attention to their own disseminative role. In their inability to deal with the disparity between claims of the Panthers' image and their actual political potential, *The Black Panthers: A Report* and *The Murder of Fred Hampton* participate in the Panthers' own errors; by contributing to the spectacularization of the Panthers, they contributed to their destruction.

The failure of these films to negotiate the contradictions in such highly politicized representation is all the more striking since it prefigures parallel ambiguities in an industrial genre that exploited a debased form of Black militancy to pre-empt the vacant space of a genuinely Black cinema: blaxploitation.

Blaxploitation Films and the Picaresque Hero

The financial success of Ossie Davis' *Cotton Comes to Harlem* (1970) spawned a plethora of generic remakes aimed specifically at the Black market. Of these genres—the western (Sidney Poitier's *Buck and the Preacher*, 1972) or the musical (*Lady Sings the Blues*, 1972), for example—the most successful was the gangster movie. The new film noir featured a Black hero as urban outlaw, usually a drug-dealing pimp, pitted against the mafia and a corrupt white police force, while its sister-genre typically constructed an equally-powerful heroine who, ironically, took an equally-ferocious vengeance on the ghetto drug-pushers. *Shaft* (1971), *Shaft's Big Score* (1972), *Shaft in Africa* (1973), *Slaughter* (1972), *Slaughter's Big Rip-Off* (1973), *Superfly* (1972), *Superfly T.N.T.* (1973), *Across 110th Street* (1972), *The Mack* (1973), *Trick Baby* (1973) and *Trick Turner* (1974) along with *Coffy* (1973), *Cleopatra Jones* and *Foxy Brown*

(1974)—these are fairly representative of the two variants. Although initially such films were produced independently by Blacks,
they were always studio distributed. As the genre proved its
financial viability, the studios took control. *Superfly*, for instance,
was independently written and financed by Blacks, with Warner
Brothers purchasing it for distribution, but the sequel was produced
inside the studio (Mason, 1972:62). While the fourteen examples
mentioned above all featured Black stars and extensive Black casts,
ten were white-written, white-produced and white-directed. Only
Gordon Parks' direction of the two *Shaft* films and the first *Superfly*,
and Ron Neale's direction of the second *Superfly* interrupt the
close-out (Klotman, 1979:passim).

Blaxploitation did provide the Black proletariat with something
no previous film had: a hero from the community who is resourceful
and powerful enough to take on and defeat its predators. But the
utility of that image was compromised and almost entirely
countered by the displacement of attention away from the properly
political analyses of the situation of Black people and from the
possibilities of ameliorating it by systemic social change. By
focusing the problems of the ghetto exclusively on local criminal
issues, blaxploitation spoke directly to the everyday experience of its
audience; but its generic conventions—the redress of wrong by the
superhero vigilante rather than by community control; the portrayal
of corruption as a police or mafia aberration rather than as endemic
and structural; the backhanded glorification of heavy drugs,
prostitution and other forms of self-destruction that sublimated
resentment rather than channelling it in socially useful directions;
and a chauvinist, macho anti-intellectualism—allowed for a vicarious
release of anger in ways that threatened the power and prejudice of
neither the state nor its local institutions. Accordingly, the
politically regressive instrumentality of blaxploitation films for the
bourgeois state was widely recognized in both the popular Black
press (e.g. Mason, 1972) and radical film journals (e.g. Washington
and Berlowitz, 1975).

While the majority of these films were entirely cynical formula
productions, some remain of interest, either because like *Across
110th Street* they take the conventions to such hyperbolic extremes
that they subvert the genre's mechanism of gratification, or because
like Melvin Van Peebles' *Sweet Sweetback's Baadasssss Song* they
struggle against the limitations of the genre strongly enough to
rupture its ideological closures. *Sweetback* is especially illuminating
because in the trials of its hero it dramatized the tensions between
the genre's need to de-politicize the Black condition and Van
Peebles' own political commitment, a tension that recurs on the

formal level in his attempts to use strategies developed in the underground to force the industrial vocabulary of blaxploitation towards a more authentically Black dialect. Thus *Sweetback* finally argues for itself a meta-generic meditation on the difficulty of the Hollywood film being made over into a genuinely Black cinema.

In *Sweetback* Van Peebles retains the full roster of generic motifs—'a detailed and graphic social anatomy of the black underworld that established credibility; a carefully segregated point of view, which unfortunately misfired because no white character was allowed a shred of humanity; a set of symbols and gestures that bore a great freight of outlaw meaning; and a ritual of mayhem that almost orgasmically released upon the film audience the picaresque urban outlaw as a mythic black redeemer' (Cripps:133-34)—almost to the point of caricature, making Sweetback himself a professional stud for example. But Van Peebles also attempts to bring these conventions into focus with the politics of Black liberation. In distinct contrast to the suppression of political self-conciousness (*Superfly*'s ridicule of political activists is typical) demanded by the entertainment industry, *Sweetback* recognizes Black Power and makes Sweetback's response to it the motive of his actions and the condition of his heroism. The implications of the opening scenes, where Sweetback is transformed from a child into a man and then from a woman into a man, are completed by the police attack on the radical, Moo Moo. That attack awakens Sweetback from his social passivity; when he defends Moo Moo, he acquires speech for the first time in the film, whose night shortly thereafter gives way to day. Free from his profession as a sexual spectacle and liberated into his role as outlaw, he jeopardizes his life for Moo Moo. Sweetback's recognition that his people's future lies with the young radical is endorsed by the representative of the Black church, who applauds him for having saved the young bud that the police would have picked off; and as Moo Moo's protector and probable heir (for the film's ending suggests that after recovering his strength in Mexico, he will return), Sweetback receives the support of the Black community and the assistance of other racial and sexual minorities.

It is on the basis of such a reading that Huey Newton was to declare *Sweetback* 'the first truly revolutionary Black film made' (Newton, 1972:113), and Sweetback himself 'a beautiful exempli-fication of Black Power' (139), a position which, while it overstates the case, is not without some justification.[9] But although the logic of the narrative does allow such a reading, the implications of the *bildungsroman* narrative in which the hero grows from the renegade stud of blaxploitation to the militant of the documentary tradition, the use of the latter role model as a comment on the former and even the suggestion that Sweetback's sexual potency carries the stigma of his political impotence, cannot be fully elaborated through the available register of narrative motifs. Sweetback cannot finally transcend his blaxploitation machismo; nor can Moo Moo, despite the terroristic pretensions of his name, be more than a cypher. Without charisma or initiative, he provides no politically useful role model, his absolute dependence on Sweetback undermining all the assertions of his primacy. Incapable of appropriating film presence, he is incapable of asserting his priority in aesthetic or political terms.

These thematic tensions, whereby *Sweetback* undermines the militancy it would valorize and falls back into the generic codes from which it would distinguish itself, recur in Van Peebles' attempts to expand the formal vocabulary of the commercial feature. The general absence of shot/reverse-shot patterns and other standard tropes, the often ungrammatical lighting patterns and the grainy image that follow from the low production budget, by and large harmonize with the decrepit urban slums, reinforcing their decay rather than producing distance. In this, as in many of its motifs, *Sweetback* recalls contemporary independent feature productions, especially Roger Corman's biker and soft-core exploitation films, but goes well beyond these in its assertion of authorship. Independently produced by Van Peebles (although perhaps with completion funds from Bill Cosby [Cripps, 1978:132]), it was also written, directed, edited and scored by him, as well as starring him in the title role. This insistence on personal vision links it with the underground in terms of its auteurist control over all stages of its production, and with the trance film, especially in terms of its structure.

Like the picaresque heroes of Curtis Harrington's *Fragments of a Seeking*, Kenneth Anger's *Fireworks*, or Stan Brakhage's *Reflections On Black*, Sweetback wanders through an urban nightmare of demonic antagonists and sexual hyperbole, seeking the resolution of psycho-sexual confusion. This structural subjectivity is reciprocated by parallel formal invocations of the late sixties psychedelic underground, especially through image manipulations—the color solarizations, multiple superimpositions and loop printing—associated in Los Angeles with Pat O'Neill and Burton Gershfield (some of *Sweetback*'s effects were done in a small company run by O'Neill). Used to punctuate crises like Sweetback's initial beating of the police and his sexual triumph over the motorcycle gang leader, these optical effects skew the film towards the first person. Yet the subjectivity effected does not distinguish the artist from the community so much as it affirms the commonality of his highly charged vision: it inscribes Blackness. The film's other main stylistic trait, the construction of a phantasmagoric mosaic out of short shots of the cityscape and brief interviews with the people, visual jazz riffs in which the continually moving and zooming camera creates a vertiginous run through the ghetto, establishes the reciprocity of Sweetback's vision with that of the community. Other underground conventions that destroy diegetic unity and transparency, like the use of black music and the quasi-surrealist chorus of voices that follow Sweetback through the desert miasma, similarly fix the individual, even in its crisis, as the product of a whole culture.

It is appropriate, then, to approach *Sweetback* as psychomachy, as the dramatization of a deep psychological, even subconscious conflict in which the polarization of the political and the sexual is only the summary vocabulary for a whole series of libidinal and social bifurcations across which the Black self in its historical uncertainty is stretched, conflicts in which the individual, Sweetback, recapitulates the condition of an entire people. Yet *Sweetback*'s existence as a commodity in Black social transactions doesn't derive from the praxis of the community, but from the isolated entrepreneurial determination of a single man to make the production methods and marketing operations of capitalist cinema the vehicle for social reform. Unlike Black music, it could find its place in the community, not as popular expression or even as a model production capable of popular imitation, but only as a commodity, indistinguishable in this respect from every other exploitation film. The opening credits, which affirm 'The Community' as its stars, thus speak to a contradiction, for while the urban Black proletariat is cast in the starring role, it is as the same time the film's dupe. Concealing the commodity relations by which it works to sustain the capitalist cinema, *Sweetback*'s very celebration of blackness, of blackness given voice, substitutes for a genuine community culture, a Black revolutionary cinema.

The Missing Cinema

The virtual absence of cinema from the most vigorously progressive social movement of the sixties must be understood as the joint effect of the establishment media's refusal to portray honestly the radicalization of the Black movement, together with the parallel failure of Blacks themselves to develop a film culture responsive to their needs. These conditions and their outcome provide a particularly clear instance of the historical and social determination of cultural production. Indeed, parallel conditions forestalled any substantial cinematic contribution to other ethnic struggles during the sixties. Hollywood did continue the modification of its portrayal of Native Americans that had been developing since the end of World War II,[10] and there were a few instances of successful collaboration between independent filmmakers and Native American groups, like that between Carol Burns and the Survival of the American Indian Association which produced the Newsreel-distributed *As Long As The Rivers Run* (1971). Sol Worth's remarkable 1966 experiment of introducing the apparatus to the Navajo, however fascinating the films and however invaluable the critical perspectives on cinema that they make available, was of little use to the Navajo themselves. Nor did collaboration between white radicals and the Latino community in Newsreel films like *Los Siete* (1969), *Rompiendo Puertas (Breaking and Entering)* (1970), *El Pueblo Se Levanta (The People Are Rising)* (1971), and *G.I. Jose* produce anything with the social momentum of the Chicago Guerrilla Theater, Fresno's El Teatro Campesino, or New York's Soul and Latin Theater. Apart from isolated instances, the disparity between the political disenfranchisement and economic marginality of ethnic minorities on the one hand, and the material conditions of cinema on the other, the resources it demanded and the social relationships it allowed, together with the antipathy of ethnic arts to those material conditions, prevented any substantial role for the medium in ethnically or racially based political contestation.

Cultural traditions aside, it is clear that the virtually unalloyed commodity consumption which occupies the position of these absent ethnic cinemas is a matter of class rather than race or ethnicity *per se*. With the exception of students, women and sexual minorities, those sixties dissident groups who theorized themselves politically, especially racial and ethnic minorities, prisoners and GI's, were all predominantly from the working class. Their common failure to produce cinema for their own purposes should be thought of, then, as an aspect of the absence of a working-class cinema. Clarifying the dominant cinema's connection with capitalism, its intrinsic and inevitable reiteration of economic and social subordination and impoverishment, this more general failure had profound implications for cinema as a whole—and for the terms by which a materialist history of it might be undertaken.

9

From Sweetback to Celie:
Blacks on Film into the 80s

James A. Miller

'In this society you have to be very skeptical about any work about Black folks that receives popular acceptance.'
Maurice Wade

Mainstream film critics are quick to suggest a causal connection between the changing image of Blacks in Hollywood films and the relationship of Blacks not only to the structure of the motion picture industry but to American society as well. In some circles, for example, Steven Spielberg's adaptation of Alice Walker's *The Color Purple* is already being hailed as a cinematic *and* social landmark, signalling a new willingness on the part of Hollywood to tackle serious explorations of Afro-American life, offering new opportunities for Black actors and actresses, and so on. At one level, statistics seem to support these claims. Nominated for eleven Academy Awards, *The Color Purple* grossed sixty million dollars in its first three months of circulation and will probably emerge as one of the top fifty box-office hits of all time (displacing along the way Sidney Poitier's 1967 hit, *Guess Who's Coming to Dinner*, currently 49th on the list). Clearly the film struck a responsive chord in its audience—Black and white—and its place in the history of Hollywood seems assured. Nevertheless, the critical accolades which *The Color Purple* has received are more indicative of the terms the motion picture industry proposes for the portrayal of Afro-Americans during the

1980s than symptomatic of any structural shifts in either Hollywood or American society.

In recent years, particularly in the context of a film industry which produces only a handful of films in which Blacks are prominently featured and offers Blacks only occasional supporting roles, virtually every film touching upon Black life has been hailed as a major event. This was as true of *Ragtime* (1981), *An Officer and A Gentleman* (1982), and *A Soldier's Story* (1984), as it is of *The Color Purple*. In a climate of scarcity, each of these cinematic events assumes an exaggerated significance, which is underscored by the critical attention these films have received in the popular press and by the reward structure of the motion picture industry itself. Academy Award nominations for films about Blacks have become *de rigueur* in Hollywood during the past two decades, reflecting a certain ideological practice within the film industry.

These recent developments are an extension of the racial liberalism which has historically encouraged a sentimental faith in progress under the auspices of the motion picture industry. As Thomas Cripps points out: 'Year after year *Uncle Tom's Cabin* (1927), *Hallelujah!*, *Hearts in Dixie*, *The Green Pastures* (1936), *Slave Ship* (1937), *So Red the Rose* (1935), *Beggars of Life* (1928), *Crash Dive* (1943), *Sahara* (1943), *Pinky* (1949), *Stormy Weather* (1943), *Cabin in the Sky* (1943), *Raisin in the Sun* (1961), *Lillies of the Field* (1963), *The Defiant Ones* (1968) and *Sounder* (1972) promised an ever hopeful future. Much like a happy ending, progress seemed at least possible on the screen if not in real life.'[1]

The symbolic representation of Blacks on screen *has* changed during the past two decades; the blatent racial stereotypes Donald Bogle has described as 'Toms, Coons, Mulattoes, Mammies and Bucks'[2] has gradually been displaced by more subtle and in many cases more insidious portrayals of Afro-American character and experience; but the residual echoes of these racial stereotypes continue to shape Hollywood's images of Blacks into the 1980s. The box office success of Hollywood's most recent ventures into Black life should therefore not be confused. with a decisive transformation in traditional modes of cinematic representation of Blacks. In fact, Hollywood films about Blacks during the 1980s represent, in cinematic terms, the images of Black life spawned and reinforced by a retrogressive cultural and political period.

The principle is a simple one: the motion picture industry, always sensitive to shifts in popular mood and political climate, has historically responded to social and financial pressure to alter its representation of Blacks with short-lived cosmetic changes; when the pressure is removed, Hollywood invariably reverts to its long established practice of resurrecting familiar racial stereotypes to both entertain and reassure white audiences. During the late 1960s and early 1970s, Hollywood temporarily shelved old racial stereotypes in the face of mounting urban unrest in the cities and economic instability and uncertainty in the motion picture industry. Now that the threat of Black revolt seems to have passed and the agenda of the new Right is clearly ascendent, stereotypes of Black life have re-emerged in Hollywood with a vengeance.

The Black Movie Market

These developments are thrown into relief by a brief survey of Hollywood's portrayal of Black life during the past twenty years, a period which roughly coincides with the belated discovery of the economic value of the Black movie-going audience. Although an independent Black cinema emerged during the early twentieth century and developed along lines parallel to the corporate picture industry until the early 1950s, Hollywood did not really begin to notice a Black movie-going audience as a potential market until the mid-1960s.

This 'discovery' occurred against the backdrop of sharply declining profits in the film industry and widespread social and political turbulence in American society. From 1946 to 1960 average American weekly movie attendance dropped sharply from a peak of 90 million to 40 million; by 1971, weekly attendance had dropped to roughly 17 million. During the same period, the number of feature films produced in the United States dropped from 378 in 1946 to 154 in 1960, to 143 in 1971.[3] At the same time, white flight from the nation's cities during the 1960s left a void in many downtown movie houses which could only be filled by Black moviegoers. According to a 1967 estimate, Blacks accounted for about 30 percent of the movie-going audience in the nation's cities, where the largest movie theaters were located.[4] And the growing political militancy of the Black community during the 1960s—the urban rebellions, the emergence of the Black Power movement, and increased demands by Blacks for greater opportunities and participation within the motion-picture industry—forced Hollywood to re-evaluate and re-fashion its images to respond to a politically aroused Black community.

Hollywood's recognition of the new mood (and box office potential) of the Black community was reflected in the gradual displacement of the screen persona of Sidney Poiter, the 'ebony saint,' in favor of images of hip, aggressive Black masculinity, personified by football star Jim Brown and, later, other Black actors drawn from professional sports (Fred Williamson, Bernie Casey and Paul Winfield, among others). The first Black actor to achieve genuine star status in the film industry, Poitier virtually personified Black achievement in Hollywood from his first film *No Way Out* (1950), through *Guess Who's Coming To Dinner* (1967). Poitier was an ideal screen hero for a social era dominated by a liberal/integrationist faith and an unquestioning allegiance to the values of the American middle class. As Donald Bogle puts it:

> For the mass white audience, Sidney Poitier was a black man who had met their standards. His characters were tame; never did they act impulsively, nor were they threats to the system. They were amenable and pliant. And finally they were non-funky, almost sexless and sterile. In short, they were the perfect dream for white liberals anxious to have a colored man in for lunch or dinner.
> Poitier was also acceptable for black audiences. He was the paragon of black middle-class values and virtues. Black America was still trying to meet white standards and ape white manners, and he became a hero for their cause ... This was one smart and refined young Negro, and middle-class America, both black and white, treasured him.[5]

In spite of the box-office success of *Guess Who's Coming to Dinner*, Sidney Poitier's screen persona was dismissed during the late 1960s by Black and white critics alike as no longer pertinent to the needs of a highly volatile political era. Jim Brown's screen presence, by contrast, exuded a newly valorized Black physical force and sexuality. Stoic and taciturn on the screen, Brown portrayed characters in worlds where men operated on the basis of physical strength and survival instincts. His first films, *Rio Conchos* (1964) and *The Dirty Dozen* (1967), established Brown's persona as a bold and decisive individualist, completely confident of his own power, and, in most cases, morally superior to whites. For all of the Black Power overtones of Brown's screen image, however, his brute strength and power were usually contained within the restraints of white power and authority. In *Dark of the Sun* (1968), for example, Brown is aligned with a group of white mercenaries whose task is to rid an African nation of a group of revolutionary 'Simbas' (a not-so-veiled reference to the Mau Mau revolt in Kenya), sacrificing himself at the end of the movie to save his white comrades and therefore revealing himself to be a team player at heart. B-grade action films, the eleven movies Jim Brown made between 1967 and 1970 were nevertheless a precursor to the images of independent and aggressive Black men which dominated the Hollywood screen during the early 1970s.

In addition to Brown's emergence as a new screen hero, other films produced during the late 1960s revealed the extent to which Hollywood had begun to re-define the formulaic and generic conventions which shaped the cinematic definition of Black life. Jules Dassin's *Up Tight* (1969) was the first in a series of movies produced during the period which sought to incorporate contemporary political changes in the Black community. An attempt to reinterpret and update Liam O'Flaherty's classic novel *The Informer*, the film was set in the Hough district of Cleveland after the assassination of Martin Luther King and offered an unusually frank portrayal of the urban ghetto—albeit in the context of a highly didactic and plodding script. Similarly, Sidney Poitier's refurbished image in *The Lost Man* (1969) was also based on an earlier movie about the Irish Rebellion, *Odd Man Out* (1947). Although Poitier donned dark sunglasses and rapped to the brothers on the street, his portrayal of a Black revolutionary was flat and unconvincing. Both of these films were noteworthy for their fascination with the gritty details of the urban ghetto and for their superficial treatment of the Afro-American liberation struggle.

Two other films produced during this period were bolder in exploring the possibilities of film genre. Both, not accidentally, were directed by Blacks. Gordon Parks' *The Learning Tree* (1969), based on his widely praised autobiographical novel, was a nostalgic evocation of a time and place far removed from the urban realities of the late 1960s. A recreation of Parks' childhood in Kansas during the 1920s, *The Learning Tree* was both unflinching in its portrayal of racism and violence, and elegant in its evocation of rural detail and pastoral beauty. Ossie Davis' *Cotton Comes To Harlem* (1970), based on Chester Himes' novel, was a freewheeling, good-natured satire which delighted Black audiences throughout the country. Such films hinted at the potential for a rapid shift in film content, as Hollywood scrambled to adjust its product to the tastes of its Black moviegoing audience. But it was the overnight success of Melvin Van Peebles' *Sweet Sweetback's Baadasss Song* (1971), which defined the dominant tendency in Hollywood films, launching a brief but significant boom in Black-oriented films.

Sweet Sweetback to Shaft

A landmark event in the history of independent Black cinema, *Sweet Sweetback's Baadasss Song* was a totally maverick production. Van Peebles financed it, produced it, wrote and directed it, and composed the music for it. He chose the distributor and carefully orchestrated the marketing and advertising, turning his production into one of the top grossing independent films of all times. Produced at the crest of Black nationalism throughout the United States, *Sweet Sweetback* effectively captured—some would say exploited—Black resentment, giving it an iconic form that had not been seen on film before. As James Murray observes, *Sweet Sweetback* 'in effect, dared white patrons to walk into the theater'.[6]

Van Peebles' hero is a Black stud who performs in sex shows for largely white night club audiences in the Los Angeles ghetto. When two white policemen burst into the club looking for a Black man they can tab as a suspect to quiet public alarm about a murder case, Sweetback is persuaded to go along with them. On their way to the station, the police stop and arrest a young Black militant whom they beat mercilessly. Sweetback watches this scene impassively at first, then suddenly attacks the police with his handcuffs, bashing in their heads. In the aftermath of this scene, Sweetback is transformed from an amoral and apolitical stud into a political outlaw whose consciousness grows with each successive episode. Pursued by a ruthless and savage police manhunt, Sweetback eludes them with the assistance of various elements of the Black *lumpen proletariat*: pimps, gamblers, prostitutes and others. Recaptured once, Sweetback is rescued by a group of Black children who set fire to the patrol car he is in. He makes good use of his sexual prowess along the way—to persuade a Black woman to remove his handcuffs, in a sexual duel with a white woman who rides with the Hells Angels, and in a knife-point rape of a Black woman to distract approaching policemen at a rock festival—before he finally makes his escape across the desert.

Sweetback was highly controversial and an astounding box office success. Although the film was widely criticized by white critics and raised the ire of thoughtful Black writers like Lerone Bennett, who took exception to *Sweetback*'s emphasis on sexual prowess as an instrument of Black liberation,[7] critical attacks on the film were overshadowed by its enthusiastic reception in the Black community. *Sweetback*'s popular and political appeal was underscored by the twelve-page, scene-by-scene analysis which the Minister of Defense of the Black Panther Party, Huey Newton, devoted to the film in the Black Panther newspaper (June 1971). Given the orientation of the Black Panther Party, Newton's fascination with the film was understandable. First of all, Van Peebles' insistence, in the opening credits, that the real star of *Sweetback* was the 'Black community', coincided with the emphasis of the Black Panther Party on the Black urban *lumpen proletariat* as the wellspring of Black revolutionary consciousness—and, in a broader sense, with a more general repudiation of the norms of the Black bourgeoisie.

One distinct tendency which emerged out of this paradigmatic shift was the glamorization of the ghetto and the elevation of the pimp and other members of the Black *lumpen proletariat* as folk heroes. Van Peebles' film glorified the pimp/stud, even as it conveniently overlooked the social/sexual context within which his hero flourished.[8] Secondly, the plot and musical score celebrated a communal mood within the Black community, touching upon a widely shared need to triumph over an oppressive system. Throughout the film, Sweetback is aided by members of the Black community wherever he goes, and his triumph at the conclusion belongs as much to the community as it does to his own instincts for survival. Black moviegoers, who comprised the overwhelming majority of the film's audience, seemed less concerned with *Sweetback*'s verisimilitude than with the vicarious satisfaction of watching a Black man strike out at the system. Finally, Van Peebles' flamboyant and outspoken behavior, and his personal triumph over the motion picture industry made him something of a folk hero in his own right.

Sweet Sweetback's Baadasss Song was a real, if controversial step towards the development of an independent Black cinema during the early 1970s. Criticized by many for its glorification of the Black man as stud and for its portrayal of women as, in Pearl Bowser's words, 'mere vessels existing along the path of the hero's flight to freedom and manhood,'[9] *Sweetback* nevertheless accurately gave cinematic expression to many of the contradictory elements underlying the mood of the Black community during this era. And Van Peebles' exploration of the themes of Black consciousness and black liberation, together with his personal rebellion against the dominant economic apparatus of the Hollywood film industry sharply distinguish *Sweetback* from other Black-oriented films produced by Hollywood during this period.

Gordon Parks' *Shaft*, released several months after *Sweetback*, combined similar images of Black urban lifestyle into more familiar and palatable fare. *Shaft*'s hero is an individualistic and rebellious Black detective who lives in an elegantly furnished Greenwich Village duplex, dresses in expensive leather coats and enjoys life on his own terms. Although Shaft lives downtown and works out of a Times Square office, he maintains close ties with the uptown Harlem community. Thus the film effects a skilful muting of the potential tensions between maintaining one's racial identity and pursuing the good life.

Physically resourceful, flamboyant, and fiercely independent, Shaft flouts the white establishment, puts Black mobsters in their place, and foils a Mafia attempt to take over Black-controlled rackets in Harlem. In its re-invigoration and updating of the detective film, *Shaft* skilfully incorporated the impulses of a Black Power era into acceptable cinematic images. For all of his arrogance and his refusal to play by the rules of the white establishment, John Shaft's life-style is governed by the same desire to enjoy the good life as his white counterparts (and his Black audience). And the anti-white sentiments of the film are skilfully deflected onto acceptable targets: a Mafia gangster, an irate Times Square motorist, an arrogant police officer. In addition, Shaft's individualism functions as a mechanism of reassurance as well. A loner and an outsider, Shaft is too committed to the pursuit of his own comfort either to spearhead or join a political movement for social change.

Although *Sweet Sweetback's Baadasss Song* and *Shaft* represented diametrically opposed tendencies in the portrayal of Black life, they were both clear box office successes. *Sweetback* grossed over $10 milion during its first year, while the commercial success of *Shaft* reputedly saved M.G.M. Studios from financial disaster. More importantly, the variations inspired by the popular success of these films triggered a stampede in the motion picture industry, leading to an unprecedented profusion of Black superheroes on film.

The 'Blaxploitation' Boom

With the popular and commercial success of *Superfly*, one of the top-grossing films of 1972, the so-called 'blaxploitation' film was established as a dominant trend in the motion picture industry. Directed by Gordon Parks, Jr., *Superfly* tells the story of Youngblood Priest, a hip Black cocaine dealer who is trying to make one final score before he retires. Priest's flashy lifestyle, his sexual conquest of Black and white women, his triumph over Black thugs and corrupt white officials, and his upward mobility—epitomized in the final scene where Priest, snorting cocaine, drives away in a shiny Rolls Royce—proved to be an enormously successful formula for young Black audiences. By 1972, Blacks had become one of Hollywood's favourite subjects. Whereas in 1970 only 14 black-oriented films were released by Hollywood, between 1970 and 1972, some 50 feature films were specifically aimed at a Black audience which was estimated to spend about 120 million dollars a year at movie box offices.[10]

The success of *Superfly* spawned a number of Black-oriented films, many of them hastily financed and poorly produced, which emphasized violence, crime, drugs and 'beating the system'. In sharp contrast to the revolutionary potential at least implied in *Sweet Sweetback*, 'blaxploitation' films like *Melinda*, *The Man*, *Cool Breeze*, *Black Caesar*, *Trick Baby* and countless others produced between 1972 and 1974 offered a pyscho-therapeutic palliative to predominantly Black audiences, deflecting the themes of Black consciousness and revolt into cinematic fantasies which implicitly reinforced the political and economic status quo. Social commentary was kept to a minimum, while Black audiences were regaled with Hollywood illusions of racial revenge in the form of Superspade, a figure who, in Daniel J. Leab's words, 'lived a violent life in pursuit of Black women, white sex, quick money, easy success, cheap "pot" and other pleasures'.[11]

Not only did 'blaxploitation' films allow Hollywood to capture the market uncovered by the financial success of *Sweetback*; the virtual glut these films created in the marketplace undercut and forced to the periphery of popular consciousness efforts to explore alternative images of Afro-American life by a handful of Black directors and by independent Black film-makers. During the same era, Sidney Poitier turned his efforts towards directing, popularizing the history of Blacks in the West with *Buck and the Preacher* (1972), and making two of the most successful Black-oriented films of the mid-1970s, *Uptown Saturday Night* (1974), and its sequel, *Let's Do It Again* (1975). At the same time, however, films like Bill Cosby's lowkeyed western, *Man and Boy* (1971), or movies based on Black literary works like Raymond St. Jacques's production of *The Book of Numbers*, Ivan Dixon and Sam Greenlee's *The Spook Who Sat By The Door*, based on Greenlee's novel, and Brock Peters's production of *Five On The Black Hand Side*, based on the play by Charlie L. Russell—all of which appeared in 1973—failed to attract the popular and critical attention which they deserved.

These failures in the marketplace were echoed in the difficulties Ossie Davis faced with his ambitious plans to establish an independent company to finance and produce Black movies. In the aftermath of his successful direction of *Cotton Comes To Harlem*, Davis, along with other Black actors, announced the formation of Third World Cinema Corporation, an organization designed to make Black films and to channel profits back into the community by providing jobs for Blacks, Puerto Ricans and other minority groups. Their first project, a film biography of Billie Holiday which was to star the late Diana Sands, was taken over by Berry Gordy's Motown Productions, the newly created film production arm of Gordy's record company. Gordy used the film as a vehicle to introduce Diana Ross, one of Motown's leading singers, and *Lady Sings the Blues* (1972), emerged as a Hollywood film, not an independent one.

In the meantime, Davis traveled to Nigeria to direct *Kongi's Harvest*, a satire on contemporary African politics by the Nigerian playwright and novelist Wole Soyinka. The first major motion picture produced in English by an African company, *Kongi's Harvest* (1971) was turned down by major distributors in the United States. Although the film was greeted by standing ovations at its premiere in Lagos, Nigeria, its theme was deemed to be too specialized for mass distribution in the United States. A similar fate met Davis's production of *Countdown at Kusini* (1974), also filmed on the African continent and financed by Delta Sigma Theta, a national Black sorority. Davis's production of *Black Girl* (1972), based on J. E. Franklin's play, was similarly ignored by the studios.

Ironically, despite Davis's sincere and self-conscious efforts to develop an alternative to 'blaxploitation' films, his most commercially successful ventures during this period were at least implicitly shaped by the cinematic values he sought to challenge. *Gordon's War* (1973), was Davis's cinematic response to *Superfly*, an attempt to undercut the emphasis on drugs so typical of films of this genre by staging an all-out war on Harlem drug dealers by a Black Vietnam veteran. *Claudine* (1974), a comedy about a Black welfare mother of six and her relationship with a genial, out going garbageman (played by James Earl Jones), scored points with its critique of an unresponsive welfare bureaucracy as well as for its sympathetic insights into the pressures of ghetto life, particularly upon the young. But one of the major ideological drawbacks of the film (besides casting Diahann Carroll as Claudine) was the confused and stereotypical conception of its main characters: Claudine as both a poverty-stricken Black woman who apparently cannot control her libido and a strict but loving Black matriarch who upholds middle-class values for her children; and Roop (James Earl Jones) as a genial but irresponsible stud who has already abandoned his own family and clearly would prefer not to assume the obligations of another.

With few exceptions, attempts by Black producers to create cinematic alternatives to 'blaxploitation' had little impact upon the practices of the motion picture industry. Instead, Hollywood effectively captured the market for Black-oriented films by developing commercially successful formulas for their growth. By 1972, some forecasts predicted that nearly one quarter of future Hollywood films would be created for predominately Black audiences.[12] But in spite of these optimistic forecasts, the production of Black-oriented films had sharply declined by 1974. Why did this occur?

Decline of Black-Oriented Films

Some critics suggest that the decline in Black-oriented films during the mid-1970s coincided with a slackening of interest among Black youth and a growing maturity and critical sophistication among Black audiences in general, spurred by a growing backlash against 'blaxploitation' films by a wide cross-section of the Black community. From the very beginning, these films had provoked the wrath of Black religious and political leaders, psychologists, journalists, political activists and artists—all of whom condemned the motion picture industry for glorifying anti-social Black images. Against a backdrop of moral condemnation, various coalitions sprang up in Black communities throughout the country to press their grievances against the motion picture industry. The Black Artists Alliance was organized in the film, television and theatre industry to serve as a pressure group for Blacks within the industry, while the Hollywood-based Coalition Against Blaxploitation (composed of representatives of local NAACP, CORE and SCLC chapters) was organized to rate films according to Black standards—with the threat of film boycotts and grassroots protests to gain concessions from the Hollywood studios. On the East Coast, Roy Innis announced the formation of the Harlem Cinema Foundation in the aftermath of an incident when the cast and crew of *Come Back Charleston Blue* were ordered out of Harlem by community activists. Innis' Harlem Cinema Foundation, organized to encourage movie production in the Black community, issued numerous demands to the motion picture industry, including the employment of more Blacks in films, payment to Black-owned banks of a share of the profits, and the establishment of an endowment fund for the training of Black apprentices in the motion picture industry. Despite promises of cooperation from several filmmakers, no Black-oriented films were produced in New York for several months following this episode.

On the national level, the Reverend Jessie Jackson's attack on 'blaxploitation' films in the Sunday *New York Times* (July 30, 1972), provided an ideological and moral rationale for the various challenges to the motion picture industry from diverse forces within the Black community. The debate over 'blaxploitation' and the responsibilities of the motion picture industry to the Black community was often confused and contradictory. Nevertheless, this debate can only be seen as one term in the socio-economic equation which shaped Hollywood's attitude towards Black subjects during the mid-1970s. While the debates over these films may have affected patterns of film consumption in the Black community, they had little immediate effect on profits.

Indeed, one of the ironies and paradoxes of cinematic history during the period 1968-1974 is that the very commercial success of Black-oriented films led to their demise. While it is true, as Clayton Riley and others have pointed out, that the profits earned from Black-oriented films during this period helped stabilize a financially troubled motion picture industry, it is also true that, once Hollywood producers recognized the economic potential of the Black audience, they also understood they did not have to make Black-oriented films to exploit it. As James Monaco points out: 'Surveys showed that as much as 35% of the audience for such blockbusters as *The Godfather* (1972) and *The Exorcist* (1973) was Black. If Black audiences were turning out in such numbers for essentially non-Black films, why cater to this particular subculture? Moreover, if white people could be attracted to movies that were based on Black themes or that starred Black actors, revenues could easily double. The success of films like *Sounder* and *Lady Sings the Blues* in 1972, starring Blacks in Black stories, but directed by whites with an overlay of white sensibility, proved the workability of this theory. The "crossover" film replaced the Black film, except for a few independent productions.'[13]

Monaco pretty well sums up the critical transition which occurred during this period, one which clearly has a direct bearing on the climate in which films are produced during the 1980s as well; but I would add that this shift in Hollywood's portrayal of Black life also coincided with the general hardening of racial attitudes characteristic of American life during the early 1970s. The theme of racial revenge, so common in 'blaxploitation' films for example, had its counterpart in a cycle of films produced for mainstream consumption during roughly the same era. Clint Eastwood's *Dirty Harry* cycle, beginning in 1972 (the same year *Superfly* was produced), expressed growing frustration with a corrupt and disintegrating society and a contempt for liberal solutions to social problems while celebrating personal vigilantism as a way of restoring social order. At the same moment, *Death Wish* (1974), glorified similar inpulses in a bourgeois context. A film like the 1973 James Bond thriller, *Live and Let Die*, symbolically re-enacted the racial struggle by pitting James Bond against a ruthless and effective Black gangster organization, driving the point home by pitting Roger Moore and Yaphet Kotto against each other in a mortal conflict for the possession of a white woman.

Rocky, the box office blockbuster of 1976, skillfully played upon the public perception that Blacks had gone too far by appropriating the same desolate urban landscape which had defined the setting for many Black-oriented films and locating its hero squarely within it. Beyond the obvious parody of Muhammed Ali in its portrayal of the flamboyant Apollo Creed, *Rocky*'s more insidious messages to at least part of its audience are established through the casual details of the film itself: the sharp contrast of the poised and elegant Black female television reporter who interviews Rocky against the background squalor of the meat-packing plant, for example, signals that Blacks have made remarkable strides towards socio-economic progress while other deserving groups have been neglected and left behind. This sense is expressed in the film not through Rocky (who is anyway too inarticulate to express his deepest feelings), but through his brother-in-law Paulie, who seethes throughout the film with the not-so-hidden injuries of class.

Such films accurately captured and encoded the conservative mood of America during the mid-1970s, displacing Blacks from the center to the periphery of the Hollywood screen. Thus, by 1977, only four major films about Blacks were released by Hollywood studios and Black actors found themselves relegated to supporting roles—when they appeared in films at all—cast as either sinister villains, threats to social order, or as trusted and loyal sidekicks to white men.

Comic Blacks: Pryor and Murphy

Just as significantly two of these four films featured Richard Pryor in his first starring roles: *Greased Lightening* and *Which Way Is Up?* It is no coincidence that Pryor emerged as a major box office attraction right at precisely the moment Hollywood discovered the economic value of the crossover formula. Although Pryor earned his spurs by working on the 'chitlin circuit' of Black nightclubs and theaters long before he was 'discovered' by Merv Griffin and television audiences, his outrageous and unpredictable humor appealed to Blacks and whites alike, virtually assuring him of a ready-made audience when he first ventured into films. An effective performance as Piano Man in *Lady Sings The Blues* (1972) launched Pryor's film career and, by the mid-1970s, he was firmly established as the Black superstar of the decade.

Pryor's first two feature films, both collaborations with Black director Michael Schultz, suggested some interesting possibilities in the exploration of Afro-American life. *Which Way Is Up?*, Carl Gottlieb's adaptation of Lina Wertmueller's *The Rape of Mimi*, allowed Pryor to demonstrate his comic range by portraying several characters in the film. At the same time, the movie's exploration of the exploitative situation of California farm workers, its realistic setting—underscored by Schultz's use of actors from El Teatro Campesino—and its examination of the theme of working-class betrayal—although muted and somewhat undercut by Pryor's comic performance—suggested the possibility of a social realism which anticipated Pryor's outstanding performance in *Blue Collar* (1978). *Greased Lightning*, a restrained and understated depiction of the story of Wendell Scott, the first Black stockcar driver to break the color barrier in a sport shaped by Southern mores, turned out to be the most financially successful film about a Black subject produced during 1977—suggesting there were audiences for films in this genre which Hollywood tended to ignore.

Pryor's debut was followed shortly by his role in *Blue Collar*, a gritty and realistic portrayal of three Detroit auto workers, one white and two Black, who rob their union and stumble into a web of union and mob corruption. The union's revenge leads to the death of one of the Blacks, the capitulation of the other and, by implication, the end of a tenuous alliance between Black and white workers. One of the last films to feature Blacks during the 1970s, *Blue Collar* was, unfortunately, a box office failure—signaling perhaps the unwillingness of Pryor's established audience to accept him in anything but comic performances.

In fact, despite his dramatic successes in these films, Pryor's screen roles (with the exception of his on-stage performances in *Richard Pryor Live in Concert* [1979], and *Richard Pryor Live on the Sunset Strip* [1982]) have been uneven and apparently shaped by a desire to appeal to the tastes of a white movie-going public. As his film career has continued through the rest of the 70s and into the 80s, Pryor's dramatic range appears to have been more and more sharply circumscribed by the stranglehold of the industry's 'cross-over' mentality. After token appearances in Neil Simon's *California Suite* (1978), *Wholly Moses* and *In God We Trust*, Pryor rejoined Gene Wilder, his film partner in *Silver Streak* (1977), in *Stir Crazy* (1980)—cast in the familiar role of comic sidekick. Since 1980, Pryor's performances have increasingly drifted towards the maudlin and sentimental. *Bustin' Loose* and *Some Kind of Hero* (1981) made gestures at social statements, but failed both in their execution and at the box office, while *The Toy* (1982) must be ranked among one of the most atrocious and tasteless films of the 1980s.

In it, Pryor plays an unemployed writer who persuades a white corporation president (Jackie Gleason) to employ him, first as a maid and later as a department store employee. While working in the toy department, Pryor meets his future 'owner' Eric (the spoiled child of the corporation president), who chooses Pryor as the newest addition to his toy collection. Pryor at first vociferously objects but relents when Gleason offers him enough money to make it worthwhile. In spite of the various humiliations to which Eric subjects him, Pryor succeeds in discovering the child's essential humanity, teaching him along the way the meaning of friendship and love. Pryor and Eric then team up to convert Jackie Gleason, an indifferent parent with ties to the Ku Klux Klan. In gratitude for having his suspect business dealings exposed, his ties to the Ku Klux Klan severed and his humanity restored, Gleason offers Pryor a writing position on a newspaper he owns—an offer Pryor unhesitatingly accepts. This final economic transaction between Pryor and Gleason unwittingly presents a perfect metaphor for the current relationship between Blacks and the motion picture industry: it asserts the necessity of sacrificing one's personal integrity and racial pride as the price of socio-economic progress.

The downward slide of Richard Pryor's film career during the early 1980s coincided with the emergence of Hollywood's newest Black superstar, Eddie Murphy. Murphy's successful transition to Hollywood films was almost exclusively a by-product of his appearances as a regular on television's *Saturday Night Live*. Following in the footsteps of other cast members—Dan Ackroyd, John Belushi, Gilda Radner and Bill Murray—Murphy first captured the attention of movie-going audiences in *48 Hours*, an action-filled comedy-drama (1981), which was quickly followed by *Trading Places* (1983), a farce of role-reversals co-starring Dan Ackroyd. Murphy's most recent blockbuster, *Beverly Hills Cop* (1984)—a film which grossed $235 million—has consolidated his claim as one of the rising Black film stars of the 1980s. Murphy's stage presence—charismatic, brash, and unpredictable—invariably provokes comparison with Pryor, but Murphy's persona lacks the social bite, the edge of Pryor's best performances, and his films suggest a return to the integrationist ethic of the Sidney Poitier era. Although Murphy's screen persona often appropriates the street-wise style of the Black urban ghetto, his hip, wise-cracking manner inevitably conveys an underlying message of racial harmony.

In *48 Hours*, for example, Murphy plays a convict who is granted temporary parole to help a white cop (Nick Nolte) search for two vicious murderers. Although Murphy's character initially rebels against Nolte's authority, he ultimately accepts it, choosing to help Nolte apprehend the murderers rather than sieze the opportunity to escape. In the process, of course, the two men learn to trust and respect one another—to the point that Murphy willingly returns to complete his sentence at the end of the film. Thus, Murphy's subversive humor is directed towards convenient and socially acceptable targets—a lily-white country and western bar in a key comic sequence in the film. *48 Hours* concludes on a note of racial harmony and the re-assertion of the social status quo.

Similarly, in *Trading Places*, Murphy dramatizes the American success myth by proving that he is worthy of acceptance in the most exclusive circles of white society. Two wealthy brothers (Don Ameche and Ralph Bellamy) argue about the influence of heredity and environment on wealth and social stature. To test their theories and settle their argument, they fire their nephew (Dan Ackroyd) from his position as a stockbroker in their exclusive firm, replacing him with Eddie Murphy, a ghetto hustler. Both Ackroyd and Murphy overcome their initial difficulties in their new roles to discover previously untapped talents and abilities. The ease with which Murphy adjusts to his new social status is particularly striking, as is the mixture of disgust and disdain with which he views his former street associates from his new vantage point. Once such an adjustment in perspective has been effected, moreover, the end of the film follows logically. The way is now clear for Murphy and Ackroyd, discovering that they have been duped, to join forces to take revenge on the two brothers, becoming—predicatably—best friends in the process.

Beverly Hills Cop extends the successful Eddie Murphy formula into the exclusive world of Beverly Hills, permitting Murphy to perform his particular brand of mayhem on the world of the rich and famous while continuing the ground base of racial harmony and cooperation. Murphy portrays a detective from Detroit who travels to Beverly Hills in search of a murder suspect. Although Murphy's brash street style immediately clashes with the pretenses of the Beverly Hills community, he ultimately secures the grudging respect and cooperation of the Beverly Hills police force and brings the criminals to justice. At the end of the film Murphy—with a straight face—asserts his love for the same detectives who have mercilessly beaten him shortly after his arrival in Beverly Hills and harassed him throughout most of the film.

A Soldier's Story

Clearly, Eddie Murphy's comedy dramas, however fast-paced and entertaining they may be, are a throwback to the proven Hollywood formulas of the past, combining contemporary humor with liberal integrationist appeals appropriate to a conservative era—appeals, that is, for social acceptance which place the burden of proof squarely on the shoulders of the Black community. So it is not surprising that Murphy's enormous popular appeal has not translated into any improvement in the bleak prospects for Blacks in Hollywood films during the 1980s—witness Howard Rollins and *A Soldier's Story*. Although Rollins' portrayal of the rebellious Coalhouse Walker, Jr., in *Ragtime* (1981), won him an Academy Award nomination, the film itself was a financial failure and Rollins spent several years as, in his own words, 'the least working leading actor I've ever seen in my life,'[14] before landing the role of Captain Richard Davenport in Norman Jewison's production of *A Soldier's Story*. And the difficulties Jewison faced in securing financing for the film, based on Charles Fuller's Pulitzer Prize-winning *A Soldier's Play*, are symptomatic of Hollwood's treatment of Black life in a conservative era. Turned down by four major Hollywood studios, the project was finally picked up by Columbia Pictures. It was allocated a budget of 6 million dollars, approximately half of the industry average for a feature film, and given a modest promotional budget. Yet despite Columbia's half-hearted commitment, *A Soldier's Story* was a popular hit, setting attendance records at theaters in the United States and Canada—a success precisely attributable to the extent to which the film bowed to the ideological concessions required by the cross-over formula.

In many respects, *A Soldier's Story* retains the dramatic integrity of Fuller's play, a murder mystery set on a segregated army base in Louisiana in 1944. Fuller wrote the screenplay, and the cast of the film was largely drawn from members of the Negro Ensemble Company, the respected Black theater group who had first staged the play in 1981. At the same time, however, the film recreates the ambience of Norman Jewison's most successful film, *In the Heat of the Night* (1967), which starred Sidney Poitier. In both films, the plot revolves around an angry but restrained Black outsider who journeys to the segregated South to investigate a murder that the local white authorities would rather ignore; in both cases, the Black outsider earns the grudging admiration and respect of his white counterparts as a result of his dogged determination to pursue the investigation to its conclusion.

The flashback sequences of the film vividly re-created the sharp antagonisms between the murder victim, Sergeant Vernon C. Waters (the late Adolphe Caesar), and PFC Melvin Peterson. Sergeant Waters is the achetypal self-hating Negro who believes that progress can only be achieved by emulating white standards of behavior, while PFC Peterson is an intelligent Black rebel whose mannerisms and appearence bear an uncanny resemblance to the late Malcolm X. As Captain Richard Davenport, the investigator delegated to discover Sergeant Waters's murderer, Howard Rollins is restrained and inscrutable throughout the film. In spite of the obvious hostility of Colonel Nivens, an unreconstructed southerner, and the resistance of Captain Taylor, the ineffectual and racially patronizing base commander, Davenport affirms his faith in the American system of justice by doggedly pursuing the truth. Much like Sidney Poitier in an earlier era, Rollins seldom allows human emotion to break through his reserve. Only after he discovers that Sergeant Waters's murderers are Black, not white—as it had been commonly assumed across the base—does Davenport allow his suppressed anger to erupt in the face of a hapless and dishevelled PFC Peterson, now revealed as the chief culprit. Davenport's controlled but angry denunciation of Peterson—'Who gave you the right to judge . . . to decide who is fit to be a Negro or not?'—offers both Davenport and the audience a convenient catharsis of the tension which has been developing throughout the film.

Several dimensions of this dramatic resolution suggest how contemporary ideological concerns have shaped this cinematic text. The surprise discovery that Sergeant Waters's murderers are Black violates the normal expectations of the genre, while simultaneously freeing white audiences from assuming any undue guilt or responsibility for the social reality portrayed on the screen. At the same time, Davenport's verbal attack on PFC Peterson echoes contemporary concerns in the Black community with 'Black-on-Black' crime, and represents, on another level, an attack on Black political 'extremism'. Against the backdrop of the larger social context of the world within which the all-Black company is confined—the racism of small-town Louisiana during the 1940's and the racism of the military itself—Davenport's statement thus deflects from the social milieu, confining our attention to the responsibilities of individuals within the Black community itself. Spoken by a self-assured individual who apparently bears none of the scars of Sergeant Waters's self-hatred, an individual who has by contrast achieved a high degree of mobility within the system, Davenport's short speech reflects the ideological essence of the film—a perspective reinforced by the concluding scene.

Davenport's solution to the murder occurs in the context of the decision of the US military to allow Black troops to fight against the Nazis, thereby allowing Jewison to stage an upbeat Hollywood finale. In the final sequence, Black troops are shown proudly and triumphantly marching off to war. Davenport, on foot, encounters Captain Taylor riding in a jeep, and persuades Taylor to offer him a ride. Sitting literally shoulder-to-shoulder, the two men converse as fellow officers, admitting that they were wrong about the case and each other. Taylor suggests that he may have to get used to dealing with Black officers, Davenport smiles one of his inscrutable smiles, and the film ends on a crescendo of martial music—suggesting that a new era of harmonious race relations is at hand. In Charles Fuller's play, however, we are informed that the members of the Black company, having won the right to fight against the Nazis, are all killed in battle—an ironic commentary which undercuts the liberal optimism of the film.

The Appeal of *The Color Purple*

The success of *A Soldier's Story*, particularly among white audiences, constitutes the immediate backdrop for the production of *The Color Purple*, the most recent entry in the Hollywood 'crossover' sweepstakes of the 1980s. Yet the film does represent—on the surface at least—an unprecedented breakthrough in the portrayal of Black women as cinematic subjects. Black women, to be sure, have suffered from decades of neglect and misrepresentation at the hands of the motion picture industry, and one would have to pore over reels of celluloid to discover aesthetically or socially satisfying images of Black women in Hollywood films: Abbey Lincoln in *Nothing But A Man* (1964), Cicely Tyson in *Sounder* (1972), but very little else. The announcement that Stephen Spielberg would produce Alice Walker's Pulitzer prize-winning novel therefore raised expectations that this film would create new space for the exploration of Black women subjects. These expectations could be fulfilled, however, only if the film managed to capture the essence of Alice Walker's fiercely anti-patriarchal and healing vision, a challenge clearly beyond Spielberg's capacities. Although Menno Meyjes's script captures some of the spirit of Walker's novel, Spielberg's direction glosses over and distorts its ideological essence.

Walker's novel is primarily concerned with charting the development of Celie's voice, a quest which is spurred on by her sexual awakening in the hands of Shug Avery. Spielberg's film often drowns out Celie's voice with the saccharine strains of Quincey

Jones' music, and it reduces the love affair between Celie and Shug to several chaste kisses between friends. Spielberg's apparent unwillingness to accept Walker's novel on its own terms is the most recent example of the ideological concessions dictated by the 'crossover' mentality, a formula which leads inevitably to the trivialization of Afro-American life. In Spielberg's hands, for example, the setting is transformed into a landscape more reminiscent of Tara in *Gone With The Wind* than it is evocative of the realities of the rural deep South. Even worse, the Africa sequences are more suggestive of *Wild Kingdom* than of a continent caught in the throes of colonialism. Shug Avery belongs more to the milieu of a Harlem cabaret than she does to the world of a down-home juke-joint, while Sofia—a model of female strength in Walker's novel—is most often (in conjunction with Harpo) an occasion for simple comic relief.

But Spielberg's most significant interventions concern his subtle re-assertion of patriarchal power: first, in the invention of a minister father for Shug, and in the stylized rapprochement between her and her father, sinners and saints, the blues and gospel at the film's climax; secondly, in Mister's decision to go to the immigration board and secure their assistance in bringing Nettie and her family home. At every critical moment, Spielberg intervenes, softening the edge of Walker's vision with Hollywood clichés and racial stereotypes. While it would be easy enough to lay these transformations of Walker's novel completely at Spielberg's doorstep (and certainly the film bears the unique imprint of his own psychobiography), it should be clear that Spielberg's choices have also been shaped by Hollywood's vision of the kind of film about Black life that would appeal to a mass audience in the American 1980s.

The commercial success of *The Color Purple* will no doubt spawn yet another 'renaissance' of films about Black subjects. A film based on Toni Morrison's *Tarbaby* is already in production, and plans are underway to produce, under Martin Scorsese's direction, another screen version of Richard Wright's explosive 1940 novel *Native Son*. (Wright was involved in the original film production, starring himself as Bigger Thomas, in 1949-1950. The film had its world premiere aboard a Pan American strato-clipper in November 1950, received favorable reviews at the Venice Film Festival in 1951, but ran into censorship problems in many cities in the United States.) Black culture can be enormously profitable—as the motion picture industry discovered during the early 1970s—particularly when it is projected into a time and space comfortably removed from contemporary social and political realities. Far from constituting a decisive leap forward in the portrayal of Black life, however, the triumph of the Hollywood 'crossover' film during the 1980s forebodes a further circumscription of opportunities for Blacks within the motion picture industry: a cinematic retreat to nostalgia and the pastoral mode as the lens through which Black life is filtered; more fantasized reconciliations between Blacks and whites through the 'gentling' subordination-assimilation of Blacks to white norms and expectations; and, in general, a flight from the depiction of contemporary social reality. To judge from contemporary trends, the long unequal love affair between the Black community and Hollywood is far from having dissolved from its final scene.

Works Cited

Baraka, Amiri (Jones, Leroi) (1963). *Blues People: Negro Music in White America* (New York) (1966). *Home: Social Essays*, (New York), (1972). *Spirit Reach* (Newark).

Collins, Kathleen (1981). 'Kathleen Collins in Conversation with Oliver Franklin,' Pearl Bowser, ed., *Independent Black American Cinema* (New York: Third World Newsreel).

Cripps, Thomas (1978). *Black Film as Genre* (Bloomington).

Crowdus, Gary. 'The Murder of Fred Hampton.' *Cineaste*, 5, 1 (1973): 50–51.

Gayle, Addison, Jr., ed., (1972). *The Black Aesthetic* (New York).

Georgakas, Dan (1972). 'They Have Not Spoken: American Indians in Film,' *Film Quarterly*, 25, 3 26–32. (1973). *Finally Got the News*: The Making of a Radical Film. *Cineaste* 5, 4: pp. 2–6.

Karenga, Ron (1972). 'Black Cultural Nationalism.' Gayle, pp. 31–37.

Klotman, Phyllis Rauch (1979). *Frame By Frame: A Black Filmography* (Bloomington).

Kofsky, Frank (1970). *Black Nationalism and the Revolution in Music* (New York).

Mapp, Edward (1972). *Blacks in American Films: Today and Yesterday*. (Metuchen, New Jersey).

Mason, B. J. (1972). 'The New Films: Culture or Con Game.' *Ebony*, 28, 2 (December 1972): pp. 60–68.

Murray, James P. (1973). *To Find an Image: Black Films From Uncle Tom to Superfly*, (New York).

Newton, Huey P. (1972). *To Die for the People*, (New York).

Taylor, Clyde (n.d.). 'New U.S. Black Cinema,' *Jump Cut* 28 (n.d.): pp. 46–48.

Washington, Michael and Berlowitz, Marvin J. (1975). 'Blaxploitation Films and High School Youth: SWAT/SUPERFLY.' *Jump Cut*, 9 (October 1975): pp. 23–24.

10

Women Writin' Rappin' Breakin'

Nancy Guevara

'Like Aretha Franklin says, who's zoomin' who?'
Roxanne Shanté

Over the past few years, a rash of Hollywood hip-hop movies, together with a spate of thirty-second hip-hop spots for Pepsi-Cola, Kodak, and Burger King, have spun a hype fantasy-image of South Bronx B-boys boogieing, breaking, and scratching records for a massified and mainly white viewing audience. This image of hip-hop is uninflected by any hint of the socio-economic or racial context in which its practices arose, or of the cultural antecedents of these practices: in its commercial representations hip-hop simply *appears* as a faddish display of male exuberance in inner-city ghettoes, a sudden inexplicable burst of color and energy in the cultural vacuum of the early 1980s.

What follows is an attempt to correct one aspect of this distorted image, by foregrounding the distinct and essential creative role of *women* in the formation and development of hip-hop—and by doing so through the testimony of some Black and Latina women themselves. But just as the elision of women from the hip-hop image (however aided and abetted in actuality by various male participants in hip-hop subculture) must be seen in the context of the overall distortion of hip-hop by and in the mass commercial media, so women's involvement with and contributions to the subculture of hip-hop must be understood in the context of its descent from the historical continuum of creative expression of Blacks and other oppressed groups in the United States. The purpose of this introduction, then, is to sketch out some of the main threads and major conjunctures about this genealogy, before moving on to the voices of some of the women rappers, breakers and graffiti writers in hip-hop.

Each of the three forms of hip-hop—rap music, subway graffiti, and breakdance—had grown out of a long history of interaction between Black and Latin urban cultures, whose most recent phase began during the late 1940s, when migrants arriving from colonial Puerto Rico started to take up jobs and live in neighborhoods alongside American Blacks.[1] Since that time, close social interaction between Blacks and Latins and their common subordination to the dominant culture have created the conditions for the development of unique alternative modes of expression. Subway graffiti, for example, descends from the 1950s street graffiti used to proclaim a Black or Latino gang's hold on its territory. During the sixties, graffiti developed into a more elaborate communications network with its own codes of behavior and aesthetics to reflect the identity and concerns of Black and Latino teenagers.[2] Graffiti became even more colorful and stylized during the early seventies with the advent of subway graffiti, which introduced spray-paint as the key artistic medium. While the graffiti of the fifties and sixties did not travel outside the immediate neighborhood, and thus remained unseen beyond the ghettoes, subway graffiti increased the circulation of names, words and messages, carrying this persistent search for identity and self-expression both across and uptown.[3]

The roots of rap music are more complex and varied.[4] Beyond its immediate historical antecedents within Black culture (from the bragging blues of Bo Diddley to the high-energy inspiration of James Brown in cuts like 'Soul Power' and 'Sex Machine', from radical prison toasts to those developed by hip-hop deejays like Afrika Bambaataa and Grandmaster Flash), there stretches a longer history, running back through street games of 'signifying' and 'the dozens' all the way to the word games embedded in Caribbean and West African cultures. The appropriation and dissemination of rap by Puerto Rican deejays like Charlie Chase was facilitated by the similarity in verbal dexterity and rhythmic use of voice prized in these Black traditions to those common to such Latin musical styles as the Puerto Rican *décima* and *plena*. The result of these convergent influences is a complex and highly innovative technique not only of 'rapping' often overtly political lines over previously-recorded musical accompaniments, but of 'mixing', 'cutting', 'scratching', and 'backspinning' the records themselves, thus producing a whole realm of empowering uses of record music for individual and collective expression.

Similarly, the acrobatic virtuosity of breakdancing has clear precedents in early African-rooted forms like the jitterbug and rumba. Here again, James Brown appears as a direct and hugely influential precursor. His spectacular stage performances together with his dancing song hits are recognized sources of breakdancing, along with martial arts and gymnastics. But the belligerent appearance of many breakdance steps, with their emphasis on leg and footwork, also characterizes other Black and Latino dance forms, such as the *capoeira* developed by African slaves in Brazil more than three centuries ago.[5]

Of course the ahistorical commercial presentation of hip-hop is neither accidental nor new. Whenever Black or Latino aesthetic innovations have been repackaged and sold to white audiences as entertainment fads, the contextual and traditional meanings of those innovations have been airbrushed out.[6] Cooptation by the dominant culture invariably involves repression; and in the case of hip-hop (as with bee-bop and bop culture forty-odd years ago), the repression comes in both hard and soft forms. We will return to this point in closing, and so for now will merely note that each year more than $9 million of the New York City budget is spent on the 'graffiti war' waged by its Mass Transportation Authority, and that only a few years ago Black and Latino teenagers were routinely arrested for breakdancing in shopping malls and subway stations.

Nor is the exclusion and/or trivialization of women's role in hip-hop culture a mere oversight on the part of the image-makers. The undermining, deletion, or derogatory stereotyping of women's creative role in the development of minority cultures is a routine practice which serves to impede any progressive artistic or social development by women that might threaten male hegemony in the sphere of cultural production. Just as the accomplishments of women in the Blues tradition or in rock 'n roll remain largely unrecognized, so in commercial representations of hip-hop, women are typically depicted in secondary roles as cheerleaders or bystanders rather than as producers and active participants. Or, when they do receive leading roles, as in most of Hollywood's hip-hop films, women come to hip-hop through romantic involvement with young Blacks and/or Latin breakers and rappers. In this role as exotic outsiders with whom the white audience is encouraged to effect a fantasy identification, their education in rapping and breaking functions to connect hip-hop to mainstream white culture.

The political challenge that hip-hop represents as an expression of oppressed groups in the United States is magnified significantly when the women involved are brought into the real picture. Through the testimony of female rappers, breakers and graffiti writers, vital aspects of the undocumented, intricate cultural contexts and contradictions of hip-hop emerge. Who are these women? What do they think is the origin or future of hip-hop? How do women use this style? Is theirs different from the style men use? What do they think of the social role of hip-hop? The best answers to these questions come from the women themselves. Let's hear what they have to say.

Lady Pink and Lady Heart: 'This *is* a Man's World'

How did 'Lady Pink' become involved in subway graffiti? 'Like any other graffiti writer. First, you're an apprentice to a master who teaches you how to tag your name properly. Then you do pieces on paper. When you have the hang of that, you're ready to go to the [subway] yards. There is so much to know before going to the yards that only masters can get away with it.' To succeed, a writer must be able to create and handle intricate graffiti forms and styles, of which 'tags' (stylized signatures) and 'pieces' (four or more bubble letters representing a name or word) are the simplest.[7] Lady Pink (Sandra Fabara) was a consummate graffiti writer by the fall of 1980, at age fifteen. She was a participant in the historic graffiti show at Fashion Moda in the South Bronx, and was the curator of an exhibit which displayed the works of twenty well-known graffiti writers. Her popularity increased after she played a leading role in the documentary film *Wild Style* (1984).

Pink came from Ecuador at age seven. In New York, she was encouraged by her seventh-grade teacher to attend the High School of Art and Design after she was singled out as the best artist of her class. There, Pink became interested in graffiti and practiced her style in the ladies' room, with her friend 'Lady Heart' (Gloria Williams), who was born in Corona, Queens, to a family that had come north from Alabama.

During her high school years, Heart and her brother devoted long hours to practicing their tags and pieces on the walls. Soon, a teacher wanted to know who was painting the school walls. The result, to their surprise, was that Heart and her brother were commissioned to paint several murals in school and throughout the neighborhood. Thanks to an early interest in painting, Heart was already accustomed to oils and acrylics, but she became more interested in graffiti when she met Pink, and went on to learn more graffiti techniques together with her.

To Pink, graffiti is a personal challenge. Her involvement is directed, as she puts it, 'against the idea that women have no brains, only emotions. That at three o'clock in the morning a girl should be sleeping.' It is not hard to imagine how her family responded to this defiant attitude, but what had been the reaction in the male-dominated world of graffiti? Pink and Heart recognize the talent of male graffiti masters, and are quick to acknowledge the support they have received from Doze, Case, Lee and Seen in particular. Nevertheless, female writers are often the target of jealous males who seek to discredit them. The competition that typically exists among writers takes on a special character when applied to women, as in the constant charge of 'biting' (copying someone else's style) brought against female writers by any number of males.

Moreover, the artistic prestige of girl writers within the hip-hop subculture too often depends less on their ability to use or create style than on their personal (meaning, as often as not, sexual) reputation. Heart explains: 'Being a girl writer you have to be brave because whether you are that kind of girl or not, they figure when a girl hangs out with all these boys [she] is this kind of girl and that. And it's up to you to handle yourself accordingly when situations like that come up.' Graffiti gossip extends to four boroughs, so 'who knows what kind of story is gonna end up in the Bronx when it really happened in Queens,' says Heart. Female writers understand that the boys' personal attacks on their reputation aim at discouraging their participation. 'The stories get so outrageous that it makes you laugh. They want graffiti for boys only. I think they figure that you say something so bad about us, it's just gonna hurt our little feelings and we're not gonna want to be bothered with graffiti. But anybody that's half way on the road to maturity knows not to let what other people say really affect them.'

Yet the negative comments about Pink and Heart are known in more recent times to have discouraged other females from becoming writers, or at least from going beyond 'tagging'. But fear also seems to keep females from going to the subway yards in large numbers. As Pink says, graffiti 'is a filthy business, and then going through creepy tunnels in the South Bronx at three in the morning . . . ' Heart agrees: 'It takes nerve to be a graffiti writer. The yards are dark, the trains make noise. Even when a train is shut-off it makes noise, and you jump and look. You gotta look under the train, and up and down the lanes. Sometimes the workers sneak up on you and they'll chase you!'

Why, then, under such unfavorable conditions, do some young women get involved in graffiti? Heart believes that 'a lot of girls want to be down with graffiti even if they don't write it themselves because there is something about graffiti that just draws people to it.' Pink thinks graffiti writing is the result of a need to make 'your mark on a city that got to be so huge,' where 'you're just a little nobody from the ghetto. You have no money, no school training, what can you do?' Heart adds: 'It is an artistic outlet, to develop your artistic qualities and to make you own little statements.' Moreover, Heart strongly disagrees with predominant accounts claiming that graffiti developed out of the desire of writers to become famous. She thinks that being a writer 'takes much more than that! It started out showing your art work, your talent'.

Wall and subway graffiti of the New York style, unlike others (e.g. bathroom graffiti), serve not merely to label but to reveal, even proclaim, the author's identity, ideas and feelings. One of Pink's graffiti pieces reads (above her signature): 'War, crime, corruption, poverty, inflation, pollution, racism, injustice . . . this *is* a man's world!' Her message not only expresses how she feels about the world, but attributes the actuality of these conditions to men, and contrasts it with a hypothetical female world. Her more overtly political works include representations of burning bodies in El Salvador, war tanks in Nicaragua, skulls after a nuclear disaster, and murals of formidable Amazons symbolizing the power of women.

There are differences in both style and subject between female and male writers. 'Men have a passion for black!' exclaims Pink. 'I sometimes exclude black altogether. I work more with light colors. Things that are a little softer, more tender, sensitive.' Her subjects also differ from those of the young men: 'I paint women. Women in distress or very strong women'. Landscape and flower scenes are other subjects favored by female writers because 'girls wanna more or less decorate the trains,' says Heart. 'Guys talk about destroyin' it, not killin' it but they want all the space for themselves. They all wanna be city kings, their names up on every train all over the city.' Pink has often used stencils to paint big lips and roses instead of writing her name. And both Pink and Heart seek to 'make a statement' by painting make-up and other female properties on the sides of many trains. To them, a style that is consciously, deliberately 'feminine' will help lead to the recognition of girl writers, and will contravert the oppressive attitude of their male peers.

But the women's struggle to establish a presence within graffiti encounters other serious obstacles in addition to male prejudice. Both the sudden commercial success of the graffiti style and increased official opposition to subway graffiti have altered the course of the graffiti movement, arguably to the greater detriment of women writers than of men. While graffiti on canvas is widely popular and marketable, subway graffiti remains an illegal activity. As Heart points out: 'Graffiti is more dangerous now that some yards have attack dogs and tall fences with double sets of barbed-wire.' Earlier on, she reminisces, 'there was none of that. The yards used to be dark and there was always a way in and out.' And the recent prospect of fame and financial rewards has also had a severe impact on the graffiti practice. Heart explains: 'A lot of new writers have the wrong perspective about graffiti. They don't know what respect is about. They just wanna write, write, write.' Disrespect among writers is manifested by crossing-out (covering someone else's name with one's own): 'Toys [apprentice writers] in New York developed a habit of crossing out other people's work to get famous,' says Pink. 'Everything is destroyed, nothing lasts. It is not worth it any more. It's a waste of paint, energy, talent, and risking your life for nothing! It is not the MTA with their dogs and fences, they haven't killed graffiti half as much as the underground battles due to jealousy.' She points out that female writers are a particular target, and often get their work crossed out especially quickly.

Called criminals by the authorities and artists by art dealers, facing danger in the yards and derision and hosility from their male counterparts, female graffiti writers are caught up in baffling contradictions. Lady Heart, for example, joined the US Army looking for the security that life in a subway yard manifestly lacks. She did not want to risk 'getting caught now that I'm no longer fifteen and will go to jail for writing'. Lady Pink has got commissions to fulfill, interviews to give, gallery exhibits to set up, and thus has little time to develop a women's subway style further, or to figure out female strategies to counteract male domination.

Yet despite the serious problems that beset subway writers, Heart is optimistic about the future of graffiti. She believes that 'graffiti is gonna be around. It will never disappear. The little kids will keep trying.' Writers will continue to try because 'their talent hasn't reached the ability where they can go on canvasses right now. So the best place to practice is on the trains, where you see it running and other people see it too and they tell you how it looked.'

Us Girls and the Revenge of Roxanne

Although there are some women deejays, they participate in greater numbers as rappers. Lisa Lee (Lisa Counts) was born in the South Bronx. Her mother is Jamaican and her father is from Atlanta, Georgia. Lisa Lee started rapping in 1976, at age thirteen. She began by writing 'rhymes' for a girlfriend rapper who later encouraged her to 'get on the microphone'. Around 1979, Lisa Lee met Sha Rock, another rapper from North Carolina who was the 'one more' in the group The Funky Four. Lisa recounts: 'Sha Rock was also rapping. Back then it was more like competition. Other people would always compare me to her. They wanted us to battle. She wasn't into it and I wasn't into it, cause I don't like that kind of stuff. So, we got on the mike together.' Soon after, Lisa Lee and Sha Rock decided to form an all-female group. By 1984, Lisa Lee, Sha Rock and Debbie Dee were well-known as the 'Us Girls'. They appeared in *Beat Street* and recorded one of the movie's theme songs, 'Us Girls Can Boogie Too'.

Lisa Lee is an experienced rapper. She rapped in male groups before the formation of 'Us Girls', and one of her recordings was produced by the famous Afrika Bambaataa in 1983. Like most rappers, Lisa composes 'rhymes' or 'raps' which she rehearses and memorizes for performance. As she explains, rapping involves a variety of steps and skills: 'A rhyme is about a situation, like, I was on the train, or about a person. You have to get a topic and put a situation into a rhyme. A routine is more for the group. I write my own rhymes; when we do routines, we all write them.' To construct a routine 'we all keep bringing our different ideas. I may see something that would sound good in a rap. What nobody else has talked about. Whatever idea comes to mind, we write it down and figure out how to put it into a rap. For example, we say let's talk about what's going on in the South Bronx. The parties, or what happens when you get robbed, or how people dress at the parties.' In a live show 'you talk about these situations. You more or less try to get the people up to party with you, you try to involve the people.' But when doing a record 'you try to get a message out to the people. You stick to one specific subject'. The popularity of rap music has encouraged its thematic development. Rappers are now more aware of the content of their rhymes. 'Before you just wanted to get the crowd to party', Lisa says, 'now you go home and you write something that makes sense. Whenever you rap, you want to relate a message to the people. Because people are more into it now, you know that they really listen to what you're saying.'

Since theirs is an oral genre, rappers are more concerned with the delivery of words than with the correctness of grammar and spelling on paper. Verbal ability and memory are emphasized over writing, and words are often altered to fit the rhythm. Lisa Lee, for example, discards the written words after she has memorized a rhyme; and Roxanne Shanté, a more recent female rapper, is known for never writing her rhymes.

But what are the rhymes about? Themes of sex, money and power predominate in rap compositions. Strong sexual imagery is frequently used to indicate personal affirmation. Like other Afro-

American musical forms, rap music is infused with sexuality. It has been said that the power of Black music is an expression of Black social struggle, its sexuality a form of rebellion against all forms of social and political oppression.[8] Certainly the use of straightforward sexual language in rap lyrics and the unreserved movements of their stage delivery express collective sexual emotion and work to liberate the performance and the performers from prevailing inhibitions.

But female rappers are often restricted in their performance. In this regard, rap music, otherwise an emancipating collective expression, becomes oppressive and discriminatory. Lisa Lee's experience illustrates this difference: 'In a show, males do different things than we can do. When they get up there, they'll say something smart to a girl in the crowd, something nasty. They like that kind of stuff and we can't. When they have emcee conventions, and all the emcees come to compete against each other, they start taking off their shirts and their pants just to win. We can't do that, we don't really get into it but the crowd loves that.' When asked why women rappers feel they cannot do the same, Lisa Lee responds laughing: 'How are we going to take off our skirts? . . . If they do it, if a male does that, the audience will say, Man they're crazy. I like that. If a girl does it, they'll say, Oh my God! they were disgusting and nasty. That's how they judge it. I don't know. That's how how it is out there.'

In the case of rap performance, the response of the audience restrains or bolsters the amount and form of sexual display in ways that reflect the dominant values and judgements of the society at large. In rap music, what a female rapper may or may not say during her performance and the ways she (physically) presents herself are much more defined than in the case of her male counterpart. 'Being that we're all female, we just dress more feminine', says Lisa Lee. Mini-skirts and high-heeled shoes guarantee a favorable response.

Style and subject matter in rap music also vary according to gender. Female rappers tend to be less aggressive (while remaining assertive) in their use of sexual language and imagery. Compare the following two rhymes by a female and male rapper respectively:

Sophisticated is the Lady Lisa Lee
to be the man in my life, you got to be my only.
I'll always hold you secure in my arms real tight,
squeeze you real good til you feel just right.
I have a heart of gold I wanna share with you,
and give you the type of loving, that you never been through.

Versus:

> I worked her body til she went insane
> she started talking like Lois Lane.
> She said, 'Hey sir. I'm your fan
> cause you did me badder than Superman.'

Similarly, explicitly political themes are more often found in the lyrics of male rappers then in those of women. The titles alone of many male rap cuts—e.g. 'How We Gonna Make the Black Nation Rise', or 'White Lines'—suggest the powerful political messages they seek to convey. Yet the same feminine 'image' whose repressive construction and projection inhibits the expression of female rappers of their own sexuality appears to constrain their ability to develop styles in the direction of political assertiveness as well.

However, more recent female rappers have begun to question this role. The case of Roxanne Shanté is an eloquent example. Lolita Shanté Gooden is from Jamaica, Queens. Her mother is from Alabama, her father from Antigua. At age fourteen, Roxanne Shanté recorded 'Roxanne's Revenge' (1984), a female 'response' to the widely popular song 'Roxanne Roxanne' by UTFO (1984). The Revenge of Roxanne answers UTFO's sexist remarks about a girl named Roxanne with Shanté's defiant rap. ' "Roxanne's Revenge" came off the top of my head,' says Shanté. 'It wasn't my major subject. It's a story. Like "Roxanne Roxanne" is the story of a girl, "Roxanne's Revenge" is saying that guys should stop talking about girls because it's not working anymore. It's played out! Talking about girls is fine as long as you've got something good to say about them. Why do you always gotta say girls are stuck up?'

The combination of UTFO's 'Call Her a Crab (Roxanne Part 2)' and 'The Real Roxanne' with 'Roxanne's Revenge', 'Roxanne Is a Man,' 'The Original Roxanne', etc., exemplifies a new development in rap music: groups or individual rappers responding to other rappers' songs. A still more recent example of sexual polemic in rap is the response by 'Super Nature', a female group, to the very popular and witty 'LA-DI-DA-DI' (by Doug E. Fresh and M.C. Ricky D, 1985). This active controversing and cross-reference creates dialogue aimed at complementing or, more often, challenging the statements made by other rappers; for Shanté, rap responses are important to 'put guys, or anybody else with a crazy ego, in their place'.

Roxanne Shanté recorded 'Run Away', 'Queen of Rock' and

'Shanté's Turn' among other songs in 1985. Her topics vary from the personal to the socially conscious: 'Out of the kitchen and into the streets. That basically sums it all up', she says. 'Men say that women are only good for cooking, cleaning and making babies. That's changing. But now if a woman goes to work, people call her a woman of the world. When men go out to work, they're just working men. Why can't they be just working women?'

With her testimony Roxanne Shanté confirms once more that female rappers are acutely aware of the prejudice against women's work. But she disagrees with other females on how to deal with the problem. While Lisa Lee worried about high-heels for a performance, Shanté now goes on stage with no make-up and everyday clothes: 'The audience is not there to see how you dress but to see how you perform,' Shanté says. Most of her fans are older women, but except for a few confrontations with male rappers, Shanté finds men appreciative of her: 'They congratulate me on "Roxanne's Revenge". I look up to Run-DMC and The Fat Boys in particular because they don't let their success go to their head, and you can say that's what I'm trying to be like.'

Baby Love: Give Us A Break

Daisy Castro, 'Baby Love', is one of the few well-known female breakdancers. Her parents came from Puerto Rico in the early 1960s and decided to settle in New York City, where Daisy was born in 1968. Daisy has practiced Flamenco since she was six, and by the time she joined the now famous Rock Steady Crew, around 1981, she had some breaking experience as well. Two of the crew members, Prince Ken Swift and Doze, lived near Daisy and were longtime friends before she was asked to break with the group. At the time there were other girls learning to breakdance and forming their own groups. Daisy remembers another young woman who was involved long before she herself arrived on the scene: 'That was when everything was going down in breaking [around 1976], but she stopped. Now there's a lot of girls breaking.'

Of the recent female crews, Daisy thinks the Dynamic Dolls is one of the best: 'It's a group of three girls. They are good. There is a lot of them that are good ... I think every girl group that's out there is good because they've got the nerve to do it. I'm very proud of them.' Actually, female breakdancers have existed all along, but have never received as much recognition as males. This neglect has itself conditioned the relation of women to breakdancing. Moreover, it is often claimed that because breaking, the most athletic of the breakdancing moves, requires a lot of upper-body strength, women are less likely to try it.[9] To most commentators, breakdancing developed exclusively as competition between males and requires this macho quality to be executed.[10] But the assumption that breakdancing draws only from male-related activities ignores other possible influences. The speedy footwork and acrobatic tricks of freestyle double-Dutch, for instance, are no less impressive than those of breakdancing. Like most breaking moves, this energetic female street game depends on how well the jumper balances her body weight, the swiftness of leg and feet movements, and the gracefulness of her performance.

The widespread notion of the dangers and difficulty of breaking does tend to discourage female breakers. But breakdancing has more to do with concentration, balance, practice and precision than with sheer physical strength. As Baby Love put it: 'Breakdancing is concentration. If you concentrate you'll get it. That's the way I actually feel about breaking for girls. Plus we got strength up here too. All you need is a lot of exercise and you get your strength.' Some breaking moves may indeed be uncomfortable for women: the handglide, for example, in which breakers spin on one hand, with bent legs spread far apart, involves positioning the elbow across the stomach in a way that can be painful. But Baby Love insists that however much they may prefer some moves over others, female breakers can do them all.

Nontheless, when girls do get involved in breaking, they are often patronized by boyfriends or big brothers who decide which steps are sufficiently safe or feminine for them to do. The emphasis on femininity from peers and others has direct implications on the style of female breakdancers. As Baby Love expresses it: 'girls got all kinds of styles. They got b-boy style, then they mix it with b-girl style or with Lock. B-girl style is more feminine. It's basically the same, just different names. The guys do it more of a man style, a girl maybe can do a little bit of turning or a little bit of jazz, and then right there you could start breaking. That would be a feminine way.' In general, slower and smoother breaking moves are considered feminine and appropriate for females.

As with graffiti writing and rapping, this conventional femininity plays a twofold role in breakdancing. On the one hand, it limits the style and form of expression. But it is also used by women for self-assertion. A 'feminine' style is stressed by girl breakers to differentiate it, and to some extent distance it, from the style of boys. 'We do a more feminine style than the guys just to show that we're not girls trying to look like guys', says Daisy. 'We're not trying to take a guy's place. We try to prove to people that guys are not the only ones that can do it. Girls can, too, and they've got rights!'

The relegation of females to a cheerleading role in breakdancing contests is also closely related to repressive definitions of femininity. In most breakdance contests women do not battle men. The Rock Steady Crew often performs without Baby Love: 'I'm always there. But sometimes I don't battle because the other groups don't have a girl for me to battle, and it's kind of weird a girl battling a guy, you know. I stand there and cheer them up and make sure they win the battle.' Daisy realizes that the increasing popularity and acceptance of breaking have encouraged greater participation from women and a restlessness with their limited function as cheerleaders: 'There are girls that are dancing as good as the guys. And they're willing to take on anyone that comes their way.'

Media and commercial success, Baby Love thinks, has given 'an opportunity to the kids to show what they got', but it also raises concerns about the future of breakdancing: 'It's gonna last in the hearts of the kids who've been doing it for a long time. But it's not gonna be something that people will keep on paying groups to do. It's gonna go right back to the streets. I think it belongs there. It belongs in people's hearts. If it does leave, it won't leave for ever. We're gonna do it in the streets. It's gonna stay here but not everybody is gonna keep on making money out of it.' For Baby Love, breakdancing is more than a fad destined to disappear after its commercial potential declines; it is part of her culture, a street form in which women will continue to participate in spite of the constant marginalization of their presence in the mass media hype.

Conclusions

COLLEGE GRAD for anti-litter/graffiti
efforts in NYC. $15,000.
New York Times classified, Oct. 20, 1985

Lady Pink, Lady Heart, Lisa Lee, Roxanne Shanté and Baby Love all attest to the presence and active participation of women in hip-hop. These Black and Latina daughters of immigrant working-class parents belong integrally to the social landscape in which hip-hop first developed. Hence their familiarity with and command of styles and techniques used in hip-hop. Through them, we learn that women elaborate styles and subjects of their own which are often very different from those of the men. Furthermore, these young women express a keen understanding of both the commercial establishment's interest in hip-hop and the official opposition to hip-hop by the political authorities, as well as the prevalent gender discrimination manifest in the expectations of their male peers and in the omission or distorted portrayal of their role by the media.

Commercial and media representations tend to conceal the strong official opposition to hip-hop of which Lady Pink and Lady Heart spoke. Subway writers have been physically abused, imprisoned and even killed (as in the widely-publicized case of Michael Stewart), while mainstream artists like Keith Haring or Kenny Scharf capitalize on their graffiti-esque painting and its exhibition in Manhattan galleries. Recent attempts to combat subway graffiti have tended to deny the common social base of hip-hop forms and pit them against one another, as in McDonald's 'Rap Against Graffiti Contest' and the 'Break Against Graffiti Coalition' project by We Care About New York, Inc. Let us remember, too, that breakdancing was also opposed when it was still a street form which, in the eyes of the authorities too closely resembled stylized gang fighting. More recently, in the wake of racial violence reported at showings of the rap movie *Krush Groove*, rap music has encountered increasing antagonism. Despite rampant cooptation and romaticizing, hip-hop is still largely treated by officialdom as a form of pollution and a public menace. Yet perhaps the most serious threat it represents to the established culture is its example of alternative artistic practice. Lady Heart's vision of art as a public act, exposed to mass scrutiny and utilizing forbidden spaces for execution, challenges the dominant view of art as a private, individual expression limited to art schools, galleries and other designated areas. Art in the hands of subway writers becomes a tool of public expression in the subversion of top-down cultural programming and the hegemony of billboard icons.

In the United States, Afro-American music once helped awaken the political consciousness of slaves in the fields and the church; while more recently in Britain, the Punk and Rastafarian alliance (working-class British and Jamaican youth) and the direct connection of the East End Punks with the British Socialist Workers Party in the 'Rock Against Racism' campaign, have given practical examples of how 'symbolic resistance can be translated into political action'.[11] So today in hip-hop, Black and Latino expressions have the same potential to provoke and accompany the social movements of oppressed groups—a potential whose political importance has already been noted by commentators as far away as Paris, where Sidney Duteil, host of a television and dance show called *Hip-Hop*, argues that reggae, African, English and American music are emerging as a configuration of styles which together constitute a 'powerful weapon against racism'.[12]

The political significance of hip-hop is extended and deepened by the presence and active participation of the women of the hip-hop subculture, who must fight not only the prevailing prejudice against racially oppressed groups and working-class art, but the critical double standards applied throughout Western culture to women artists. The traditional belief that women do not have the physical capacity to engage in certain high art practices (e.g. sculpture) is mirrored in the denial of women's ability to breakdance. The jealousy of male graffiti writers shows up in hostile and belittling comments towards the work of female writers like Lady Pink, and in the attempt by the graffiti boys to discredit Pink and Heart through personal sexual aspersions. Moreover, abiding notions of female delicacy and the ideal of feminine purity crop up thoughout all these women's testimony, and have had noticeable impact on their styles. While some women develop alternative styles that draw on such notions, for example, the use of predominantly soft colors by Lady Pink, and the jazzy moves of Baby Love, Roxanne Shanté, as we saw, refuses to comply with demands for feminine out-fits in rap performances.

Far from being submissive and accepting, the female rappers, breakers, and writers strike back; but their resistance takes on a number of complex and contradictory forms. The actual variations of style and subject chosen by most of the hip-hop women to state their claims do not appear to defy stereotypes of femininity. To paint big red lips on subway trains as a statement of female independence tends to reinforce sexist ideas about women's artistic expression. Similarly, the 'Us Girls' effort to project a feminine image by wearing mini-skirts during a performance, and Baby Love's search for 'delicate' breaking moves, indicate signs of confusion between expression and its stereotype. But these manifestations of distinctive female styles are initiatives undertaken by the hip-hop women to counter male supremacy. They represent important acts of resistance when considered within the gender structure of hip-hop practice.

Women obviously experience an even more intense opposition for their involvement in hip-hop than do men. On top of official harassment come family and peer demands for composure in the name of femininity. In addition, women's struggle for recognition in hip-hop is sabotaged by the tendency of the media to ignore, negate or stereotype their participation. The testimony presented here should help to dispel the illusion, propagated by Hollywood and Madison Avenue, that girls are involved in hip-hop only as cheerleaders, bystanders and exotic outsiders. The young women's dual struggle, both with the media images and within hip-hop itself, represents the movement's most radical challenge: just as hip-hop poses a menace to dominant white bourgeois culture, women's participation in its supposedly masculine rituals threatens still another haven of male hegemony.

11

Notes on an Alternative Model: Neither/Nor

Hortense J. Spillers

'Language has always been the companion of empire.'
Antonio de Nebrija, 'The Year of the Other' (1792)

In an inventory of American ideas, the thematic of the 'tragic mulatto/a' seems to disappear at the end of the nineteenth century.[1] Even though certain writers in the United States have pursued this configuration of character well into the twentieth, with varying and divergent purposes in mind,[2] it is as though both the dominant and dominated national interests eventually abandoned the vocation of naming, perceiving, and explaining to themselves the identity of this peculiar new world invention. A retrieval of this topic will, therefore, appear anachronistic and irrelevant to African-American critical projects at the present moment. Furthermore, the term itself and the issues that it raises are so thoroughly circumscribed by historical closure and are so apparently bankrupt in the situation of their origin that my attempt to revivify them is burdened from the outset with doubt, with the necessity to prove their revised critical point. But it seems to me that the mulatto figure, stranded in cultural ambiguity, conceals the very strategies of terministic violence and displacement that have enabled a problematic of alterity regarding the African American community in the United States.

Created to provide a middle ground of latitude between 'Black' and 'white', mulatto being a neither/nor proposition—inscribed in no historic locus or materiality—could therefore be only evasive and shadowy on the national landscape. To that extent, the mulatto/a embodied an alibi, an excuse for 'other/otherness' that the dominant culture could not (cannot now either) appropriate or wish away. An accretion of signs that embody the 'unspeakable', of the Everything that the dominant culture would forget, the mulatto/a as term designates a disguise; covers up, in the century of Emancipation and beyond, the social and political reality of the dreaded African presence. Behind the African-become-American stands the shadow, the insubstantial 'double' that the culture dreamed *in the place of* that humanity transformed into its profoundest challenge and by the impositions of policy, its deepest 'un-American' activity.

To understand, then, the American invention of the mulatto, a term imported from the European lexicon,[3] is to understand more completely, I feel, the false opposition of cultural traits that converge on the binary distribution of 'black' and 'white'. My further aim in exploring this topic, however, is to try to discover how 'mulatto-ness', the covering term, explains the workings of gender as a category of social production that has not yet been assimilated to women of color. Rather than definitive proof for this point, these notes are a trial of it.

Before pursuing these observations further, I should point out certain difficulties inherent in this analysis. Those historical subjects subsumed under 'mulatto/a' cannot be so easily banished to the realm of the mythical. I am drawing a distinction throughout between historical figures like Frederick Douglass, or Lemuel Haynes, Vermont preacher of the early nineteenth century, and the *appropriation* of the interracial child by genocidal forces of dominance. The latter concerns a violence, or fatal ignorance, of naming and placing that is itself paradigmatic of the model of alterity.

To compare, then, historical subjects with idea-forms or iconographic content or characters from novels might suggest an incommensurability, or even incapacity in a critical method, but the comparison could be instructive, since it alerts us to the subtleties that threaten to tranform the living subject into an inert mass and suggest the reincarnations of human violence in their intellectual and symbolic array. The 'mulatto/a', like the 'nigger', tells us little or nothing about its buried subject, but it reveals a great deal about the psychic and cultural reflexes that invent and invoke them. I am suggesting that in the *stillness* of time and space eventuated by the 'mulatto/a'—its apparent sameness of fictional, historical, and auto-biographical content—we gain insight into the *theft* of the dynamic principle of the living that distinguishes the subject from his/her objectification. Such difference remains evident in the institution of new world enslavement and the captivity and production of, for example, William Faulkner's narrator's 'wise supine' female of *Absalom, Absalom!*

The contradictory paternity of the mulatto character in fiction, like its parallel in the historical sequence, demarcates the beginning and end of cultural and symbolic illegitimacy. We shall try to see more fully how and why that is the case. America's historic mulatto/a subject plays out his/her character on the ground of a fiction made public and decisive by dimensions of the spectacular and the specular. In his/her face, the deceits of a culture are mirrored; the deeds of a secret and unnamed fatherhood made known.

Faulkner and the Grammar of Racism

'My father was a white man. He was admitted to be such by all I ever heard speak of my parentage. The opinion was also whispered that my master was my father, but of the correctness of this opinion, I know nothing . . .'[4] Frederick Douglass by any other name would tell the same tale over and over again with frightening consistency. But mulatto-ness is not, fortunately, a figure of self-referentiality. Neither the enslaved man/woman, nor the fugitive-in-freedom would call *himself/herself* 'mulatto/a', a special category of being that isolates and overdetermines the human character to which it points. A semantic marker, already fully occupied by a content and an expectation, America's 'tragic mulatto' exists *for others*—and a particular male other—in an attribution of the illicit that designates the violent mingling and commingling of blood lines which a simplified cultural patrimony wishes to deny. But in that very denial, the most dramatic and visible admissions are evident.

The site of a contamination, this marked figure has no name that is not parodic. Joe Christmas, for example, connected with the realm of immanence, of pure nature, makes no claim to rational force in the eyes of his maker.[5] Standing outside the ruined house of Joanna Burden, at the broken gate, in thightall weeds, Christmas, in an erection scene, engages gestures of alienation that overlap the erotic: 'watching his body, seeming to watch it turning slow and lascivious in a whispering of gutter filth like a drowned corpse in a thick still black pool of more than water' (p. 100). Shortly following this bizarre moment, a car comes into Christmas's hearing, as he observes his body 'grow white out of the darkness like a kodak print emerging from the liquid'. Just as the photograph results from a biochemical process, Christmas materializes the unarticulated, unaccomodated American identity—raw and fundamental in a portrayal of basic, unmitigated urges. We cannot even call Christmas's compulsion 'desire' yet, since it is untouched by the mediations and remediations of culture. Transformed into naked, grotesque, hungry man at the world's margin, Christmas speaks the radical disjuncture of human experience as his own private chaos. Christmas's narrative takes hold of a conscious infinity of pain as we see him refracted through an endless regression of events in the *rencontre* of former selves. We observe a figure drowning in a sea of phenomena, enacting and re-enacting a purposeful purposelessness of movement that is bizarre to the point of madness. Animated by forces beyond his knowing, Christmas embodies the deracinated person, fixed in cultural liminality. Time passes for him, over and around him, but it has no subjective properties that he might call his own.

A 'unanimity-minus-one',[6] who assumes the terror and cruci-fixion of natal community's 'expendable figure', Christmas is Faulkner's powerful effort to give grammar to American racial ideology. But 'race' itself is already a mystification by 1929, which year also witnesses the publication of Nella Larson's *Passing*, another sortie into the intrigues of genetic determinism. 'Race' becomes for Faulkner, as for Larson and Jessie Fauset, a metaphor through which the chaotic and primitive urges of human community find systematic expression. In that sense, 'community' comes weighted with the heft of irony, since, in Faulkner's case, its ultimate embodiment is Percy Grimm, one's 'perfect kamikazi'. It is therefore both stunning and only to be expected that, for Grimm and his kind, Christmas's jugular relocates in his genitals: the flight of Joe Christmas, arrested in the kitchen of the outraged Reverend Gail Hightower, ends in a bloodbath. Grimm pursues him through the mob that wants his flesh for the death of Joanna Burden. More precisely, his killing is a castration, as Grimm hacks away at the forbidden 'cargo' in the name of white women's honor.

It would seem, then, that the mulatto in the text of fiction provides a strategy for naming and celebrating the phallus. In other words, the play and interplay of an open, undisguised sexuality are mapped on the body of the mulatto character, who allows the dominant culture to say without parting its lips that 'we have willed to sin', the puritan recoil at the sight and the site of the genitals. In that regard, Percy Grimm is his culture's good little factotum, who understands on some dark level of unknowing that the culture—more pointedly, the culture of the Fathers—can never admit, as Joe Christmas's wildness reminds them, that the law is based on phallic violence in an array of other names and symbols. The term 'mulatto/a', then, becomes a displacement for a proper name, an instance of the 'paradox of the negative' that signifies what it does not mean. In Faulkner's work, at least, sexuality is literally monumental, with none of the antiseptic saving grace that psychoanalysis lends. The unavoidable bedrock of human and fictional complication, sexuality is here put back in proximity with the terrible.

If, as old man Doc Hines in enraged and consistent babble contends, Joe Christmas—his probable grandson—describes 'the mark and the knowledge', then Christmas is the first and last victim on his way out, given the peculiar occasion to understand history and culture, or those economies of violence that carefully differentiate 'inner' and 'outer', 'order' and 'degree'.

In his *Conquest of America*, Tzvetan Todorov distinguishes three fundamental dimensions to alterity: 1) the *axiological* level—'the other is good or bad, I love him, or . . . he is my equal or my inferior (for there is usually no question that I am good and that I esteem myself)' 2) the *praxeological* level, the placing of distance or proximity between oneself and an imagined other—'I embrace the other's values, I identify myself with him; or else I identify the other with myself, I impose my own image upon him; between submission to the other and the other's submission, there is also a third term, which is neutrality, or indifference'; 3) the *epistemic* level—'I know or am ignorant of the other's identity. Of course, there is no absolute here, but an endless gradation between the lower or higher states of knowledge.'[7]

As an instance of the exterior other in *negative* identity, Christmas, on Todorov's levels of analysis, is made the absolute equivalent of anomie. At no time in his fictional development do we see him in clear association with wild, untamed plenitude, from Faulkner's version of terrifying sexuality in the figures of Joanna Burden and Burden's good double in the pregnant Lena Grove, to the unspeaking and unspeakable neologism of filth—the 'woman-shenegreo' of a particular Christmas nightmare—to the moonscape of urns, associated with the menses and Christmas's initiation into the rites of the sexual and sacrificial, to the cosmic infinity of days and space that swallow him up in a hideous repetition-compulsion that precedes his end. We observe in Faulkner, paradoxically, instances of the exterior other in *positive* identity, one whose laws of behavior are much harder and more challenging to detect.

The Narrative as Sexual Violence

The exterior other in positive identity is, for Faulkner, a female. In the Faulknerian situation of the female, we gain insight into the processes of gender-making as a special outcome of modes of dominance. But even more importantly, we observe gender as a special feature of racialist ideology. In other words, the African-American female, in her historic identity, robbed of the benefits of the 'reproduction of mothering', is, consequently, the very negation of femaleness that is the peculiar cultural property of Anglo-American women. Faulkner's *Absalom, Absalom!* might be looked at as a study of the case.

This novel renders a fiction of misplaced incestuous longings and the play of homoerotic motives by way of a Freudian family romance.[8] It is key that the children of unreconstructed Thomas Sutpen, the great obsession of Rosa Coldfield's furious speaking, are actually and symbolically 'white' and 'colored'. In effect, this character out of the Virginia wilds, with a crucial stop in Haiti, represents the Fatherhood that founds a 'civilization' but culminates in a return of the repressed—French *Bon*-become-black *Bond*, what Faulkner's Luster says the law puts on you when it catches up with you. The route from Haiti, to New Orleans, to Sutpen's Hundred in Yoknapatawpha County, is purposefully and gravidly suggestive, as it involves the worlds of sub-Saharan Africa, the Caribbean, and the United States in the replay of an economic triangulation whose wealth is built solidly on the backs and with the blood of captive human cargo. It is, then, not at all accidental in the scheme of history implied by Faulkner's fiction that the savage and dangerous denial of Charles Bon's paternity has precedent in the cultural institution of new world enslavement (as attested by Frederick Douglass, for example) and that this enslavement has a special place, meaning, and economics for the female, as witnessed in the narrative of Linda Brent.[9]

Absalom, Absalom! concerns most directly a man who had two sons, one of them the would-be morganatic byblow of an obscure white male on the run (except that Sutpen did marry the mother of Charles Bon only to discover, after the fact, that he had been 'betrayed' by the makers of this contrived connubial arrangement). The overseer of a sugar plantation on the island of Santo Domingo—branded in historical memory by the successful revolt of Touissant L'Ouverture—Sutpen tells his version of his fiction to his contemporary, the grandfather of Quentin: that, heroically, singlehandedly, he had quelled a siege of insurgent African captives on the Haitian land. The reward for his 'bravery', the dowry of the marriage bed, so to speak, is the hand of the master's daughter, whose mother, in turn, is Spanish, the dark suggestion, not French. When Sutpen discovers that the woman to whom he is married has 'Negro blood' in her veins, that single most powerful drop of dexyribose nucleic acid, he decides simultaneously that she cannot, for that reason, contribute to the increment of his 'design'. He then abandons her and her son, repudiating them in the name of a higher social and moral purity. But he compensates, he imagines, by relinquishing his legal right to various Haitian properties accruing to him as marital lagniappe. These properties revert to the plantation owner's daughter, who remains unnamed, like all mulattas (with the exception of Clytie, Sutpen's other daughter).

Leaving the West Indies for other new world territory, Sutpen arrives in Mississippi to take up land and build his 'empire'. With white Ellen Coldfield, of the indubitable blood, Sutpen has a daughter and son, Henry and Judith. But in Haiti a full decade before, Charles, the Good—forced into being a prodigal—has been denied the *name*, if not the connubial inheritance, of the father. At 'Ole Miss' on the eve of civil war, brother and brother meet—the marked and the untainted—their consanguinity unknown to either. This disastrous encounter that possibly ends in fratricide bears the earmark of sexual attraction, incestuously linked. But parallel to it is the complementary sybaritic tale, staked out in massive erotic display, of Charles Bon installed with his mother in New Orleans under conditions of severe and privileged privacy. In the narrative of Quentin Compson's father, not definitively informed by the apposite 'facts' of the case, a probable fiction is hatched—or a fiction 'true enough'—concerning Bon's unnamed octoroon mistress and the intricately manufactured arts of pleasure that distinguish the fictive New Orleans whorehouse.[10]

Compson's social and political sense makes several things evident at once: He imagines himself the embodiment of the 'heritage peculiarly Anglo Saxon—of fierce mysticism' (p. 108). The world that he narrates through his son Quentin is permeated by notions of caste and hierarchy. This order of things, eminently linear, is fundamentally identified by its interdictive character, whose primary object of desire and placement is the female. But in this instance, 'femaleness' is abstracted by legal practice and social custom into an idea that may be sealed off at any concrete point as forbidden territory. In other words, female, in the brain of the creating male narrator, allows access only insofar as she approximates physical/sexual function. A curious split of motives takes place here so that on the one hand the last women in this hierarchical scale of values—the 'slave girls' for instance—are both more and less female, while, on the other, the same may be said for the first 'lady', albeit for radically different reasons. Compson's 'ladies, women, females' specify an increasingly visual and dramatic enactment of male heterosexuality along three dimensions of female being—'the virgins whom gentlemen someday married, the courtesans to whom they went while on sabbaticals to the cities, the slave girls and women upon whom the first caste rested and to whom in certain cases it doubtless owed the very fact of its virginity . . . ' (p. 109).

In this economy of delegated sexual efficacies, the castes of women enter into a drama of exchange, predicated on the dominant male's self-deceit. The third caste robs the first of a putative clitorial and vaginal pleasure, as the first purloins from the third a uterine functionality.[11] *Only* the latter gains here the rites and claims of motherhood, blind to its potential female pleasure and reduced, paradoxically, in the scale of things to a transcendent and opaque Woman-hood. In fact, we could say that whatever 'essence' or 'stuff' of the female genitalia that is lost in Compson's first estate of females is more than compensated by the third estate, inexorably fixed in the condition of a mindless fertility, just as bereft as the first of the possibilities of its own potential female pleasure.[12] But quite obviously the ways and means of domination are not adopted with cultural/historical subjects-become-objects in mind, nor is 'gender' here any more than, or other than, an apt articulation of a divided male heteroclite eros.

Inside the split ego of the dominant male falls the 'mulatta', or the 'octoroon', or the 'quadroon'—those disturbing vectors of social and political identity—who heal the rupture at points of wounding. Allowing the male to have his cake and eat it too, or to rejoin the 'female' with the 'woman', the mulatta has no name because there is *not* a locus, or a strategy, for this unitarian principle of the erotic in the nineteenth-century mentality of Faulkner's male characters. Bon's unnamed female forebear and his unnamed octoroon mistress, the unvoiced shadowy creatures who inhibit the content of the narratives of three male figures in the novel, suggest both the vaginal and the prohibitive pleasure.

The patriarchal prerogatives outlined by Compson are centered in notions that concern the domestication of female sexuality—how it is thwarted, contained, circumscribed, and above all, *narrated*. Not a single female character here escapes the outcome, from the infantilized, doll-like women of the master class, to the brutalized women who serve them. Under these conditions, sexuality is permissible, but silenced, only within the precincts of the father's house. We should say in the place of the *permissible*, that sexuality is *clean* only in the father's house. Beyond the sphere of domesticity, the sexual—tenaciously named—effects synonmity with the illicit, the wild, the mysterious, without permutation.[13] One of its signs is the 'mulatta', who has no personhood, but locates in the flesh a site of cultural and political maneuver. Unlike African female personality, implied in her presence, the 'mulatta' demarcates those notions of femaleness that would re-enforce the latter as an object of gazing—the dimension of the spectacular that we addressed before as the virtually unique social property of the 'mulatto/a'.

The Mulatta as White Fiction

Noted for his/her 'beauty', the 'mulatto/a in fiction bears a secret, the taint of evil in the blood, but paradoxically, the secret is vividly worn, made clear. Unlike Joe Christmas, whom we designated as an instance of the exterior other in negative identity, the mulatta, in positive identity, has value for the dominant other only insofar as she becomes the inaccessible female property that can be rendered, at his behest, instantly accessible. Teasing himself with her presence, the dominant other re-intersects the lines of sexuality and 'civilization' forced to diverge by the requirements of the family, private property, and the state. 'Virility' reveals itself in the whorehouse as the scandal that is not only sufferable, but also primarily applauded as the singular fact and privilege of the phallus.

It doesn't matter if the principle of virility is, among the living historic male subjects, an engagement fraught with chance, or the erection that occasionally fails, or the sporadic impotence about which the living historic female subjects remain loyally silent. We are talking about myth here, those boundaries of discourse that determine belief, practice, and desire. To that extent, all gendering activity—'male', 'female', and their manifold ramifications—constitutes the Grand Lie about which novels are written and against which the necessary 'hurt' of history presses.[14]

Even though Compson the narrator does not entirely grasp the political and ironic implications of his own conjecture (as *reported* to Shreve by Quentin at Harvard), nor know in those recalled narrative moments that Charles Bon is *not* an Anglo-Saxon male, he adequately identifies the complementary relationship between chattel slavery and a eugenics of pleasure. Imagining what young Henry Sutpen, the Mississippi provincial, might have observed in his exposure to certain peculiarities of New Orleans life, Compson draws out the hidden exchange-value of female use here as a commodification of the flesh that takes place according to intricate rules of gallantry. The caste/cast of octoroon females (in which Bon's pregnant mistress is installed) literally belongs to a class of 'masters', who protect their 'property' by way of various devices that cluster in notions of 'honor'. It would not do, for instance, for Henry Sutpen to call Bon's mistress a 'whore', since he or any other male committing this *faux pas* would be 'forced to purchase that privilege with some of [his] blood from probably a thousand men' (p. 115). The protection of chattel property in this instance occasions the ethics of the duel as the *vertical* version of the tumescent male. In other words, maleness is centered here almost entirely in displaced forms of sexual activity manifested in acts of courtesy and carefully choreographed through an entire 'field of manners' from a certain architectural structure and accoutrements of the interior, to modes of dress and address.

This relocated mimesis of European courtly love traditions places 'gender' squarely within the perspective of a cultural invention whose primary aim is gratifying the appetites of the flesh. This materialist philosophy, modulated through various points of human valuation, would suggest that culture itself elaborates a structure of production and reproduction, positing, quite arbitrarily, 'higher' and 'lower' reaches of human society which are in turn immersed in the principle of desire in the Dominant Other. But it seems that powers of domination succeed only to the extent that their permeation remains silent and concealed to those very historical subjects— 'higher' and 'lower'—upon whom the entire structure depends. In other words, the fictions and realities of domination are opaque (not everywhere and at once visible) not only to the subjected (and *narrated*) community, but they also remain elusive in their authentic character as raw and violent assertion to the dominant (and *narrating*) community. Compson, for example, as a materialized fictive presence, assumes a piacular function of female use. His hyperbolic sense of the 'Anglo-Saxon' male mission is grammatically similar to Perry Miller's classic analysis of the puritan colonial's 'errand into the wilderness'.[15] That Compson's grammar crosses its wires with the 'religious impulse' suggest not only the vanities of self-deceit, but also the implicit obscenities of an unironized view of any human and social arrangement. Further, his shortsightedness would problematize the 'religious' itself as a special means of domination; as a dominant discourse hiding its hand, veiling its baser motivations.

But Compson initiates the first half of his analysis with a substantially correct assessment: the structure of the octoroon mistress represents the 'supreme apotheosis of chattelry . . . human flesh bred of the two races for that sale . . . ' (p. 112). That the sentence does not finish itself, overwhelmed by intervening and obstructing periods, ambiguates meaning: 'that sale' *of?* '*that* sale,' period? And no presumption of ignorance on the hearer's part—'we all' know *which* sale *that* is. 'Apotheosis' proximate to 'chattelry', however, give rise to an untenable—one might even say godless—

oxymoron. It is also a filthy joke. But none need call it 'sacrilege', since, in Compson's view at least, this very discourse of contiguity has been ordained by God himself.

A divine prosthesis, the narrator's 'thousand, the white men, made [the octoroon mistress], created and produced them; we even made the laws which declare that one eighth of a specified kind of blood shall outweigh seven eighths of another kind' (p. 115). This refined prattle of a pseudo-human science is not entirely misleading since it designates the *bestial* character of human breeding. If 'mulatto' originates etymologically in notions of 'sterile mule', then mulatto-ness is not a genetically transferable trait. It must be calculated and preserved as a particularistic project in 'race'. The Southern personality's historic fear that the binary 'races' might come together in the spawn of the 'miscegenous' is absolutely assured and pursued in the presence of the 'mulatto'. In fact, it would seem that this presence describes that point of intersection between the fulfillment of the prohibitive wish and the prohibition itself,[16] so that the energies of the narrator's recalled text are part and parcel of an enormous struggle to ward off a successfully *willed* and *willful* compulsion:

> the white blood to give the shape and pigment of what the white man calls female beauty, to a female principle which existed, queenly and complete, in the hot equatorial groin of the world long before that white one of ours came down from trees and lost its hair and bleached out—a principle apt docile and instinct with strange and curious pleasures of the flesh '(which is all: there is nothing else)' which her white sisters of a mushroom yesterday fled from in moral and outraged horror—a principle which, where her white sister must needs try to make an economic matter of it like someone who insists upon installing a counter or a scales or a safe in a store or business for a certain percentage of the profits, reigns, wise supine and all-powerful, from the sunless and silken bed which is her throne. (pp. 116-117)

What Compson imagines concerning 'the hot equatorial groin of the world' can be guessed only too well and has, embarrassingly, no historic basis. Nor need it have any for the narrator, since the subject, one narrator removed, is addressing its own over-determined sexuality. In the process, 'black' remains unnamed, except by implication in an imagined metonymic substitute. To return a moment to Todorov's dynamics of alterity, we observe that the narrator: 1) has *epistemically* no valuable or enviable knowledge of the female subjects in question; 2) distances himself *praxeo-logically* from the subjects so that they reveal to him no dynamic historical movement, remaining for the reader the fictional counters that they are; 3) accomodates himself *axiologically* to those subjects in a stunning act of obverted condescension that objectifies an other at the same time that the latter is isolated as a potentially sacred feature.

What has been 'created' here is not so much a fiction of the octoroon heroine as a text of an evoked 'Anglo-Saxon' male presence *having*, essentially, a creation myth, related to the act of giving birth. But this behaving as though the fictive text were 'real', that it *ought* to give the reader valuable information about the historical sequence, contravenes the assumptions of our present critical practice. The misstep is useful, nevertheless, in what might be abstracted from it. 'White' women and those historical subjects trapped in the figuration of 'hot equatorial groin of the world' modulate into the very same economic, if not cultural, principle by sheer semantic proximity. The distinction that I wish to make here between 'economic' and 'cultural' is meant to identify in the latter those social and political uses to which the subject is put, while 'economic' defines the translation of such uses at once into actual cash value, but also in the symbolic and figurative currencies released by such translation. The processes that I would keep discrete here overlap in actual social practice such that a distinction seems wrong. But the narrator's insistence on the 'economic matter' of, by implication, a hired vaginal substance, make clear that dollars and ledgers are what *he* means as the materialized figurative value of the 'white sister'. It is less clear, from his point of view, although doubtlessly true, that the reign of the 'wise *supine*' is just as costly and dear for the very same commodity, even if a 'sunless and silken bed' carries a richer poetic and visual reverberation than counters and scales and stores and business.

Thrown down into the narrator's sentences as extended parentheses, these abrupt elaborations yoke 'white' and 'not-white' female in a figurative alliance and a historic alignment that only the ahistoricality of 'color', or the 'proud fierce mysticism' of 'Anglo-Saxon' racial ideology, has excised. If the Compsons of the world enforce 'order' and 'degree' in their 'casting' of women, then at least they suspect that fundamentally the female substance—everywhere the same—acquires *different* value according to the very same standard of measure: its *imagined* and *posited* worth to a superior buyer, made supreme by his competence to command desire.

The missing *persona* from Compson's scheme is already there in what the metonym conceals. But 'equator', in its coterminousness with portions of the sub-Saharan African continent, proclaims the narrator's suggested meaning. Indirection in this case, which is itself a mode of figurative elaboration, brings us to a crucial point.

In attempting to articulate a theory of difference regarding African-American women's community, we have begun by looking at the semantic 'processes of appeal' that occur in certain textual evidence, including fiction. The Faulknerian excerpt, although isolatable in its persistent stylistic mannerisms, provides, in that regard, points of concentration in what we might call the historical narratives that refer to this community of women. I have in mind here not primarily those written texts of history, or those texts based in self-conscious historiographical pursuit. I mean, rather, those configurations of discursive experience *about* which appear dispersed across a range of public address and which may or may not find their way to topics of the historical discipline. These configurations, embedded in public consciousness, enact a 'symbolic behavior' that is actually metatextual in its political efficacy, in its impact on the individual life-narratives of the historical subject.

Though 'African-American women's community' and 'mulatto/a' may appear to be widely divergent structures of human attention, the one claimed by the historical dimension, the other stalled on the terrain of the reified object, they share common ground in two crucial ways. First, there is the proximity effected between *real* and *imagined* properties. The 'mulatto/a' appears historically when African female and male personality become embedded as American political entities, at that moment when they enter public and political discourse in the codes of slavery, the rise of the fugitive, the advertisement of the run-away man/woman.[17] Second, both effecting a radical alterity with the Dominant One, they demonstrate the extent to which modes of substitution can be adopted as strategies of containment. In other words, if the African American women's community can be silenced in its historic movement, then it will happen because the narratives concerning them have managed successfully to captivate the historical subject in time's vacuum. By denying the presence of the African American female, or by assimilating her historical identity by giving her precisely a false body, ventriloquized through a factitious public discourse concerning the 'blood' and 'breeding', the dominant mode succeeds in transposing the real into the mythical/magical.

The situation of the 'mulatta' in the same field of signification with the African American female juxtaposes contrastive social and political uses. I am less interested in the class implications of this cultural phenomenon than its symbolic processes and their outcome. Subsequent to the intrusion of a figurative middle term or ground between the subjugated and dominant interests, public discourse gains the advantages of a lie by orchestrating otherness through degrees of difference. Eighteenth-century philosophy's 'great chain of being' ramifies now to disclose within American Africanity itself literal 'shades' of human value, so that the subjugated community refracts the oppressive mechanism just as certainly as the authoring forms put them into place. This fatalistic motion that turns the potentially insurgent community furiously back on itself proceeds by way of processes we might call 'archaizing'. Faulkner's narrative voices provide examples of this trait when Quentin Compson posits in the 'hot equatorial groin of the world' and 'those white ones of ours [come] down from trees and . . . bleached out' aspects of the magical, or the ahistorical, not at all responsive to context or altering agency. The 'mulatta' isolated from the living subject which incarnates her, just as, it is hinted, 'black' and 'white' women are, exemplifies the position occupied by those utterly outside the circuits of social power. 'Power' in this instance consists in the prerogative to name human value, to distribute and arrogate it.

The world according to captives and their captors strikes the imagination as a grid of identities running at perpendicular angles to each other: *things* in serial and lateral array: *beings* in hierarchical and vertical array. On the serial grid, the captive person—the chattel property—is contiguous with inanimate and other living things.

Alterity and Dehumanization

Anamboe 1736
Nov. 24th Sold Capt. Hammond 4 women for Recd. the following goods

		Oz.	A.
Viz.16	perpets	5	
7	half Says	3	8
3	half Ells		
1	ps. Niconee	1	8
4	qr bb powder	2	
14	sheets	2	14
2	paper Sleties		5
112	galls rum	7	

This itemized excerpt from an agenda for commodity[18] exchange vividly illustrates the dehumanization of African personality. Frederick Douglass, however, provides a narrative a full century later for such a scenario, remembering the division of property upon the death of one of his former masters. Having to return from

Baltimore to the site of Captain Anthony's estate, he writes of the occasion: 'We were all ranked together at the valuation. Men and women, old and young, married and single, were ranked with horses, and sheep, and swine. There were horses and men, cattle and women, pigs and children, all holding the same rank in the scale of being, and were all subjected to the same narrow examination.'[19]

From Donnan's account of the slave galley's logs and bills of lading, as well as actual sales, to Douglass' *Narrative* of the 'peculiar institution', we discover time and again the collapse of human identity adopted to the needs of commerce and economic profit. But even more startling than this nominal 'crisis of degree' (which renders an equality of substances not unlike the figurative collapse of disparities in metaphorical display) is the *recovery* of difference in a hierarchical and vertical distribution of being, as though this cultural 'disarray' stood corrected, or compensated. In the inter-section of these axes, at the point of 'mules and men'—the human ownership and possession of other human beings—the notion of property so penetrates the order of things that the entire structure is undermined by a simple overwhelming paradox: those subjects located at this incredible juncture of saturation are both more and less human. More human because they enter into a wider ecumenicalism with named and claimed things, or vocabularies of experience; less because it is their destiny—by virtue of Christ's church and the spirit of national insurgence and constitutionality—to *be* human first and only. That we find no comparable 'list' of being, as we do the carefully accounted one for commercial items, suggests that 'laterality' has done its job. No more needed to be said once it were possible to rank human with animal. In effect, the humanity of African personality is placed in quotation marks under these signs and problematized as a leading public and philosophical issue.

Alterity, therefore, describes not only an inauthentic human status, but also the locus of an outright relationship between non-historical elements that come to rest beyond the veil of humanity and its discourses; this lack of movement in the field of signification seems to me the origin of 'mulatto-ness'—the *inherent* name and naming, the *wedge* between the world of light and the step beyond—into the undifferentiated, unarticulated mass of moving and moveable things.

Between these dualities, the 'shadow' of the 'mulatto/a' is interposed. It is surprising that there is between William Faulkner, writing in the twentieth century, and Frances E.W. Harper, writing in the nineteenth, a certain lexical recurrence that initiated my observations in the opening pages of this essay. Quentin Compson the narrator describes Charles Bon in terms of appropriation that are just as apposite to his octoroon invention. In fact, Charles Bon is also thrice made—once by the attenuated concepts of history that haunt his characterization; once by the structure of mimesis that the character purports to display; and yet again by the appropriating speaker as a 'shadowy' presence. 'A myth, a phantom: something which [Ellen and Judith Sutpen] engendered and created whole themselves; some effluvium of Sutpen blood and character, as though as a man he did not exist at all'. (p. 104).

Frances Harper entitled her 1893 novel *Iola Leroy, or Shadows Uplifted.*[20] It is not altogether clear what dramatic and rhetorical function the topos of 'shadow' serves in the novel, this very ambiguity complements the text's topic: the fate of Iola Leroy, mulatta girl remanded back into slavery and overcoming, at last, the pain and confusion of her biography. But the novel just as certainly concerns the reunion of mothers and children—the blood line of slavery—divided across the cleavage of 'race'.

In each instance of re-encounter, the pilgrimage that precedes it seems compelled by the mulatto status of the character, as though, in comic resolution, the peace and order of the world were returned in their happiness. For Harper's narrator *only* the mulatto characters can ascend. These agents, 'too white to be black, too black to be white,' share with Bon and Christmas the magical status of liminality, but in the case of Harper's eponymous heroine, the piously sacred overtakes her. She assumes the equally ambiguous estate of the blessed: 'The shadows have been lifted from all their lives; and peace, like bright dew, has descended upon their paths. Blessed themselves, their lives are a blessing to others' (p. 281).

In effect, the law and the order of this world have been fully regained, but at a price. This world has ended as the character slips away from earth into the non-historical eternity of unchanging, transcendent things. This false movement takes us back to the notion of the intruded wedge between opposed dualities. In this instance, the mulatta mediates between dualities, thus suggesting that mimetic movement, imitating successful historical movement, is upward along the vertical scale of being. The only 'Black' in this case who can move is not quite 'black' enough, or certainly not enough that the people who need to know can tell. We observe for the female a similar structure of assumptions at work in the Faulknerian instance.

The 'shadow' as a center of ambiguity in Faulkner's and Harper's works discloses the dramatic surprise that unites these otherwise divergent writings. By way of concluding these notes, I would observe three crucial moments: the lifting of the shadows from the one-dimensionsality of Harper's characters' lives; the phantom-like, shadowy aspects that cluster around Compson's version of Charles Bon; the terrible, ascensive epiphany of Joe Christmas's slaughter:

> Then his face, body, all seemed to collapse, to fall in upon itself, and from out the slashed garments about his hips and loins the pent black blood seemed to rush like a released breath. It seemes to rush out of his pale body like a rush of sparks from a rising rocket; upon the black blast the man seemed to rise soaring into their memories forever and ever. (p. 440)

In all three instances, the character achieves, at last, the superior talismanic force: his or her difference from the recognizably human. This attribution of extraordinary humanity obviously works in contrastive ways: as we have seen in the case of *Iola Leroy*, the closural device points towards a divine and beneficent ground of potentialities; in the case of *Light in August*, towards a sacrificial torture. In *Absalom, Absalom!*, Charles Bon, immersed in the secrecies of origin, is invested by effects of adoration, as he becomes the veritable love object of brother and sister Sutpen. But these opposing indices—pointing upward and downward—mobilize character to the very same region of finality. 'Hell' is 'heaven' turned upside down, as 'heaven' comprehends 'hell' in the classic cosmogonic schemes.

That the semantic field here clings tenaciously to notions of the transcendent without openly declaring them as such is a perfect instance of Foucault's 'enunciative field'.[21] In this type of discursive relation between what I would call a founding concept and 'forms of succession', 'quite different domains of objects' are involved that 'belong to quite different types of discourse.' Concomitance is generated 'either because they serve as analogical confirmation [of the founding concept] or because they serve as a general principle and as premises accepted by a reasoning, or because they serve as models that can be transferred to other contents.' The founding concept here may be generally regarded as a religiously discursive pointer, as we have observed in Compson's blank parody of the creation process. But the analogues to a religious discursivity in these works fracture in contradiction: the 'sacred' mulatto figure simultaneously repels and attracts because of his/her blood-crossed career. Faulkner's narrator attributes to Joe Christmas the 'pent black blood' and to the octoroon female 'seven-eighths' of the *right* blood type. It is not until Bon's blood connection is revealed that

Henry Sutpen most probably commits fractricide on the 'blood brother' whom he has loved.

Throughout Harper's work the narrator refers to blood in various charged phrases: the 'tainted blood' of 'white Negroes'; the 'trick of the blood'; 'outcast blood in the veins'; 'traditions of blood' and the human estate; 'the imperceptible infusion of Negro blood', etc. As the life essence, human blood, for all that scientific knowledge teaches concerning it, persists in notions of the mysterious. At least one tends to regard it mysteriously, as if its scientific definition were insufficient to exhaust its range of figurative possibilities. The blood of which these fictive narrators speak has little to do with the scientific, even when they hint, and perhaps all the more so, mensurative dimensions of the substance, as in one-half, one-fourth, one-eighth 'black'. It appears that medical and scientific knowledge, after all, are not the arbiters of the blood *where we live*, nor yet the origin of recourse when geneaologies, or the 'transfer' of time through children and properties are concerned. Blood remains impervious, at the level of folk/myth, to incursions of the 'reasonable'; it inscribes the unique barrier beyond which human community has not yet passed into the 'brotherhood of man' and the 'Fatherhood of God'. But this very difficulty of the blood is the hinge upon which the concept of community, as we now understand it, appears to turn.

Like the pharmakon, blood is both the antidote and the poison, as the intrusion of mystery in its place segregated the menstruating female, banished the outraged maternity of the unhusbanded woman, and rendered 'femaleness' itself the site of absence. On this basis, American Africanity was assigned to the axis of 'thingness' in a vision of human community that replicates time and again notions of hierarchical and linear display. If there is mystery—or spirit drooping down in the midst of things—then someone must safeguard its secrets; traditionally, the offices of the priestly function (and here I mean any structure of the esoteric), of the recondite in general, of the Dominant One, of a hyperbolic phallic status have fallen to the lot of the male. It is this inner and licit circle of a coveted and mystified knower and knowledge that determines the configurations of the law and the order—the name, the law of the Father.

But the mystery apparently yields its secret, despite the covering names, as the glorification of a male heteroclite sexuality, which designates the only 'maleness' that can lay claim to the phallic principle. Under these conditions of culture and acculturation, we regard the 'mulatta' as the recovery of female gender beyond the

Father's house, beyond the lights of the female who falls *legitimately* within its precincts. The borders of the exogamous arrangement are extended without guilt. But the 'master', not always sufficiently protected against the burden of incest, might well have discovered his daughter (by African female personality) when he took to the bed of his wife. The invention of the American 'mulatta' virtually assured his success.

SECTION THREE
Crisis in the Hemisphere

12

Culture and Community: The Language of Class in Guatemala

Carol A. Smith

When asked who are their oppressors, what is their class position, what is the nature of stratification in their society, Guatemalan Indians will invariably point to the structural polarity between ethnic groups—Indians and Ladinos—rather than to any other division that the outside analyst might see or want to impose. If further pressed about particulars—relations of an Indian worker to a wealthy Indian artisan or landholder, or about a neighboring community of Ladino smallholders whose economic conditions of existence seem indistinguishable from those of the Indian community—the Indian speaker will doggedly maintain that ethnicity overrides class, that the oppressors are Ladinos not capitalists, that the wealthy Indian is still a member of the community while the poor Ladino is not. This essay seeks to explain why Guatemalan Indians think the way they do about social relations. To do so it will have to deal with the material and objective conditions of Indians and Ladinos as well as the historical and subjective meaning of these social and cultural categories. Since the objective and subjective categories do not coincide, issues of ideology and class consciousness are central to any such explanation.[1]

My purpose in exploring these issues is to inform a political question of considerable significance in Guatemala: why Guatemala's Marxist-Leninist revolutionaries have failed, once again, to mobilize Guatemala's Indian masses. Moreover, it is essential to understand why this failure has occured despite concerted efforts to incorporate Indian interests and goals in the revolutionary struggle between 1978 and 1982, despite the long history of revolutionary organization and practice (this is Guatemala's third revolutionary failure)[2] despite the fact that Guatemala's economic, political, and cultural contradictions are greater than those found in the other

Central American countries (two of which—Nicaragua and El Salvador—have sustained revolutionary organizations much longer), and finally despite the obvious dedication and general organizational skill of the Guatemalan revolutionary leadership.[3]

To deal with this question requires a prior consideration of two others: 1) why Mayan Indian *campesinos*[4] have not differentiated into classes, but remain unified in corporate communities of resistance, even though they have participated in a well-developed commodity and wage-labor economy for more than 100 years; and 2) why political protest in rural Guatemala takes on ethnic rather then class coloration and is mobilized (and usually limited to) local ethnic communities rather than classes. Indian culture is not a minor issue in a country where native-speakers constitute fully half the population. Nor is the existence of so many self-identified Indians a simple accident of fate. Indians have maintained their identity over four centuries of struggle against considerable odds, when most Indians in the Americas have lost that battle. In doing so, Indians have created the particular political and economic features of Guatemala that have made its transformation an intractable problem for Guatemalan revolutionaries.[5]

These issues will be addressed by examining the usefulness of the category 'class', as employed in most Marxist discourse and as employed by the Guatemalan revolutionary leadership, for analyzing the present political divisions and struggles in rural Guatemala. We can situate this particular problem by considering a recent debate among British historians (E.P. Thompson, Perry Anderson, and Gareth Stedman Jones) about whether or not class is properly a transhistorical concept or is limited to capitalist (possibly western capitalist) social formations.[6] Applied to the case at hand, this debate forces us to question the epistemological grounds for the Guatemalan Marxist argument that the Indians have 'false' consciousness because they do not have a revolutionary class vision that trancends their immediate (commonsense) ethnic experiences. If the category of class is relevant only to developed western capitalism, one could just as easily argue that Guatemala's revolutionary leadership shows a false understanding of the historical situation of Guatemala and its potential for a particular kind of revolution in their attempt to impose western capitalist (and Marxist) categories of capitalist/proletariat on their particular political reality.

This argument, in turn, raises a further methodological question: the degree to which Marxist analyses of any kind can be taken out of the social and historical context that produced them as a discourse. Underlying the Thompson/Anderson debate about class is the issue of whether one can use *any* categories derived from an analysis of capitalism in non-capitalist (or non-western) contexts. Concrete manifestations of this problem can be seen in the difficulties scholars have encountered in defining twentieth-century peasants as a class, developing theories of ideology or fetishism for non-capitalist societies, or even developing a critical standpoint (such as that of the proletariat) from which the truth or relevance of a political analysis of non-capitalist or non-western societies can be evaluated.[7] Most scholars who have analyzed non-western, non-capitalist formations and who are sensitive to the problem of importing categories from capitalist society tend to reduce all non-capitalist forms to a single instance, the simple negation of capitalism, neglecting the historical particulars basic to a critical Marxist analysis.[8]

In the following argument I try to show a way out of this dilemma. The solution proposed draws heavily from Pierre Bourdieu's *Outline of a Theory of Practice.*[9] Bourdieu constructs an implicit 'method' of Marxist analysis of political power, opposition, and struggle that does not impose universal categories of analysis, but still attempts to find commonalities of social structuring across history. The method forces one to consider the historical residue as expressed in thought and ideology, as well as to consider the constant remolding of that residue (i.e., culture) through interaction with a given set of material circumstances—as expressed and realized in social practice. In this regard, then, the method is radically historicist and non-teleological, resembling in many ways what Gramsci termed the 'philosophy of praxis'.[10] Applying this method to Guatemala, I try to establish, and to explain why, class as defined for capitalist society is *not* the appropriate category or concept for analyzing political struggle in Guatemala. But I also try to show that the kinds of struggles and groups-in-struggle extant in Guatemala *bear on* the formation of class and on the possibility for revolution in Guatemala. In my view, until Guatemalan revolutionaries understand the basis and meaning of 'Indian' in Guatemala, there will only be more tragic failures of the sort we have just witnessed.

The Debate on Class

E.P. Thompson, in a well-known article subtitled 'Class Struggle without Class', questions the usefulness of applying a nineteenth-century concept, 'class', to earlier periods of western history and (implicitly) to non-capitalist, non-western societies. At the same time he enjoins us to retain the concept of 'class struggle', with the proviso we understand that groups in struggle and the issues over which they fight may be quite different in other epochs and places from what we expect them to have been in nineteenth-and twentieth-century Europe. Perry Anderson argues that Thompson has gone too far in deconstructing the nature of class, while Gareth Stedman Jones claims Thompson has not gone far enough. The present essay defends Thompson's formulation, but on grounds somewhat different from those proposed by Thompson himself. The difference in my approach stems from treating class in a non-western context in which capitalist relations of production exist but are not fully developed.

According to Thompson:

> 'Class, as it eventuated within nineteenth century industrial capitalist societies, and as it then left its imprint upon the heuristic category of class, has in fact no claim to universality. Class in that sense is no more than a special case of the historical formations which arise out of class struggle ... Class struggle is the prior, as well as the more universal concept ... (for) people find themselves in a society structured in determined ways (crucially, but not exclusively, in productive relations), they ... identify points of antagonistic interest, they commence to struggle around these issues and in the process of struggling they discover themselves as classes, they come to know this discovery as class-consciousness. Class and class consciousness are always the last, not the first, stage in the real historical process.'[12]

In Thompson's formulation, *classes* do not exist if class consciousness does not exist; yet, class *struggle* can exist without either fully formed classes or class consciousness; at the same time, class struggle—which is 'universal and manifest'[12]—leads to the making (whether always or only in the right circumstances is not made clear) of *both* fully formed classes and class consciousness.

Perry Anderson suggests that Thompson's radical approach to class—equating class with class consciousness—is 'fatally circular' in that one is unable even to judge the relationship between objective class position and subjective appreciation of that position if one assumes that whatever group considers itself to be a class necessarily *is* a class. He argues: 'It is better to say, with Marx, that social classes may not become conscious of themselves, may fail to act or behave in common, but they still remain—materially, historically—classes.'[13]

Anderson's criticism becomes all the more important in light of Gareth Stedman Jones's observations about the language of class struggle among the early Chartists (Thompson's 'made' working class). Jones notes that the language of protest used by the Chartists was not that of class but politics. He goes on to argue that the Chartists were neither an objective nor a class-conscious 'working class' either before or after their movement. They were instead a multi-class coalition, brought to political struggle by deteriorating economic circumstances, and unified by a particular political (radical) analysis of these circumstances. Radicalism, however, 'could never be the ideology of a specific class. It was first and foremost a vocabulary of political exclusion; whatever the social character of those excluded.'[14] 'Attention to the language of Chartism suggests that its rise and fall is to be related in the first instance not to movements in the economy, divisions in the movement or an immature class consciousness, but to the changing character and policies of the State—the principle enemy upon whose actions radicals had always found that their credibility depended.'[15] This being the case, Jones suggests, one can understand the Chartist struggle as a class struggle only by assuming that it *should have been* a class struggle (by the standards of twentieth-century class analysis), thereby distancing oneself from the actual language and demands of that particular struggle.

According to Anderson, if Jones is right about the Chartist movement, then we would have to believe that the English working class, which 'made' itself during the late eighteenth and early nineteenth centuries, 'unmade' itself later. We would also have to accept the fact that 'real' classes may never have existed, insofar as there has rarely, if ever, been a close correspondence between the so-called objective features of class, a class's consciousness of itself, and the political analysis or knowledge of the nature of class oppression that comes out of class struggle. Thompson, in other words, had continued along 'orthodox' Marxist lines about the necessary development of proletarian class-consciousness (as opposed to that of any other oppressed class), by insisting that the development of the proletariat and its consciousness was necessary to the very conceptualization of society in class terms. But he has thrown out most of the 'orthodox' understanding of the objective determination and relevance of class in all societies, by denying that class is a concept of universal, trans-historical importance. Anderson, it should be pointed out, does not really seem to disagree with Thompson about when, where, and how class consciousness emerged in England; he is more concerned about abandoning the universal concept of *class*.

What Jones concludes about the concept of class is not entirely clear from his analysis. But if we take him to represent the extreme deconstructionist position on class and power (a position represented by Foucault, for example),[16] we would conclude that nothing from the Marxist vocabulary developed to analyze nineteenth-century social conditions could be used to explain past epochs—or to understand (perhaps even to envision) future ones. The only possibility open to us is to discover and, where feasible, mark the limits of the mutually conditioning objective and subjective factors that imprison all analyses within a bounded discourse. In the case at hand, then, we might use such an analysis—the cultural/societal domination of a general political discourse that was not, strictly speaking, class-based—to explain the limited revolutionary potential of the English working class.

The issues at stake here go to the heart of the dualism inherent in Marxist analysis—the claims to a universal view and explanation of human experience (that the 'history of all hitherto existing society has been that of class struggles'), with the opposing claim that human nature and social reality are only to be understood within particular, historically conditioned experience in which 'men make their own history'. Anderson's argument, that class is a theoretical concept with pertinence to all human social behavior, does not entail the usual reflectionist view of consciousness summarized in Marx's famous formulation: 'It is not the consciousness of men that determines their being, but, on the contrary, their social being that determines their consciousness.' Anderson in fact disavows such a simple view. But his argument forces him to defend a rather meaningless vision of the Marxist project. For if there is no direct relation between consciousness and social being, as Anderson and most other Marxists now concede, why retain as one's basic anchoring point a universalist class analysis which can neither be true to the interior (cultural/cognitive) conceptions of social reality of all times and places, nor be relevant to explaining historical change and political struggle in all times and places? Is the objective merely to measure differences in the lack of fit between man's social being, based upon a 'mode of production of material life', and the 'social, political and intellectual life process in general' supposedly 'conditioned' by the mode of production? Or is the objective to understand specific cases of historical change and political struggle, and, perhaps, to change them?

The opposing (deconstructionist) view, which I have attributed to Jones, severs the connection between material life and conscious-ness altogether, such that members of different or even opposing classes are assumed to share identical world views, political vocabularies, and basic idioms of social discourse. People are still 'brought to' consciousness by political conflict and struggle, but the consciousness they attain may not only fail to reflect their material circumstances, it may lead them to no more than a reinterpretation or reappropriation of an ideology they share with the opposition. The content of political consciousness, on this account, is not rooted within differing material circumstances so much as within a general culture, a bounded social discourse. In this way deconstructionists escape from the uneasy dualism described above, but only to be trapped by other problems: an obscure depiction (and perhaps understanding) of historical change, an inability to explain political struggle (unless it stems from incomplete socialization within the discourse), an assumption that one can attach the same meaning to political language despite differences in users and context, and nearly total political pessimism. The consciousness uncovered by these assumptions is not only detached from class conditioning, it is not only emergent by no particular rhythm, but it can play no 'conscious' role in transforming the social and material conditions of life. This project, too, gives us a rather meaningless vision of the Marxist project. For why, if this is so, should class consciousness be considered an instrument in class struggle at all?

We must, I believe, stick with Thompson's awkward resolution to the problem, but think through its implications for other times and places, especially those times and places where the emergence of a militant or semi-militant working class is not a foregone conclusion. The problem is not so much the indeterminacy that Thompson's resolution to this problem has produced (which may, in fact, be a positive feature), but rather his continued assumption that particular material circumstances will yield only one 'correct' subjective interpretation. One can allow various subjective interpretations (or consciousnesses) of material reality to emerge without assuming that material circumstances play little role in determining the form and content of a given political struggle.[17]

The approach taken here to the problem of consciousness departs from Thompson's principally in its attempt to link the subjective interpretation of social and material reality that emerges in a particular political struggle *back* to the material circumstances themselves. The interpretation that becomes dominant achieves this position because it reinforces or reproduces those material circumstances that make it believable. Subjective beliefs in this way remain attached to material circumstances, but dialectically rather than in one-to-one correspondence. Revolutionary consciousness, in this formulation, is never directly or solely the outcome of specific material (or even political) circumstances. It emerges from the interplay of material and ideological practices as these are worked out in the political conflicts of a given class relationship whose political alternatives are evident in large part by the practices of the other. And all of these processes in turn condition the material world.

The classes that emerge from such struggles may or may not hold a single objective interest with respect to their material circumstances, but they will hold a single and opposed interest with respect to those classes that emerge in opposition to them. These classes do not necessarily correspond to those one would define by using the universal concepts of a materialist conception of history.[18] But neither are they or their interests detached from their particular (historically given) material circumstances. In this way, the revolutionary potential of a class is given by material circumstances. But this potential cannot be assessed by a formula that divorces material circumstances from the subjective interpretation of those circumstances. From this perspective one need not accept that the proletariat alone bears the burden of coming to a truly revolutionary consciousness. But one could still argue that it is only when the proletariat comes to consciousness as a class that a truly revolutionary transformation of its (our) world is possible.[19]

In the next section I illustrate this concept of 'class struggle without class' by describing: the way in which Indians in western Guatemala use the language of culture and community to define the boundaries of political conflict; how the Indians conceptualize themselves as a class in struggle with the Guatemalan State and a system of ethnic domination; and the way in which Indian class consciousness affects the material circumstances of Guatemalan life. After describing this case, we can then reassess the questions discussed above in this non-western, and only partially capitalist, context in the following ways: the degree to which one can consider the Indians of Guatemala a class; if through struggle Indians have achieved a reasonable (as opposed to false) consciousness of their position and the sources of their oppression; and the revolutionary potential of militant Indians, who do not objectively constitute a class.

Class and Community in Totonicapan

Before dealing with local class and ethnic relations, a few words must be said about Guatemala as a whole to provide a general context for local struggles and political interpretations.[20] Guatemala's eight million people divide into equal numbers of Indians and Ladinos. Indians are people who retain traces of Mayan culture, although these traces presently bear little resemblance to the pre-colombian Mayan civilization; Ladinos are non-Indians in cultural terms, who may be of Indian, partly Indian, or non-Indian race. The country is governed by an extremely repressive state, entirely Ladino in composition, which has been relatively unified and coherent, especially vis-à-vis Indians, since the Conquest. Guatemala's economy has always rested upon coercive control of Indian labor, mainly for the production of export crops. In recent years the major plantations have utilized mostly wage labor, yet even now they obtain labor through indirect coercive means. The rural economy, which is the economy relevant to Indians, cannot be considered capitalist, insofar as it still does not rest upon the existence of a 'free' proletariat. Virtually all Indians produce some food for themselves on very small plots of their own (privately titled) land, although this constitutes usually less than half of the food they need. Virtually no Indian rents or sharecrops land. They gain additional income from various sources: about 20 percent from waged work on plantations; about 30 percent from production of food for market sale on their own land; and about 50 percent from production and sale of artisanal goods for consumption in the region.[21]

We shall concentrate on beliefs and practices concerning social divisions in Guatemala in one particular Indian community, Totonicapan in western Guatemala. This exclusive focus is necessary not only because of space, but because the Indian language of social division is based on the particularity of specific communities, not on abstract, general oppositions.[22] This fact, which I think Totonicapan exemplifies in a vivid form,[23] has been the greatest stumbling block to revolutionaries striving to unite all Indians against the state in Guatemala. Understanding the nature, meaning and specificity of community, therefore, is basic to understanding the potential for revolutionary change in Guatemala. It is also essential to any discourse about the nature of appropriate revolutionary goals. Guatemala's Indians have not only preserved their distinctive culture(s), but they have more effectively resisted proletarianization than most other *campesinos* in Latin America. That this is the ultimate Indian goal, pursued at all costs and with almost infinite communal tenacity, is the central fact that must be borne in mind by any person or group who wants to understand contemporary Guatemala.

Totonicapan's most distinctive characteristics are that it is large (more then 60,000 people organized into 48 dispersed hamlets), militantly Indian, and relatively wealthy. Totonicapan's 55,000 Indians live mostly in rural areas, but they make up the majority of people living in the small administrative town, also known as Totonicapan.[24] Totonicapan's 3,000 Ladinos live exclusively in the town of Totonicapan (with a total population of some 6,000 people), and control the local bureaucracy which represents the national government. Ladinos also hold positions in the professions and in wholesale commerce (as have some few Indians since about 1950).[25]

The Indians of Totonicapan are in a relatively privileged economic position, their condition similar to that of other Indians in some 20 of the 150 Indian communities of the region.[27] Few work seasonally on Guatemala's large lowland plantations (the economic mainstay of poorer Indians in Guatemala). Most are artisans, producing with a simple, non-mechanized technology items for domestic consumption (such as clothing) which are sold throughout the country. Most also farm, but they obtain less than 10 percent of their income from agriculture. Totonicapan was fully commodified (obtaining all factors of production from the market) by about 1880, and had used wage labor in both artisanal and agricultural production from at least that date. As I have argued elsewhere[27] economic activity in Totonicapan met for one hundred years all the conditions that Lenin thought would inevitably 'enrich the few, while ruining the masses.' i.e., that would create permanent class differentiation among peasants. Yet no permanent proletariat has emerged in this community (or any other Indian community), inasmuch as wage workers are youths who develop independent artisanal enterprises (which may or may not depend on wage labor) upon marriage or shortly thereafter. At the same time, approximately 10 percent of Totonicapan's artisanal firms hire Indian wage labor on a regular basis.

Two 'economic' factors appear to impede class differentiation in Totonicapan: the low development of the forces of production and the high local wage rate. The two factors are related in that petty capitalists, because of the prevailing wage rates, extract insufficient surplus from wage labor to improve the forces of production. Wage rates in Totonicapan are about twice as high as those of other communities in the region (both Indian and plantation). The decisive factor that prevents differentiation in Totonicapan is a non-economic one: Totonicapan producers refuse to hire non-local labor. As I have shown elsewhere, this maintains the scarcity of labor and high wage rates in Totonicapan, which maintains production in the community on a petty, artisanal scale, thus retarding class differentiation.[28]

Why do Totonicapan producers not hire outside labor? They are, after all, petty capitalists, if one accords them a class position by objective criteria, for they do extract some surplus value from wage labor. The explanation they gave to me was posed in 'class' terms, but not those an 'objective analysis' would readily identify. They considered their class interests the same as those of their local workers, an interest opposed to an 'outside structure of [class] domination'. We cannot provide the texts of their argument here.[29] But the gist of what they said is as follows: Bringing in outside workers would dilute Totonicapan political solidarity. Totonicapan's political solidarity, in turn, rested upon its cultural unity, which would be destroyed if outsiders were allowed in. The oppressors against whom the community needed political unity were, essentially, those Ladinos who represented outside authority and the state. The best means by which Totonicapan could struggle with outside authority and the state was by maintaining local cultural (ethnic) solidarity.

Totonicapan's cultural solidarity is more mythic than real: it rests on no unchanging 'peasant' tradition. Totonicapan is divided not only into incipient classes, holding different material interests, but it is divided as well into many dispersed local communities and kin groups, many different religious congregations, many political factions, and countless forms of competitive social relations. Totonicapan's cultural traditions, moreover, have changed significantly over time, each generation reinterpreting the 'necessary core' of Indian tradition. The fact that Totonicapan is divided and constantly reinterpreting its cultural tradition, however, does not override the fact that the Indians of Totonicapan have long held an overwhelming sense of themselves as a 'community of interest'. And the myth, with its language of cultural identity, is significant in and of itself. For the myth supports a general sense of Indian class solidarity (based on culture and race) versus the Guatemalan (Ladino) state, who is seen as the oppressor. The myth, in other words, forges political solidarity in the absence of 'real' cultural unity and unchanging tradition.

As far as 'reality' is concerned, Totonicapan has engaged in more or less continuous resistance against the state ever since the Conquest, most often but not always non-violently. Totonicapan often won the political rights for which it was willing to struggle, even though its demands (e.g., allowing Indian youths to enter the local secondary school, refusing to join the local militias) have rarely been 'revolutionary' in nature. The language of conflict and struggle in Totonicapan has almost always emphasized political rights rather than economic oppression. The oppressors are seen largely as representatives of the state or as groups given special economic privileges by the state rather than independent economic exploiters. Inasmuch as they see oppression in ethnic (cultural/racial) and political terms, Totonicapan Indians think its remedy necessarily lies in the political rather than the economic realm. This 'political' analysis reinforces the emphasis on cultural unity in the community.

Totonicapan's belief in its cultural unity (and the importance of that unity) is not without material effect on local class structure, however; for it creates a reality of action in face of the potential recruitment of outside workers. Because they are committed to the maintenance of Totonicapan's cultural unity—the commitment itself the source of unity rather than any unchanging cultural tradition—rich Totonicapan producers do not employ cheaper outside workers, even though it might benefit them substantially. The material result of this aspiration to a continuum of cultural practices and communal identity is that the 'objective' classes of worker and owner in Totonicapan have not solidified into real or permanent classes, conscious or unconscious. Indians of Totonicapan (and of Guatemala generally) remain not only resistant to proletarianization, but are actually not proletarianized in a real sense.

The Logic of Ethnic Conflict

The Indians of Totonicapan do not see everyone in the outside world as equally oppressive. They link the source of their oppression directly to the state, seeing their oppression in ethnic terms because the representatives of the state are exclusively Ladino. They can ignore the fact that many poor Ladinos are not part of the state apparatus because ethnicity is relevant to their lives mostly in the relations Indians have with the state. In similar fashion, the state ignores the fact that Indians have many different positions in production, because Indians have relevance to the political process only insofar as all of them can be defined as a pool of potential (rather than actual) free labor, inasmuch as they can be prevented from holding certain political powers and rights.

What, then, is the real basis of ethnic relations in Guatemala and how does this bear upon class? The historical evidence is clear on this question. Guatemalan Indians have *never* formed a single class, if one uses objective economic criteria to define class position. But they have *always* been treated as a single class by non-Indians, and thus have always been a class in relational terms. Even today Guatemalan social scientists and revolutionary leaders rarely question the class homogeneity of Indians, whether they consider them a peasantry, a semi-proletariat, a disguised proletariat, or a full proletariat. And in its political actions, the Guatemalan state has consistently treated all Indians as if they belonged to a single, subordinate and exploitable class, regardless of the actual economic position of the particular Indians confronting it. The real basis of ethnic relations is the relation of the state to potential labor-power.

The ideological basis of the Indian/Ladino division, however, is rooted in racism, a belief system which reinforces differences in the material conditions of Indians and Ladinos. Ladinos, whether members of the national bourgeoisie (who are Ladino or European) or members of the proletariat, see Indians as racially and culturally inferior. At the same time, all Guatemalans know that there is virtually no racial difference between Indians and the Ladino proletariat, the latter being mostly 'recent' or 'redressed' Indians who have given up Indian cultural markers. (Only the Guatemalan bourgeoisie, in fact, can claim a non-Indian racial heritage—and then not uniformly.) Yet it is clear that in treating communities as undifferentiated, subordinate wholes, which it does as much as it did in the past, the Guatemalan state makes certain general assumptions about all Indians. Understanding these assumptions helps us understand how ethnicity had become the language of class struggle in Guatemala.

In the past Guatemalans assumed a simple correspondence between race and class: that subordinate groups were all Indian, 'middle' groups were partly Indian, and upper groups were not Indian.[30] The correspondence between race and class was upheld and reinforced by the state, which put up barriers to the cultural assimilation of Indians—thus reinforcing the 'real' correspondence between race and class. The current ideology emphasizes culture over race: Indians are people who retain their past, while most poor Ladinos are people who do not; both groups may be racially Indian. Indians require special (and uniform) treatment not because of their racial inferiority, but because the dead weight of their traditions prevents them from taking an active role in Guatemala's modern economy. The latter argument—that Indians are merely *culturally* backward rather than racially inferior—remains racist in its assumption that only people of lesser capacity would retain Indian customs.

But it resolves the contradiction that Indians can 'become' Ladinos—a transformation now encouraged by the Guatemalan state. The resolution rests on a new myth: that one can change class position through ethnic change:—that 'smart' or capable Indians can 'become' Ladinos and thereby improve their material con-ditions. The myth that one can improve one's economic position through ethnic change is a powerful justification for the special treatment of Indians and the special relation between Indians and

Ladinos. At the same time, however, ethnic change is also a material reality and therefore reflects a real change in economic position—a class transformation in fact. The recent Ladino is no more than the fully proletarianized Indian. Seen in this light, the material condition of the recent Ladino can be considered *worse* than that of the Indian, for it implies full dispossession of precapitalist forms of community and property.

The Ladino proletariat also assumes the racial/cultural inferiority of Indians and consider themselves to be a cut above Indians in at least cultural terms.[31] Most have rejected Indian cultural identity in the belief that the source of oppression in Guatemala is racial and political. They assume that they will be able to rise above the 'class' oppression of Indians, becoming one with the Ladino bourgeoisie, by 'becoming' Ladinos. In other words, like most Guatemalans, regardless of class position, race, or ethnicity, they believe that class position in Guatemala is determined by race, culture, and history: the least Indian and least Mayan in historical distance are the bourgeoisie (along with state bureaucrats); the intermediate groups are in the process of historical transition, their placement in the social order determined by their distance from the Indian heritage; while the most Indian and most Mayan people remain the lowest subordinate class. Ladino beliefs about Indian inferiority reproduce the subordinate material position of Indians (through the agency of the state and ethnic discrimination, which actively prevent Indians from changing many of their constraining material circumstances), thereby reinforcing the belief. The correspondence between belief and material circumstances can only exist, however, in the context of a political rather than a class analysis of society. The emphasis on ethnicity (based ultimately on racism) reinforces a political over a class analysis, reproduces material differences between Indians and Ladinos, and allows the 'dispossessed' Ladino to feel superior to all Indians in material as well as in political terms.

Indian attitudes about race, racism, and culture are more complex.[32] Most Indians believe that Indian culture is rooted in both race and tradition, even though all understand and acknowledge that the Ladino proletariat consists mostly of their direct descendents. They define the Ladino bourgeoisie and state (rather than all Ladinos) as 'the' oppressors, while they see the Ladino proletariat as people like them who have 'given up the struggle'. (In Indian eyes, Ladinos are defined negatively as those who lack Indian communal unity and cultural tradition.) Thus, on the one hand, Indians believe that retention of their distinctive way of life and cultural symbols exposes them to a double oppression: economic, insofar as Indians cannot transcend certain material constraints as long as they remain Indians; and political, insofar as racism and the power of the state reinforce these material constraints and add to them the indignity of social discrimination. On the other hand, they believe that one can struggle against economic and political oppression in Guatemala only as a community of interest, and that such communities form and retain sufficient unity for political struggle only through the retention of this source of double oppression: Indian cultural identity. They do not feel a unity of interest with the Ladino proletariat mainly because they consider the source of oppression in Guatemala to be political (based on racism and cultural oppression), rather than economic (based on class exploitation).

Guatemalan revolutionaries decry both positions—the Indians' class-consciousness/separatism and the Ladino proletariat's racism/ethnocentrism—considering both to be clear cases of 'false' consciousness that divide and weaken the 'real' class struggle in Guatemala. They believe that when the present class order in Guatemala is overturned and class oppression is eliminated, facism and cultural oppression will wither away. But in their programs for uniting the Indian and the Ladino proletariat in revolutionary struggle, they ask Indians to show unity with the cause by 'becoming' Ladinos rather than asking Ladinos to 'become' Indians.[33]

Political Struggle in Guatemala

From the case of Totonicapan and the more general discussion of the logic of Indian-Ladino conflict, it remains to consider how the debate on class is directly relevant to the crisis of revolutionary strategy in Guatemala. Let us recall the central questions posed earlier: (1) Do the political struggles between Indians and Ladinos require us to consider these groups as 'classes'? (2) Are Guatemalans in general imprisoned in a 'false' discourse that disguises class relations as ethnic relations? (3) Are Guatemalan revolutionaries, in their desire to overcome ethnic division, captive to similar but inverted myopia that sees class relations as the only relevant (or 'real') arena of political struggle? (4) Is the social war in Guatemala a 'class struggle without class' or are classes emerging from the struggle? (5) What are implications for revolutionary strategy of considering this as a 'class struggle without class'?

The first step in answering these questions is to consider the general context, economic *and* political, of the Indian/Ladino struggles. I have argued here and elsewhere that rural Guatemala cannot be considered to have fully capitalist relations of production, even on plantations, because the economy is not based on the existence of a free (dispossessed) proletariat. Most rural workers in Guatemala, Indians in particular, are only marginally proletarianized, their labor only partially rewarded by wages. Not only must Indian workers supplement wages with other sources of income, because wage labor is insufficiently rewarded; but most rural capitalists cannot replace living labor with congealed labor (workers without capital), because labor is not free (dispossessed). The economic resources of capital under these circumstances are spent maintaining a repressive political apparatus which attempts to create more dispossessed labor and which ensures that the labor which does exist remains extremely cheap. Most rural capitalists extract absolute surplus value rather than relative surplus value. The existence of an extremely repressive state is directly tied to this system, for in the absence of a fully dispossessed proletariat, only a repressive state can deliver cheap labor when and where needed.[34]

To deny that this is a fully capitalist economy is not to say that it is a feudal economy. Nor would it solve our problems were we to consider it a feudal economy, with plantation owners as 'lords' and their workers (or just their Indian workers?) 'serfs'. After all, Thompson's eighteenth-century England was also far from a fully capitalist economy, but it was hardly feudal. That both economies, Guatemala in the present and England in the eighteenth century, are 'transitional', however, may be relevant to the issues under discussion. For by now it is clear that most transitions, during which peasants are slowly but relentlessly proletarianized, are accompanied by the development of centralized and repressive (if nonetheless unstable and vulnerable) states. Small wonder that proletarianization is interpreted by those suffering it to be the result of state action and political repression.

How can we consider this a false perception? And how can we continue to argue for the universal relevance of objective 'class' analysis, once we recognize that societies like modern Guatemala and eighteenth-century England are neither fully capitalist nor still feudal? Neither case provides social classes fitting the mold of a universalistic class analysis. Nor are we helped in understanding the nature of class struggle in these societies by comparing what does exist to what we would expect to exist under feudalism or under fully developed capitalism. We do much better by looking at the social relations that actually exist, identifying the points of antagonistic interest, and asking how these relations are both materially grounded and ideologically supported.

Yet does this allow us to consider *political* struggles over *political* issues by relatively inchoate multi-class coalitions as specifically *class* struggles? Thompson argues that it does because it is the process whereby 'real' (objective) classes form (in both a material and political sense) and become conscious of themselves *as a class*. He argues the point primarily by emphasizing the historical process of class formation and its relational basis—resting his case on historical teleology—that an English working class *did* eventually emerge (was proletarianized) and did become (arguably) a conscious class. Had the groups that Thompson identified *not* become fully proletarianized—had they successfully overturned the state and set up a non capitalist economy (whether socialist, or simply backward)—it is doubtful that Thompson would have considered England's future working class as *a class* during the process of struggle.

Where does that leave Guatemala's Indians and Ladinos? In quite a different situation, obviously. One could argue that the struggle between Indians and the Guatemalan state has been engendered by the same slow, relentless pressures of proletarianization which Indians have tried to resist in many ways but mainly by using symbols of ethnic identity to unify communities of interest. One could provide good evidence that most recent Ladinos do represent the Indian 'losers' in this struggle, i.e., those people who lost both the material and cultural bases for resistence to full proletarianization. From this one would conclude that Guatemala's working class 'in the making' is the Ladino proletariat. Guatemala's revolutionary leadership reached just this conclusion, only to find that the Ladino proletariat has even less in the way of a revolutionary consciousness than Indians (partly because of their belief in the possibility of class mobility through cultural change, reinforced in daily life by the even more oppressed economic and political conditions of Indians). Although they eventually found Indians to have a more militant consciousness of their oppression than poor Ladinos, the revolutionary leaders considered Indian militancy to be dangerously sectarian, because it failed to achieve solidarity with the Ladino proletariat. It is understandable, therefore, that the revolutionary leadership, given their assumptions about class and class consciousness, accuses both Indians and Ladinos of false consciousness.

But let us consider for a moment what it would mean to accept that the Indian 'commonsense' understanding[35] of the source of their oppression in Guatemala (racism and the political actions of the state) is *not* false. Let us assume, in addition, that as long as the specially disadvantaged situation of Guatemalan Indians remains, the Ladino proletariat will feel no more solidarity with them than

Indians at present feel for poor Ladinos, i.e., that the Ladino proletariat will lack a generalized class consciousness. Finally, let us assume that the present struggle between Guatemala's Indians and the Guatemalan state is revolutionary and will, regardless of the outcome, transform present class relations (in an 'objective' sense). Can we consider contemporary Guatemala a case of class struggle without class?

I believe we can and should do so for the following reasons. The unified position of the state against the Indians has produced a unity of interests among Indians against the state.[36] This unity is self-conscious, readily verbalizable and often put into concrete action, even though it expresses itself in symbolic (cultural or ethnic) form. And while it is often based in community rather than in general ethnicity, this unity can and has expanded beyond the community under circumstances where collective action is both feasible and more effective than a local response. That the state has construed 'class' in ethnic terms (or ethnicity in class terms) makes it quite reasonable for Indians to believe that their oppression is rooted in racism and culture. That they have interpreted their reality in this way such that 'ethnic' interests override 'class' interests (to the point of materially affecting class divisions within Indian communities), reinforces the state's perception of Indian class identity.

It is not surprising, therefore, that virtually all Guatemalans, Indian and Ladino alike, believe the basic division in their society—culturally, socially, economically, and politically—is between Indians and non-Indians, and that they interpret this division as a class division. This interpretation creates a *de facto* class division—in a material and political sense as well as in a perceptual sense. To remain Indian is more or less successfully to resist proletarian-ization. This is true of all Indian communities; Totonicapan is just a more sophisticated variant on a general theme. To 'become' Ladino is to join the proletariat. Those who resist proletarianization and those who have capitulated to it have quite different interests vis-à-vis other classes and the state, although an understanding of those differences could be used to overturn the present social order and its class relations. Class struggle in Guatemala has always taken the form of ethnic struggle. The material basis for equating class and ethnicity is no more false today than it was in the past. Because the symbols of ethnicity have become the symbols of resistance to proletarianization, Indians and Ladinos continue to belong to different classes. The ethnic struggle is the predominant force for preserving these class differences.

It should be clear at this point that not all forms of ethnic conflict are instances of class struggle. Symbols of ethnic identity can be appropriated by different groups for many reasons other than class struggle. One of the problems with most studies of ethnic relations is that they assume a universal form to these relations—an indefensible position. The particular case of ethnic conflict considered here exemplifies class struggle (without class) because it clearly involves a material relation between groups and affects those material relations: as a struggle it seeks to overturn or transform them. That this struggle seeks other things as well, such as an end to racial oppression, does not prevent it from also being a struggle about class. Indians see their oppression as Indians in class terms— as does, reciprocally, the Guatemalan state.

In a fashion similar to students of ethnic relations, most Marxists assume a universal form to class struggle: already formed classes (things) see their oppression in purely material terms and struggle to transform those material relations which oppress them as a class. This position is equally indefensible. As Thompson has argued, classes form in struggle and begin to see their oppression as a class in the course of struggle. The original basis for struggle may not be directly material, in England it may be for political rights. But if the basis of struggle is rooted in material relations relevant to class, the process becomes over time a determinedly class struggle. In contrast to Thompson, one must see such struggles as class-based whether or not they eventuate in the formation of fully formed 'objective' classes. If this were not the case, we would have to wait for an outcome before we could diagnose a case, during which (if we are revolutionaries) our patient might die. Political implications aside, we should consider such struggles class struggles (without class) because of their material effect on the formation of classes (as well as their effect on class consciousness).

To take the position outlined here requires no teleological assumptions. In the case at hand, for example, there can be little expectation that Indian struggles will do more than delay proletarianization in the long run. But because of these struggles, the long run may be very long indeed. Class relations and the nature of capitalism in Guatemala, moreover, will be mightily affected by these struggles, so that the ultimate outcome assumed by most students of Guatemala—full proletarianization associated with the death of Indian culture—cannot be a foregone conclusion. After all, quite a number of major social revolutions have occurred in social formations where the proletarianization process was far from complete.

This brings us to a final question: what are the revolutionary implications of the present class struggle in Guatemala? This question has two parts. First, would a social transformation that sought simply to redress the 'class' oppression experienced by Indians be a revolutionary transformation? In other words, could one have a revolutionary transformation that ignored the class oppression suffered by the Ladino proletariat? And second, would a social transformation that sought simply to redress the oppression of 'objective' class relations in Guatemala be a revolutionary transformation? In other words, could one have a revolutionary transformation that ignored the racial/ethnic oppression suffered by Indians? My answer to both questions is yes, but the revolutionary process would in either case be far from complete, since certain 'class bases' of oppression in Guatemala would remain.

An ending to the class oppression suffered by Indians would have revolutionary implications, in my view, because it would end the process of proletarianization in Guatemala and in doing so totally transform extant class (as well as ethnic) relations. The traditional model of Guatemalan capitalism could not survive if Indian demands were met, for the Indians would end not only the process of proletarianization but the coercive control over non-proletarianized labor as well. One must concede that what would emerge to replace traditional capitalism in Guatemala in such circumstances is not clear. It is even doubtful, without eradicating other forms of class oppression, that such a transformation could occur at all. But the argument about the revolutionary implications of Indian demands reinforces the point that the Guatemalan Indian struggle *is* a class struggle, one with revolutionary implications. To make this argument, one need not believe that Indian demands or analyses are sufficient for a revolutionary transformation, only that they are necessary parts of a revolutionary program.

Should Guatemala's revolutionary leadership convince Indians to take up the cause of class oppression alone, on the basis of an analysis which sees all Guatemalan workers as proletarians oppressed by capitalists, a revolutionary transformation in Guatemala is also possible, but it would be equally incomplete. There is no reason to expect that with the eradication of capitalism in Guatemala all other forms of oppression—racial, ethnic, gender, or that practiced by the state (whether a 'revolutionary' state or not)—would disappear. We have seen enough of revolutionary societies that have eradicated 'objective' class differences to know that other forms of oppression can and do remain, not least that practiced by the state.[37] The Indian analysis of state oppression is as relevant to a socialist society as it is to capitalism.

But what of the fact that the Indian language of resistance includes no clear vision of a future society? Can we accept as revolutionary the demands of a 'class' allegedly on the margins of history? To make this argument is to accept that proletarianization is a necessary precondition to revolutionary transformation, a conclusion premised upon an evolutionary view of the world and its transformations that gives absolute privilege to material life over its interpretation. Capitalism gives a future vision of socialism, only because socialism is the negation of capitalism. But all revolutionary visions are negations of the present in that they are hopes for a life without a particular form of oppression, whether of class, race, or gender. The future can only build upon the contradictions and language of the present, and there is nothing in the present that should privilege class oppression over all other forms of oppression. That Indians have not found an intellectual tradition to defend their vision—life without the oppression of race, culture, and state power—comparable to that offered by the Marxist tradition to the proletariat, does not mean that their goals are any the less revolutionary, or visionary.

One may accept, then, that all forms of class oppression must be eradicated in Guatemala for a truly revolutionary society to emerge without concluding that other forms of oppression should be considered secondary and derivative. For if one is persuaded by the argument made here, that the Indian struggle in Guatemala is a 'class' struggle, one would have to recognize that even class oppression would not be eradicated in Guatemala were only capitalist exploitation eliminated. If a socialist society were to emerge in Guatemala that ignored the demands for full equality within the society for Indians (or for women)—further proletarian-izing them for the surplus needed to build a society free of necessity—class oppression would remain. This, of course, is the great contradiction, dilemma, and tragedy of modern socialist societies. Political oppression in the name of 'primitive socialist accumulation' might be less virulent than traditional forms of class oppression but it would not necessarily be any more justifiable. If Marxism is to become truly the theory of liberation in Latin America it must break free of the dogmatism that reduces age-old cultures of resistance and ethnic identity to mere epiphenomena objectivized class categories.

13

A New International Division of Labor? The Caribbean Example

Marc W. Herold
and
Nicholas Kozlov

A prominent feature of both left and mainstream analyses of recent trends in the world economy has been the development of theories which propose the arrival of a new stage of capitalism characterized by a 'New International Division of Labor' (NIDL). Such politically diverse writers as Samir Amin, Pedro Vuskovic, Gerald Helleiner, and James Leontiades all share the view that developments in high technology (microcircuitry in particular), transport, and information processing have allowed multinational corporations (MNCs) to break apart complex production into distinct components, to parcel out the latter among different regions, and finally to sell the finished output on the world market.[1] Indeed, among left circles the 'NIDL' thesis has so deeply permeated the work being done that entire clusters of authors (e.g., at *Monthly Review* and *NACLA*) are able confidently to repeat and reinforce each other to such an extent that criticism no longer seems necessary.

But there should be something bothersome about the fact that a conservative business economist (Leontiades) and a radical former minister in the Allende government (Vuskovic) approach the analysis of foreign investment from precisely the same theoretical perspective. For example, when discussing the 'NIDL', Leontiades contends that high labor costs in the developed countries have pushed MNCs 'to set up production facilities in countries whose major attraction is an abundant supply of low-cost labor. They are producing there not for the local market but for export. . . .'[2] Similarly, Vuskovic finds low-cost labor, a 'factor' which is abundant in developing nations, to be the 'essence of the phenomenon'. The internationalization of capital (both 'old' and 'new') is best understood as being in 'strict accordance with the theory of comparative costs' (or its alter ego, the Heckscher-Ohlin-Samuelson factor endowments theorem). So it seems that the only difference is one of ideological preferences: Leontiades has eyes only for the 'efficiency' of the 'NIDL,' while Vuskovic is deeply troubled by the continuing poverty of workers in the developing nations.

Recently, however, some left analysts have become increasingly aware of the need for alternative approaches to the study of economics and society to distinguish themselves sharply from orthodox analyses along more than merely ideological lines.[4] There is a growing recognition that the approach followed so often in the past, viz., an eclectic fusion of progressive rhetoric and barely transformed (or disguised) orthodox methods and categories, leads at best to an impasse: orthodox theoretical concepts will eventually make their presence felt.

Analyzing the Internationalization of Capital

In this study, we seek to pull together the results of a substantial amount of previous work[5] by undertaking a theoretical and empirical case study of foreign direct investment (by US-based MNCs) generally and in relation to the particular cases of Central America and the Caribbean. Since our approach is quite critical of the 'NIDL' hypothesis, we will begin by explicitly formulating our methodological differences and suggesting alternative premises.

The positivist bent of traditional theory leaves it poorly equipped to comprehend the necessity of integrating analyses conducted on several levels of abstraction. Much of the work being done on the left is also infused by the positivist theoretical heritage, so that writers frequently tend inductively to theorize (generalize) transient empirical trends into a bewildering array of 'new' general theories and 'new' stages or indices of world economy.

During the ascent of the dependency and 'development of underdevelopment' theories during the 1960s, it became commonplace for left analysts to explain the dynamics of developing social formations in terms of external causes. Despite the disfavor into which dependency theory has fallen, its major and characteristic weakness—the neglect of internal class relations—continues to plague much of the work being done.

Another by-product of dependency theory is the now well established custom of distinguishing among various 'types' of accumulation according to the supposed presence or absence of 'development' or 'linkage' effects. The approach leads to a conception in which the process of accumulation in 'core' nations appears to be intrinsically different from accumulation in the 'periphery'.

Modern epistemology considers science to be the discovery and explanation of generative mechanisms. Empirical phenomena, in this view, are (complex) consequences of those mechanisms. Any approach which is tied to positivist epistemology, however, necessarily stresses the irreducibility of empirical phenomena, and, as such, can 'explain' empirical trends only in observational terms. An adequate, modern approach to social science requires a theoretical procedure in which tendential laws of motion comprehended at a high level of abstraction are integrated (but not conflated) with concrete analysis. Consequently, insofar as one seeks to understand developments in present-day capitalism, it is necessary to situate empirical phenomena within a general theory of the capitalist mode of production. Otherwise, observed phenomena are treated as no more than observed regularities or, worse yet, become themselves inductively theorized into 'new' laws of development.

It is not difficult to find examples of analyses (and subsequent prescriptions) marred by the failure to integrate concrete research with a firmly grounded theoretical perspective. For instance, nineteenth-century Russian agrarian populists correctly observed increasing rural poverty, but failed to situate this observation in a theory of incipient capitalist development. Instead, they went on to generalize the empirical 'fact' of impoverishment of the rural masses into a 'theory' which precluded capitalist development in countries late to embark upon industrialization. Similarly, dependency and 'development of underdevelopment' theoreticians in the 1960s observed (again correctly) economic stagnation and poverty in the developing nations and went on to theorize the general impossibility of capitalist development in the periphery.[6] When economic growth (capitalist development!) resumed in many Third World nations (i.e., the stagnation witnessed by the *dependistas* was conjunctural, not structural), the dependency school was unable to provide explanations and lapsed into desperate notions such as the 'active development of ultra-underdevelopment'.[7]

More recently, the 'NIDL' writers have taken a perfectly appropriate observation and inappropriately theorized it into a new stage of capitalism. High technology and developments in transportation have supposedly made possible the breakup of production processes, and MNCs parcel out the labor intensive components to low wage developing nations. The output is then sold on the world market: 'This process, which is based on the increasingly wide-spread internationalization of capital and production, has redefined the geographic location of plants producing for the world market.'[8] To be sure, it is possible to identify examples of such activity, although we demonstrate below its very limited dimensions. We seek to stress, however, that observation of particular empirical events gives no grounds for generalizing the phenomenon into a 'theory' of the alleged 'NIDL'. The internationalization of pro-ductive capital can be conceptually located as a moment in the international self-expansion process of capital. This is stated at a high level of abstraction, but the *particular forms* such international-ization assumes become clear only at a more concrete level of analysis. And here is the *main point*: no doubt the form of internationalization in a specific conjuncture might be that of low wage industrialization, but in other concrete instances the form (i.e., the manner in which the production process passes through the sphere of circulation) will be different. The adverse theoretical and political implications of theorizing transient empirical pheno-mena should be clear from the few examples cited above.

In addition to avoiding such a confusion or conflation of levels of theoretical analysis, our approach also seeks to affirm the effectivity of contradictions and developments *internal* to social formations, as opposed to the dependency and 'NIDL' perspectives, which stress determination by *external* forces. Whereas for the dependency school, the relevant external factor was the state of dependency imposed by one *nation* on another, the 'NIDL' theoreticians believe they have found a new 'dependence' rooted in the activities of *multinational corporations*.[9] Moreover, we avoid the commonplace distinctions among 'types' of accumulation processes, i.e., those which supposedly provide 'linkage' or 'development' effects and those which do not.[10]

This is not to say that the *concrete* differences (economic, political, and ideological) between developed and developing social form-ations should not be analyzed and understood—we merely object to the development of 'theoretical' models which are no more than inductions of those concrete differences. The latter approach produces a descriptive generalization as its best result, but more usually provides an illusory theoretical cognition that leads to a false sense of confidence.

The political implications of the approaches we reject may now be clear: the focus on external determination, the absence of a rigorous formulation of exploitation and class conflict, and the consequent primacy of contradictions between nations (or regions) 'confers on dependency theory a nationalist character' and a 'nostalgic longing for a frustrated autonomous development.'[11] Furthermore, the supposed dichotomy between 'core' and 'peripheral' accumulation processes leads to the characterization of accumulation in the 'periphery' as inherently disruptive, uneven, 'disarticulated,' etc.[12] By contrast, accumulation in the 'core' is seen as smooth, deliberate, 'autocentric', etc. The problem, therefore, is visualized as a particular 'type' of capital accumulation, rather than the process of capital accumulation per se. The ideological corollary of this logic in the developed nations has been support for the not insignificant revival of working class protectionism.

Further methodological differences involve the conceptualization of the capitalist firm—particularly as it bears on the issue of the determinants of foreign investment.

Naturally the 'aim' of the capitalist firm is the appropriation of profit; this follows from the very nature of capital as self-expanding value. Many left analysts, however, persist in seeking to understand this reality with terms and concepts which are taken over from neo-classical theory. Especially in the 'NIDL' literature, the firm appears as a 'profit maximizer' and 'rational allocator of resources'. This approach is from the outset precluded from grasping the (specific and hierarchical) articulation of the processes of production and circulation, and also implicitly adopts the idealized neo-classical notion of competition.

The concept of the capitalist firm (an individual capital) can and must be formulated at different levels of abstraction. At the highest level of abstraction, that of capital in general, analysis of the individual capital provides insights with regard to the investigation of, for example, the labor process. In fact, the concept of capital as self-expanding value is produced at this level of abstraction, with the attendant implications for the 'aims' which a particular capital 'chooses' to pursue.

Insights of a different sort are provided by a descent to lower levels of abstraction, from capital in general to a multiplicity of capitals and the action of capital upon capital, i.e., competition. The accumulation of surplus value now becomes 'problematic' because the accumulation of a particular capital takes place (can only take place) in proximity to other capitals[13] which are all trying to drive away and exclude each other from markets, i.e., to destroy each other. As Anwar Shaikh has ably demonstrated, the imagery of competition as a war is not merely figurative.[14]

By contrast, the traditional theory of capitalist firm behavior is elaborated *exclusively* at a very high level of abstraction: the firm, considered in isolation, is assumed to desire the maximization of profit and accomplishes this via the optimal allocation of factors.

Competition (other firms) enters the scene again as an 'assumption,' and even then only as a mechanism to ensure harmony, mutual benefit and equalization—in short, rather than the destructiveness of a war, in the traditional view of things competition 'renders capitals identical'. All capitals become equalized, with the weak rising to the level of the strong.[15]

For us, competition is a derived concept that follows from and is dominated by the very starting point of the analysis: the production of surplus value and the self-expansion of capital. The 'maximization of profit' does not proceed via tranquil marginal adjustments of the level of output. Nor does an infinitely divisible and malleable 'capital' peacefully seek out profit opportunities only to be continually thwarted by equilibrium (much as the liquid at one end of a manometer automatically adjusts itself to the level of the liquid at the other end).

No doubt many (but not all) of the 'NIDL' writers would object to the preceding characterization of the method, pointing out that their analysis is motivated by a genuine concern for miserably paid workers in developing nations, etc. Our point, however, is that good intentions will not absolve the 'new international division of labor' theorists from eventually having to accept the implications of their essentially neo-classical endeavor. For what else can their approach be called when they argue that the phenomenon of low wage industrialization is *best explained* in terms of the 'theory of comparative costs' and the abundance of the low cost 'labor factor' in the developing countries?[16] Similarly, the neo-classical heritage also reveals itself in efforts to explain investment patterns according to 'cost, labor skill, and transportation factors'.[17]

The 'NIDL' chickens are coming home to roost, and nothing makes this clearer than the ease with which the theory is co-opted into respectable reformist channels. Since it is no longer the process of capital accumulation itself which is seen as responsible for the misery of workers in the developing nations, but only a particular 'type' of accumulation (i.e., the 'disarticulated' variety), the doctrine of the 'NIDL' is neatly adaptable to the endless discussions surrounding the reforms of tariff (and non-tariff) barriers to trade, technology transfers, etc.[18] The good intentions and honesty with which some 'NIDL' writers approach their analysis in fact requires them to note the process of co-optation has already begun.[19]

In short, there can be no doubt that capitalist firms seek to increase profit and to reduce labor costs (there is nothing 'new' in capital's search for cheap labor). It does not follow, however, that we should accept the doctrine of comparative costs. We of course recognize that capital accumulation involves the expansion of capital (albeit in different forms historically) beyond national boundaries and produces both the internationalization of capital and international competition. An adequate theory of the determinants of the capitalist firm's international investment behavior in the current stage of development of capitalism must integrate the concept of the individual capital (in a milieu of many capitals) with the notion of the self-expansion of capital during the stage of the internationalization of the circuit of productive capital. Rather than the alleged 'new' low wage export-oriented industrialization, we believe that the form of internationalization is far better represented by projects such as those of the Ford Fiesta in Spain, the Iran-Japan petrochemical complex in Iran, G.T.&E.'s electrical goods project in Algeria, and the huge metallurgical-petrochemical complexes being built at Al Jubail and Yenbu in Saudi Arabia.[20] These are hardly labor intensive projects, although the output is sold on world markets.

The Industrialization of the 'Periphery'

As the material reality of industrialization via import substitution unfolded in many developing nations, the left provided a critique of this industrialization in the form of dependency theory. Now, with orthodox development literature and policy pushing export promotion (bolstered by heavy doses of IMF medicine), the left has responded with the theory of the 'NIDL'. In other words, the left has consistently refused to acknowledge that a 'genuine,' autonomously propelled industrialization has been occurring in many developing nations.

Among other things, we suggest below that industrialization of a 'genuinely' capitalist sort has been underway in much of the periphery. Is such industrialization uneven, brutal, and 'exploitative'? Of course! What else would one expect from the mode of production which has made raising exploitation of the immediate producer its historical mission? Disappointment will almost surely be the result of a search for a 'better type' of capital accumulation. Indeed, we feel that the 'exceptions' to be explained are those instances of capitalist industrialization that proceeded on the basis of relatively 'high' wages (e.g., the USA and the 'white dominions').

The currently observed fragmentation of the Third World into groups of nations with different socio-economic features[21] as well as trade structures reflects capital's historic task of developing the forces of production through the increasing specialization and socialization of labor. All this socialization proceeds, so do the engendered class struggles in the various momentary nodes, furthering capital's drive for new sources of surplus value. In other words, rather than stressing discontinuities or stages in the process of capitalist industrialization of the periphery, we focus on the unfolding unitary global, yet contradictory and uneven, process of capital's self-expansion.

During the golden post-World War II years, intensive capital accumulation centered in the developed countries proceeded on the basis of extensive opportunities for valorization in both the producer and consumer goods branches. During the 1960s a crisis emerged: the fall in the rate of profit led to stagnation in the mass of surplus value realized by additional increments of investment.[22] It is in the scramble to overcome this crisis that one locates the post-1965 rising share of international trade in total capitalist production, including the 'search for cheaper wage zones'.[23]

But the resulting enclaves of low wage export-oriented production are not self-sustaining. 'At first, the subcontractor states tried to solve the [labor supply] problem through such "bloody" methods as the forced sterilization of the Malaysian women. But now their aim is to raise the technological level of their exports. . . .'

Whether it was based on an old-style import-substitution drive, or on an import-substitution program combined with classical export-promotion, local capitalism had become a not insignificant force by the early seventies in a number of 'newly industrializing countries.'

A two-pronged program of import substitution has opened up, with one prong an 'attempt to integrate more advanced technological links in the chain of the relevant export branch (South Korean textile machinery)', while another prong 'involves an attempt to assimilate higher stages in the production of local consumer goods'.[25] There is no question of simply using Third World labor reserves as a base for re-exporting activity.

The large Ford of Spain project (1972)[26] is a classic example of such import substitution plus export promotion, as is the recent Mexican drive to reconstructure its automotive industry. It has become commonplace for host governments to permit new foreign investment on condition that it generate foreign exchanges. Mexico announced in September 1983 that it will require automobile manufacturers as well as makers of parts to balance foreign income and expenditures beginning with the 1984 model year.[27]

Other writers have observed that industrializing, indebted, developing nations have emphasized diversified export expansion programs as a way of servicing their mounting debt.[28] Is it then surprising that manufactured exports from the developing nations have been rising? Such export diversification has meant that the share of total Third World manufactured exports accounted for by the chemicals and machinery-transportation branches has grown with respect to the more traditional exports (textiles, apparel, and electronics). We truly are seeing the autos and chemicals branches outstrip the bras and calculators branches![29]

In the Third World, the new state industrial bourgeoisie—an outgrowth of the internationalization of the circuit of money capital—is determined to increase its role in the world economy, hence the calls for a 'new international economic order' and the 'new forms' taken by international productive capital. This international production activity is by no means any longer the exclusive domain of the MNCs, but is increasingly the result of Third World bourgeoisies seeking to integrate themselves into the world economy.[30] True, such internationalization of the circuit of productive capital implies that certain developing nations produce a new array of (international) products and commodities, but did not the original turn of the century boom in foreign investment also result in altered trade patterns?

The state in the less developed countries thus joins the national bourgeoisie and foreign MNCs in production activities reflecting the internationalization of productive capital, e.g., in Brazilian or Mexican petrochemicals, Saudi metallurgical complexes, Jamaican bauxite processing, etc., often (but not always) producing for the world market. As Peter Evans has suggested, capitalist development in Brazil has required some redefinition of what is meant by capitalist development, but this is precisely what must occur if we want to get away from a teleological conception of capitalism's evolution. The result (in Brazil) has been the gradual construction of an increasingly state-capitalist framework with strong interpenetration of the local state and the MNCs.[31] It implies continued accumulation directed by a small minority and the domination of the accumulation process by capital. This, rather than the alleged 'new' low wage export-oriented industrialization is, we believe, the present stage of imperialism, reflecting a higher socialization of production.

Naturally, we do not deny that MNCs adjust their business strategy to changing competitive conditions. The point is that such adjustment can be comprehended only at a very concrete level. Greater competition in world markets for manufacturers raises questions of whether the affiliates of MNCs will continue to respond to a global strategy, drawing on a common pool of resources and exhibiting the same centralization of control at headquarters.[32] A tendency to joint ventures is unquestionable, although one should not automatically infer that greater 'control' is exercised by the host government. A foremost apologist for the MNCs notes that the adoption of world models for products may enhance corporate control; likewise, software and communications systems allow firms to retain control over finance and production.[33]

The strategies adopted by MNCs to cope with the growing conflict between the requirements of 'adequate profitability' and the adjustments made necessary by the demands of governments have varied.[34] Some companies pursue the economic imperative and follow a worldwide (or regional) business strategy where the activities in various countries are integrated and centrally managed. The aim, of course, is to enhance the firm's international competitiveness. The production process is broken down by geographic area, turning out components and subsystems in plants scattered (often) in 'newly industrializing countries' around the world, and then doing final assembly in the ones that hold out the most promise as markets. Other companies forego the direct benefits of such integration and let their subsidiaries adjust to the demands of host governments (just as if the affiliates were national companies). *Fortune* magazine recently pinpointed the difference between the two strategies as having to do with the degree of *central coordination*, concluding that 'to keep up with competition, a company . . . must adopt a global strategy'.[35]

On the other hand, some firms try to leave their business strategy unclear and opportunistically reap the benefits from economic integration or national responsiveness. Each strategic management decision is judged on its own merits in 'a series of limited adjustments made in response to specific developments, without an attempt made to integrate these adjustments into a consistent comprehensive strategy'.[36] Such administrative coordination trades off internal efficiency for external flexibility, when compared with a strategy of multinational integration.[37]

One can generalize that *three main factors* affect which type of strategy will suit a particular MNC: 1) the market types being served; 2) the competition encountered; 3) and the technology used by the firm. Thus, changes in the openness of international markets, industry structure, or the technology of an industry all foreshadow a likely change in a firm's overall strategy. Finally, a global strategy of integration requires considerable financial outlays and willingness to tolerate a long payback period.[38]

Whereas in the first two postwar decades, conjunctural circumstances made the particular axis of accumulation center upon the reconstruction of war-torn economies with incidental import substitution in the periphery, one finds that different circumstances in the 1970s favored in depth industrialization of the periphery. At the abstract level, the movement can be captured in the advance from the internationalization of the circuit of money capital to that of productive capital. The precise timing of the shift must, however, be examined concretely at the level of social formation(s). The highly schematic diagram below summarizes our view of the recent axes of accumulation:

FIGURE 1

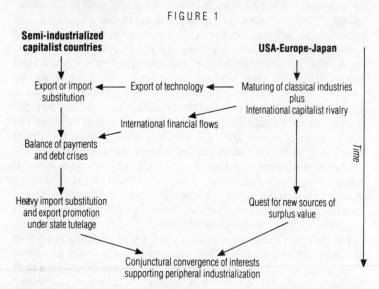

The Pattern of U.S. Investment

We will now present evidence, drawn from our previous investigations, on the overall foreign investment trends of US multinationals, the position of US multinationals in the Caribbean Basin, and the investment patterns of selected major corporations. The following salient characteristics of the US direct investment stock since the late 1960s serve as a backdrop to a fuller understanding of the specific investment trends in the Caribbean Basin:

(A) While the rate of growth of US foreign direct investment activity has slowed markedly since the mid–1970s, more than offsetting increases have been registered in indirect (portfolio) investment in the form of private bank loans to public entities in developing nations.[39]

(B) US investment in the *developed* countries has grown *more rapidly* in relative terms than that in the developing countries.

(C) us mining and smelting direct investments have not risen as rapidly as total us foreign direct investments. Nonetheless, the share of developing nations' output in capitalist world metal mining has been rising. us corporations have been particularly active in Brazil, Chile, and Colombia.[40]

(D) Between 1950 and 1980, two major characteristics of us direct investment in the petroleum branch were that it grew at a lesser rate than overall us direct investment and that the developed countries were the major recipients of new petroleum investments.[41]

(E) A truly major burst in trade and finance-related us investment has occurred, as firms in these branches followed their clients abroad and invested in growing markets. Such finance related investments have been particularly significant in Latin America, the Caribbean Basin, and Singapore.[42]

(F) A slight relative shift toward manufacturing investment in the developing nations' during the 1970s is observable, after a very rapid increase in Europe during the previous decade. The share of us manufacturing foreign direct investment in the developing nations rose from 17.6% to 21% between 1973 and 1981.[43] Naturally, nearly four-fifths of the increased us stake abroad in manufacturing during those years was in the developed countries, reflecting the far greater initial position there. The somewhat *faster growth rate* of us manufacturing direct investment in the developing nations does not support the 'NIDL' thesis. Rather, the growth rate occurred because markets in some developing nations were expanding rapidly and because the 'newly industrializing countries' began promoting indepth industrialization.

(G) Among the developing regions, Latin America received the bulk of us manufacturing foreign investment, a share which rose slightly between 1973 and 1981 from 77% to 79%. In Latin America, the 'ABM' countries' (Argentina, Brazil, Mexico) share increased from 77% to 79.5% during those years. This suggests that we are seeing the rising relative importance of certain countries within the overall configuration of us foreign direct manufacturing,[44] which is rather surprising given the accounts in the business press which decry the relatively inhospitable climate there.

(H) These manufacturing direct investments have been oriented towards serving host country markets, more so in Latin America than in the eec and Canada (see Table 1).

(I) During the 1970s, a new element appeared in us manufacturing direct investment. In an exact replay of prior investment shifts towards the us South (1940s), Puerto Rico (1950s), and the us-Mexican border (1960s), us firms set up export-oriented plants in

Table 1

Destination of Sales by Majority-Owned Affiliates of US
Corporations by Area for 1976 (in per cent)

	Local Sales	Exports to USA	Exports to Third Countries
Europe (EEC 9)	69	2	29
Canada	74	21	5
Latin America	94	2	4
Asia & Pacific	79	8	13
TOTAL	100	100	100

Source: Chung, W. K. 'Sales of Majority-Owned Affiliates of US Companies, 1976',
    Survey of Current Business, March 1978, p. 35.

Southeast Asia's 'four little tigers' as well as in other selected low
wage areas of the world (including some Caribbean islands).

(J) As regards the distribution of US direct investment across
manufacturing branches, one finds a relative rise in the food,
machinery, and chemicals branches, with the most active US
manufacturing during the 1970s in the food and kindred products
and machinery branches of the developing nations (followed by
investment in developed nations' chemical industries).[45]

(K) While the bulk of US investments remain oriented to final
products for local or regional markets, it is true that the share of
foreign-controlled firms' output in the total manufactured exports
of certain countries (Brazil, Colombia, Mexico, Argentina) has been
estimated at between 25% and 40%.[46] Such exports as there are to
the USA are increasingly partial manufacturers and intermediate
products. From the viewpoint of the MNC, such semi-processing
abroad offers certain obvious advantages, in particular higher rates
of exploitation (since the productivity differences between developed and developing nations are smaller than the money wage
differences).

(L) By way of closing the discussion of investment stock data, it is
important to observe that most investments are market-(i.e.,
competition) oriented, and, insofar as export-oriented activity is
present, it is concentrated in the raw material or other extractive
industries. Proponents of the 'NIDL' thesis might note that there
has indeed been an upward trend in export-oriented industrial
activities, but that these were *not* in the low wage industrial
branches.

In sum, a slight increase in the developing nations' (and

especially the larger Latin American countries') relative importance as hosts to US manufacturing investment took place during the 1970s, yet the bulk of US manufacturing direct investment remains in the developed countries. Such investment as exists in the developing nations is more oriented towards the internal market than that in the developed countries.

In this context we simply cannot fathom why such a huge fuss is presently made about low wage direct investment and subcontracting. Surely a glance at American economic history would reveal that subcontracting has a long domestic and international past (recall Puerto Rico, the US-Canadian automotive agreement, the US-Mexican border industrialization program, etc.). Indeed, the US South, once the haven of low wage runaway industry, is now at the center of dynamic industrialization, while the Rustbelt languishes (the unevenness of capitalist development prevails in the 'core' too, not just in the periphery). Nonetheless, much recent literature stresses the 'new' importance of cheap labor. But this is hardly something new: well over a decade ago, such different observers as the late Stephen Hymer and *Fortune* magazine were in agreement that during the 1950s American companies went to Europe, attracted by the lower wages there.[47] As *Fortune* noted: 'The companies went abroad in large part because they saw an opportunity to flee the U.S. wage structure. . . .[B]y going overseas, then, many of these companies were able to establish an edge in costs over the foreign competition—and also to neutralize their domestic cost disadvantage.'[48]

Is a 'NIDL' Empirically Demonstrable?

We now will analyze the incidence of foreign investment and low wage investments, contrasting our conception of the axes of typical developing nation industrialization with the view proposed by the advocates of the supposed 'NIDL'. The uneven development of global capitalism asserts itself in the patterns described. Rather than the traditional investments in public utilities or plantations, or subsequent horizontal import substitution, the MNC is more likely to produce services or sophisticated industrial products for both local and export markets. In fact, as regards MNC investment behavior, one observes any number of particular, conjunctural differentiations across time and space.

We believe that proponents of the 'NIDL' hypothesis must be able to support their proposition empirically with both *investment stock and international trade data*. Our review of investment stock data does not lend support to the coming of a 'NIDL'. We shall now review the sales data of majority-owned foreign affiliates (MOFAs) of US MNCs for which U.S. Department of Commerce data is available.

Empirical evidence supports our contention that the much touted low wage export activity of MNCs is a minor phenomenon, a mere addendum to the ongoing process of internally oriented Third World industrialization.[49] We find that:

(a) Growth rates of the stock of US manufacturing foreign direct investment (see Table 2) and the destinations of MOFA sales (see Table 3) do not warrant the claim of a recent massive industrial relocation. Moreover, the sectorial convergence in the distribution of US manufacturing direct investment between Europe/Canada and Latin America has elsewhere been noted (is Europe also part of the outlying world for the 'NIDL' writers?).[50]

Table 2

Average Annual Growth Rates of US Manufacturing Direct Investment by Area, for Selected Four-Year Periods

	1962–1966	1966–1970	1970–1974	1974–1978	1978–1981
Canada	9.7%	7.6%	10.7%	7.0%	4.0%
Southern Dominions	15.8	14.0	10.4*	5.7	7.6
Europe, total	16.5	11.6	14.8	11.0	7.8
the EEC 9	15.4	10.6	14.6*	11.0	8.9
others	32.9	19.9	12.8*	11.2	−1.0
Latin America and other Western hemisphere	14.3	11.2	13.5	11.5	10.4
Other developing nations	20.7	14.1	15.4	10.0	12.3

Reported direct investment figures represent book value
*Data for 1969–1973

Source: US Department of Commerce, *Survey of Current Business*, various issues.

(b) The relative importance of developing nations' manufactured exports is minor both in relation to total industrial output and the share of the developed nations' manufactured imports (the latter rose from 6.1% in 1961 to 9.1% in 1979).[51] In those countries which adopted export promotion policies, the share of manufactured exports in manufactures output has been rising between 1960 and 1973, although it exceeds 40% in only a handful of countries (Hong Kong, Malaysia, Singapore, Taiwan).[52] In the larger Latin American nations (Argentina, Brazil, Colombia,

Table 3

Sales Destination of US Majority-Owned Affiliates

	ALL SECTORS			MANUFACTURING		
	Local	Exports to USA	Exports to Third Countries	Local	Exports to USA	Exports to Third Countries
1957	n.a.	n.a.	n.a.	82.28%	4.01%	13.71%
1966	75.05%	6.44%	18.50%	81.39	5.66	12.96
1972	71.54	6.62	21.83	77.70	6.97	15.33
1974	63.18	7.27	29.55	76.67	6.39	16.94
1975	66.15	6.82	27.03	77.00	5.91	17.09
1976	65.10	6.98	27.92	75.64	6.63	17.73

Sources: US Department of Commerce, *Survey of Current Business*, 1966, p. 9.
Ibid., August 1972, p. 27.
Ibid., March 1978, p. 35.

Mexico) the ratio has been *falling* during the 1970s. Moreover, the *destination* of such manufactures is usually opposite to that predicted by the 'NIDL' writers, except in the case of certain Southeast Asian nations.[53]

(c) The commodity composition of LDCs' manufactured exports is such that MNCs might be expected to play a minor role.[54]

(d) It is necessary to stress the rather minor overall importance of US manufactured imports under the special US Tariff Code provisions (806.3 and 807.0).[55] Although the growth rate of such imports from LDCs has risen rapidly, even those who argue that international subcontracting 'appears to signal a significant shift in MNCs' method of penetrating less developed countries' concede that the absolute significance of such imports is low.[56]

(e) Equally, those branches most prone to 'running away', namely the apparel and electronics branches, have a minor significance in the economies of developed countries.[57]

(f) And lastly it is important to note the very active role of western MNCs in the sales/export of *advanced* technology to socialist nations, for which payment was sometimes made in future output produced by the project.[58]

We do not deny that the Third World has become a significant actor in the world trade of manufactures.[59] The rising share of manufactures in developing nations' total exports is particularly vivid in the case of the semi-industrialized countries, explicable in part by export promotion incentives adopted by these nations after the 1960s.[60] United Nations data indicates that developing countries' exports of manufactures (defined as SITC 5 through 8 less SITC 68) grew at an annual rate of 23.9% between 1971 and 1981 (and 26.9% between 1966 and 1976).[61] A notable feature remains the very high concentration of exports *from a few countries*— some Southeast Asian nations, India, and three large Latin American republics—which account for an increasing share of total Third World manufactured exports.[62]

The extent to which MNCs partake of this rising trend as a result of their past massive investments in industry is still being debated. Nayyar[63] has written the most comprehensive review of this matter, finding that MNCs in Latin America play a much more important role in the total of their host country's exports than in Asia. MNCs have been able to take best advantage of *regional markets* in their exporting activities, a fact we find reflected in the much greater relative importance of MOFA exports to third countries than to the USA (see Table 3).[64] Comparing foreign-controlled to national firms in Latin America, Willmore found that foreign firms export more to regional neighbors, the CACM countries.[65]

While it is true that the share of total merchandise imports from LDCs accounted for by the MOFA's US parents has been rather high (32% average for 1966-1975) and rising, it is equally true that the share of MOFAs in the manufactured exports from developing

Table 4

The Share of Developing Nations' Exports of Manufactures Accounted for by US Majority-Owned Affiliates, by Area

Year	Latin America	Africa	Middle East	Other Asia & Pacific	Total
1966	52.6%	.3%	1.4%	7.3%	11.8%
1967	56.3	3.1	1.3	8.0	12.8
1968	45.5	6.8	1.0	8.5	12.1
1969	39.5	7.1	1.1	6.7	10.1
1970	26.5	7.5	1.0	9.1	11.8
1971	27.9	7.4	1.1	6.2	10.2
1972	25.7	8.7	2.3	5.0	9.1
1973	21.9	6.8	2.5	5.5	8.6
1974	23.3	7.2	2.4	5.8	9.0
1975	23.0	7.3	3.0	5.0	8.5
1976	23.4	7.7	4.0	3.9	7.4

Sources: For 1966–1973, Nayyar 1978, op. cit., p. 63
        For 1974–1976, *Survey of Current Business*, February 1977, p. 33 and March 1978, p. 36
        Nayyar, op. cit., p.82 United Nations, *Monthly Bulletin of Statistics*, May 1979, pp. xliv–lii.

nations has been small (about 10%) and *decreasing* between 1966 and 1976.[66] Helleiner believes this is explained by the conscious 'delinking' policies of many developing nations, leading to the phenomenon of non-US owned firms exporting from developing nations to the US, and thereby lowering the measured proportion of US imports originating with US MOFAs.[67]

The majority of US MOFA exports of manufactures from the Third World originates in Latin America. The share of US MOFA products in total Latin American exports *peaked* in 1967 and has been *declining steadily since*, contrary to popular belief (see Table 4). Nayyar suggests that this trend might be attributable to the increasing export activities of domestic firms in Latin America and/ or the newly arrived non-US MNCs.[68] The former might well be the case since the growth of indebted industrialization and the rising fortunes of the domestic bourgeoisies are accompanied by a diminished relative role of the MNCs.[69]

The number of producers of standardized intermediate and industrial goods has been growing at a rapid rate. Many of these new entrants are seeking to develop dependable foreign outlets, both in the capitalist and socialist nations. In the Middle East and in Latin America, majority state-owned enterprises have emerged in chemicals, petrochemicals, fertilizers, and non-ferrous metals. These companies are intensively cultivating foreign markets, the success of which is indicated by the rapid rise of non-petroleum developing nation exports. The developing nations share of total world non-petroleum manufactured exports rose from 6% to 10% between 1960 to 1976.[70] In manufactured products with low international marketing barriers, national firms are proving to be successful exporters (e.g., textile, certain apparel items, shoes, and leather products).

Beyond the evidence presented by Nayyar, we find that while the absolute value of exports by MNC MOFAs located in developing nations rose rapidly between 1966 and 1976 (at an annual rate of 18.3%), it is also true that over the same period the total manufactured exports of developing nations rose at the much higher annual rate of 23.4%.[71] We infer the likelihood that *the MNCs' share of manufactured exports from the developing nations has not been rising.* (A word of caution is in order here: the data we have employed include only majority-owned foreign affiliates of US parents, yet it may be that minority-owned joint ventures are on the rise and could have different trade orientations.[72])

Hellieiner has noted the extent of intra-firm trade in total US imports and exports. The share of total US imports originating with US MOFAs has risen from 25% to 32% between 1966 and 1975, largely as a result of increasing imports from Canada and 'other Asia and Africa'.[73] The latter is largely due to petroleum imports from Africa. When one excludes such petroleum imports, the picture changes markedly. The share of total US non-petroleum imports originating from US MOFAs implanted in the LDCs *has fallen from 21.5% in 1966 to 12.1% in 1976*. International sourcing by US parents is not yet a runaway phenomenon.

This does not mean that both the absolute and relative magnitude of US imports under special US tariff provisions has not been rising. The share of such imports in total non-petroleum imports went from 1.1% in 1966 to 15.5% in 1980.[74] Or, put another way, intra-firm imports from LDCs have not been rising as rapidly as have imports from *un*affiliated foreigners under the special tariff code provisions.

It has been observed elsewhere that the export performance of MNC affiliates (particularly in Latin America) when compared to domestic national firms is hardly impressive.[75] Legitimate doubt may be cast upon the belief that US MNCs make an above average contribution to the development of Third World exports. While it is true that the small share of MOFA sales outside local markets is generally rising, it is *not* rising in Latin America and 'other Asia Pacific'—which should be a perplexing statistic for the 'NIDL' theorists. The tendency for serving the internal market is greatest in Latin America, and the share of output value exported to the U.S. has oscillated around a paltry 1% to 3%. Further disaggregation of Latin American data by branch shows that the exported share of output in the transportation and electrical goods branches has risen, while that in processed foods has fallen. We expect that this rising relative (although in absolute terms small) share of the transportation and electrical goods branches in Latin America results from the active export promotion efforts of governments there in the post-import substitution era. Not least has been the response of US MNCs, which have been led to pursue a strategy of geographic (regional) specialization, reflected in intra-firm trade (particularly in the EEC nine countries) and for total manufacturing in all branches.[76]

In our research we have looked carefully at the outward-orientation of US manufacturing direct investment. While the data is not as good as one might wish, we construct the ratio of MOFA export sales to the reported book value of US manufacturing investment for the years 1965 through 1976. In other words, the figure measures the dollar value exported per dollar of book value. We find that US investment *in Europe and Canada is the most outward-oriented, while that in Latin America is the least*. We suspect the difference has precisely to do with US affiliates in the former exporting to regional markets, while Latin American affiliates are domestic market-oriented. One also notes the rising outward-oriented direction of US manufacturing direct investments in the Middle East.

Lastly, a sectoral breakdown of the sales destination of US MOFAs reveals the greatest growth: in developed countries' chemicals, paper, and non-electrical machinery branches; and in developing nations' non-electrical machinery, chemicals, and transportation equipment branches.[77] These are not the branches traditionally associated with low wage labor industrialization.

The Case of the Caribbean Basin

We shall conclude our empirical presentation with an examination of evidence on the Caribbean Basin as it pertains to our critique of the 'NIDL' hypothesis. The sectoral distribution of US investment in the Caribbean Basin is presented in Table 5. The US stake in Central America and the Caribbean can be summarized as follows: 'Agriculture, manufacturing, mining, tourism, and commercial holdings account for $6.2 billion in productive investment, and another $16.9 billion is tied up in banking and financial operations. . . . This constitutes about 9 percent of total U.S. investments abroad . . . [which] put the Caribbean Basin in second place in economic importance to the United States, surpassed only by the rest of Latin America.'

Overall, one can say that during the 1970s the Caribbean and Central America accounted for a constant share of worldwide US direct foreign investment, specifically about 4%. In the last three years, there has been a very rapid rise in this ratio due largely to increasing finance and bank-related investments in the Caribbean proper (see Table 6). This reflects a continuation of major post-World War II developments in the region, which involved restructuring old sugar plantation economies into systems based on tourism, oil processing, mining, and finance.[79] Much of the investment in banking and finance in a country like the Bahamas consists of loans to affiliates of banking-finance MNCs that are essentially internal accounting transactions undertaken to avoid regulations and taxes.

From the formation of the Central American Common Market (CACM) until 1969, about 60% of the increase in total direct foreign investment in the five republics was directed towards the manufacturing sector. As a consequence, by 1969 nearly one-third

238

Table 5

US Direct Investment in the Five Central American Republics, Panama, and the 'Other Western Hemisphere' (excl. Bermuda) in US $ millions

	1973	1974	1975	1976	1977	1978	1979	1980	1981	1982
TOTAL	4580	4835	5386	5547	n.a.	7179*	11171*	13365*	17051*	23141*
Mining & smelt.	510	423	489	461	460	425	256	350	400	n.a.
Petroleum	981	n.a.	1389	1201	1402	n.a.	1502	2104	2405	2435
Manufacturing	571	644	n.a.	741	766	n.a.	935	1109	1232	1256
Trade	497	621	732	701	913	997	n.a.	n.a.	1224	n.a.
Fin., Ins.	n.a.	936	1168	1579	n.a.	2512**	5609**	7809**	10894**	16917**
					In Percent of Total for Each Year					
TOTAL	100.0	100.0	100.0	100.0	100.0	100.0	100.0	100.0	100.0	100.0
Mining & smelt.	11.1	8.7	9.1	8.3	n.a.	5.9	2.3	2.6	2.4	n.a.
Petroleum	21.4	n.a.	25.8	21.7	n.a.	n.a.	13.4	15.7	14.1	10.5
Manufacturing	12.5	13.3	n.a.	13.4	n.a.	n.a.	8.4	8.3	7.2	5.4
Trade	10.9	12.8	13.6	12.6	n.a.	13.9	n.a.	n.a.	7.2	n.a.
Fin., Ins.	n.a.	19.4	21.7	28.5	n.a.	35.0	50.2	58.6	63.4	73.1

Notes: The data for 1977 and thereafter are corrected for the negative values reported in the finance, insurance, and banking branch.
*Equals Central America + Other W. Hemisphere—Bermuda + Global Correction.
**Equals [Total banking, finance, insurance in Central America and Other W. Hemisphere] minus [Finance and insurance in Mexico and Bermuda] plus Global Correction

Table 6
US Direct Investment in the Caribbean and Central America Relative to Worldwide Investment (in US $ millions)

	1973	1974	1975	1976	1977	1978	1979	1980	1981	1982
Panama	1549	1604	1907	1957	2249	2394	2874	3171	3784	4404
5 Cen. Amer. Republics	578	683	704	677	740	793	848	1037	1046	813
Bahamas	632	766	763	1059	1229	1790	2254	2712	3015	3393
Jamaica	618	609	654	577	556	n.a.				
Other W. Hemis.*	1202	1269	1357	1277	n.a.	n.a.	7146	6443	9207	14529
(1) Subtotal	4579	4931	5385	5547	n.a.	n.a.	13122	13363	17052	23139
(2) Worldwide US Inv.	103675	118819	124212	137244	149848	167804	191612	233384	240182	248601
(1)/(2)	4.42%	4.15%	4.34%	4.04%	n.a.	n.a.	6.80%	5.70%	7.10%	9.30%

Notes: The data for 1979–1981 have been adjusted to correct for the large negative entries in the reported entries by the Department of Commerce.
*Excludes Bermuda.

of total investment was in manufacturing, as compared with only 4% in 1959. The US accounted for a large but declining proportion of direct foreign investment in the region (90% of book value in 1959 to 80% in 1969).

One would expect to find a growing *relative* share of manufacturing in total US direct investment in Latin America, given the slow growth of new mining, smelting and petroleum investments in the region. Data for US investments indicates that the relative importance of manufacturing in Central America rose from 23.7% in 1973 to 54.2% in 1983.[81] By disaggregating the manufacturing industry into branches, one finds that branches of greatest growth between 1973 and 1983 have been chemicals, 'other manufacturing' (presumably textiles and related items), food products, and, to a lesser degree, electronics. The first three branches alone accounted for 85% of the increased US manufacturing stake between 1973 and 1983. A recent study on MNCs in Caribbean countries noted that in Jamaica and Trinidad-Tobago, manufacturing activity was oriented mainly towards the internal market, whereas in Haiti and the Dominican Republic such MNC investment was often directed towards export-oriented manufacturing using indigenous low cost labor in such branches as textiles and clothing.[82]

As competitive pressures continues to affect US MNCs, it seems that the preferred roles of the Caribbean and Central America *for us business* will be four-fold (in order of decreasing importance: (1) as a haven for low wage labor operations (light industry); (2) as a continuing source of raw materials (bauxite, sugar); (3) as a base for offshore banking; and (4) as an area of deepening import substitution.

The 1970s witnessed a veritable explosion of countries seeking to attract MNC assembly operations. A recent count indicated over seventy nations offering so-called 'investment incentives'.[83] Whereas the established MNC giants rationalize their worldwide production systems, relocating in such areas as Southeast Asia, Portugal, or along the US-Mexican border, it appears that *smaller us firms*, largely domestic, are seeking out the low wage areas of Central America and the Caribbean. Naturally, exceptions arise: Texas Instruments in El Salvador and Motorala in Costa Rica, for example. The basic attraction is well summarized by the chief executive of a small US computer parts firm which had just set up an assembly operation on St. Kitts in 1980: 'they work more minutes per hour', at 10% higher labor productivity than in the USA, at one-tenth the wages.[84] In other words, the attraction is the potential to extract large amounts of absolute surplus value.

The listing of the types of operations favored by us firms in the region is indicative of their nature: assembly of electronics, producing paper boxes, stuffing toys, making leather dog chews and 'Aris isotoner' fashion gloves, sewing baseballs (Haiti produces 80% of the world's output), and making women's undergarments. Typically, the us parent transfers part of an operation to an offshore site, say, in the Caribbean, while it maintains other operations back home.

Finally it remains to be asked whether some of the Caribbean free trade zones and low wage manufacturing platforms cannot attain more dynamic and increasingly self-financed level of dependent industrialization. In fact, it is highly improbable that such a 'Singapore' model will develop in depth anywhere in the Caribbean Basin.[85] In the first place, the area is a late starter in low wage activity, facing the formidable resistence of protectionist interests in the developed countries against the rise of further Singapores or Taiwans. Secondly, there will be little us assistance for such a project, certainly nothing equivalent to the levels accorded Puerto Rico in the 1950s and 1960s. Finally, confronted with more militant labor movements, there is no dynamic entre-preneurial strata comparable to the Korean or off-shore Chinese bourgeoises.

Thus while the number and variety of low wage operations will increase, given their low capitalization and instability they will continue to account for a very minor share of us direct foreign investment, and will be principally oriented towards large local markets. Far from a New International Economic Order, we see the continuation of familiar trends in the uneven movement of capital accumulation.

14

Puerto Rico Under the Reagan Doctrine

Aline Frambes-Buxeda

A poignant measure of the current relationship between the United States and Puerto Rico is the fate of a shanty-town called Mameyes. In October 1985, as tropical storms lashed at the island, Mameyes was engulfed in an enormous mudslide. At least five hundred men, women and children were killed—although the exact number will never be known since Governor Rafael Hernández Colón, citing cost amongst other considerations, called off the search and sealed the hillside. Although the victims were all theoretically 'US citizens' the US press treated the Mameyes catastrophe with the conventional indifference reserved for 'natural disasters' in remote parts of the third world. Even the *New York Times* buried its solitary story on Mameyes in a back column (indeed, the *Times Index* lists Mameyes under the category 'weather').

But Mameyes was not in the Himalayas or the Sahel, but right on the 'backporch', so to speak, of the United States at the height of the Reagan 'boom'. And the disaster was hardly 'natural'. If the October rains caused such havoc on the island (aside from Mameyes, there was also a fatal collapse of a bridge on the principal expressway), it was because a decade of municipal cutbacks and fiscal austerity have allowed Puerto Rico's infrastructure to deteriorate to the point of collapse.[1] Even more significantly the very existence of delapidated and vulnerable shanty-towns like Mameyes points to the increasing immiseration of a large mass of Puerto Ricans.

Reaganism, and its local allies, are responsible for a new and more extreme social polarization in Puerto Rico. At one pole, there are endless rows of tinny shacks on dirt streets with wooden snackbars advertising 'creole fried' fast-foods; at the other pole, sumptuous new subdivisions of $200,000-$500,000 homes guarded by private police. After forty years of exemplary 'modernization', sixty to seventy per cent of all Puerto Rican families still depend on some form of federal subsidy, particularly foodstamps. Agriculture has collapsed and 60% of the island's fertile land is dormant or expropriated for other purposes (including new US bases).[2] Officially unemployment is at 20% but most serious analyses raise the figure to nearer 40%. Two-fifths of the population has been forced to emigrate over the last forty years to the United States, including many intellectuals and professionals, creating the great Puerto Rican diaspora that now outnumbers the island's resident population. The public debt is over 60% of the GNP, the highest in the hemisphere, and the island faces an acute ecological crisis, largely due to the petrochemical and pharmaceutical industries and the military.[3]

Yet at the same time drugs and guns have sponsored the rise of a significant *nouveaux riches* stratum. In wake of the Reagan Doctrine military spending has become the fastest growing sector of the official economy; collaterally, a 'black economy', mainly organized around drugs and connected to Contra gundealing, generates a tax-free $3 billion annually. Over the last year members of many rich and prominent families, including leading bankers and doctors, have been indicted for drug-related offenses: the tip of a much larger iceberg of elite venality and corruption.[4]

In face of such extremes of profiteering and profit, it may seem amazing that Puerto Rico is still touted by Washington as *the* model of 'democratic modernization'. The propaganda status of Puerto Rico in US foreign policy, of course, has a long history, starting with the New Deal's attempt to provide a reformist justification for the continuation of US colonialism in the Caribbean. With total disregard for the consequences of their policies in the 1940s and 1950s—i.e., forced emigration on a scale comparable to nine-teenth-century Ireland—the regime of Luis Muñoz Marin and his Popular Democratic Party has acquired legendary status. 'Operation Bootstrap', which turned Puerto Rico into a dependency of multinational corporations and the Pentagon, was the prototype for Kennedy's overarching and shortlived 'Alliance for Progress'.

In the 1980s these statist and New Deal precedents have been deemphasized to stress the new Puerto Rican 'miracle' of free enterprise and deregulated investment. As the revamped model for the Caribbean Basin Initiative, Puerto Rico has been alloted the role of steering the rest of the region into closer interdependence with the United States—and, especially, with the Sunbelt states and hemispheric financial centers like Miami and Los Angeles.[5]

'Capital' of the Caribbean?

Free trade zones are the linchpins of this new ideology of regional 'puertoricanization'. The proliferation of FTZs in the Caribbean and Central America over recent years is striking, and Puerto Rico supplies the 'official' assurance of their success in catalyzing development. (Costa Rica is the other privileged 'model' increasingly singled out for recommendation by the Reaganites.) As the Caribbean Basin Initiative has proven basically void of any large-scale financial commitment from Washington—cruelly disappointing such loyal supporters as Seaga in Jamaica who were expecting the gift of mini-Marshall Plans—the hard pressed regimes in the region have turned towards new US or Japanese investment, however insecure or piratical its form (e.g. blood plasma, baseballs and Rambo Dolls in Haiti).

Puerto Rico is the crucial commercial and financial relay point in this prospective restructuring of the circum-Caribbean economy, and its business and political elites are enthusiasts in the campaign to tame other small states to adopt the neo-liberal development model. Their specific interest is in creating a production branch division of labor that concentrates technical and financial services in Puerto Rico while exploiting the rest of the region for its cheap labor reserves (in a conscious attempt to attract investment away from East Asia).[6] As Governor Rafael Hernández Colón put it with unusual candor in his inaugural address (Januray 1985): 'In order to achieve the valuable goals of President Reagan's Caribbean Basin Initiative we shall become an active and creative instrument of political stability and democracy in the region. Our "936" funds provide a stimulating method towards developing manufacturing in the region: The first phase of production starting in fellow Caribbean countries and the last and advanced technical phase of production to be completed in Puerto Rico.'[7]

The '936' funds are tax-exempt deposits of American and foreign banks, held in Puerto Rico and relent to 'favoured' regimes in the region: Grenada, El Salvador, Guatemala, Costa Rica, Panama and Venezuela. When congressional tax reformers threatened to remove this exemption Governor Hernández Colón retained Michael Deaver to fight for its preservation. Indeed the Puerto Rican government visualizes the $7 billion of financial capital held off-shore in San Juan as the principal lever for promoting private investment in the Caribbean Basin. A key proposal, designed to reinforce the new branch division of labor, is to create so-called 'twin plant' partnerships between Puerto-Rican-based firms and counterparts in other Caribbean or Central American countries. Dominica, Grenada and El Salvador—the most 'Reaganized' regimes in the region—have been the most vocal champions of this scheme, while Hernández Colón has campaigned to make it an integral part of the Caribbean Basin Initiative.[8]

In tandem with this economic strategy, Puerto Rican officials, vigorously supported by business, are supporting the island's claim to be the 'capital' of the Caribbean. Hernández Colón has proposed making San Juan the seat of a 'Caribbean Parliament', and Secretary of State Hector Luis Acevedo has won endorsements from Costa Rica, the Dominican Republic, Grenada, Honduras, El Salvador, and the speakers of the assemblies of Venezuela and Colombia. (Venezuela's interest may reflect a shrewd strategy to secure a larger tariff-free foothold, via Puerto Rico, in the US market.) Puerto Rican leaders have also scouted the possibilities of joining the Caribbean Common Market (Caricom) and other regional organizations—although their potential membership has become controversial because of their simultaneous insistence on the ousting of Nicaragua and Cuba.[9]

Another aspect of the US-sponsored effort to portray Puerto Rico as the hegemonic model (and capitalist alternative to Cuba) is the new, official emphasis on 'Hispanic identity'. Hernández Colón in his inaugural address prioritized more extensive relations with Latin America via such cultural activities as the planned celebrations on the quincentenary of Columbus's landing (1992). This is partially geared towards internal consumption, using pro-Hispanic rhetoric to pacify the yearnings of Puerto Rican intellectuals for closer ties with Spain and fellow Latin American nations. Moreover, various local groups hope that the new programs and fund allocations, dedicated to research and congresses on Hispanic traditions, will generate additional employment and prestige for the intelligentsia. Although it is too soon to say who has bought into this transparent game, with its caricatural substitution of *'Hispanidad'* for nationalism, it has useful political fall-out for the governing Popular Democratic Party.[10]

Washington has licensed San Juan to pursue its own limited 'sub-diplomacy': thus Puerto Rico's 'official' endorsement of the economic boycott of Nicaragua in May 1985. The island's government also maintains particularly close contact with sympathetic regimes in Costa Rica and Venezuela. Ex-president Monge of Costa Rica, the former ORIT head (the regional worker's organization under the influence of the CIA), visits Puerto Rico regularly to see his old friends in the Popular Democratic Party. Meanwhile, in the spring of 1985, President Jaime Lusinchi of Venezuela sent an official delegation to meet Governor Hernández

Colón to discuss closer commercial ties. Venezuela hopes, by the end of 1986, to reopen the bankrupt petrochemical complex in Ponce as a free-trade zone. It is hoped that this project will be seen as a model of the kind of economic integration promoted by the Caribbean Basin Initiative.[11]

Militarism and Repression

The ideological and economic roles of the Puerto Rican 'model' are complemented by the island's ever increasing importance as a military base and staging area for the 'Reagan Doctrine'. Although it has always been the Gibraltar of the US imperium in the Caribbean, the overt and oppressive militarization of daily life has increased dramatically since 1981. Even in the most rural hinterlands, warplanes, military transport and armed personnel are now ubiquitous. Taking advantage of the huge reservoir of unemployed youth, the military have launched a massive recruitment campaign, which in 'Rambo' stridency and blatant appeal far exceeds anything conceivable in the United States. Recruiting tables are brazenly set up in front of schools, shopping centers, colleges, movies—anywhere young people congregate. Meanwhile, for those who resist the propaganda, there remains the dismal fact that the Pentagon is, more than ever, the employer of the last resort on the island, creating one of the largest streams of menial and service jobs. It has become the fashion for the governor, or members of his cabinet, to pose in press conferences with generals and admirals promising to increase Puerto Rico's share of military spending and employment.

Meanwhile, Puerto Rico is actively the 'granite aircraft carrier' for US programs of destabilization and counter-revolutionary warfare in the circum-Caribbean region. The invasion of Grenada was extensively rehearsed on the Puerto Rican island of Vieques (whose despoilation as a bombing range and practice invasion site has long been contested by nationalists). The frequency of military manoeuvres—now most obviously designed as trial runs for the invasion of Nicaragua or 'horizontal escalation' against Cuba—is such that the island's press virtually ignores even the most ominous exercises. Thus in at the end of summer 1985, while Puerto Rican public opinion was preoccupied with FBI operations against local nationalists, the US Navy and the Puerto Rican National Guard, together with units from Honduras, Great Britain and Holland, carried out 'Readex-3-85', a major war game involving extended operations in Puerto Rico and throughout the Eastern Caribbean. While the local press devoted hundreds of column inches to the FBI capture of 'terrorists', it scarcely noted the mock war being fought off the coast in preparation for the next stage of Reagan's 'roll back' of revolution. The commander of the Puerto Rican national guard, General Mora Medina, in a contemptuous gesture, even denied knowledge of the exercise.[13]

Because of its language abilities and ethnic complexion, the Puerto Rican National Guard has been assigned a key role in the Reagan Doctrine. This 'native' unit is continuously being sent to Honduras, Panama, and neighboring islands on special 'cultural' missions as well as military manouevres. The growing imbrication of Puerto Rican governmental structures with the Pentagon is also reflected by the large number of bureaucrats and public officials holding commissions in the Puerto Rican National Guard. At the same time, there remains a latently racist social chasm between the higher reaches of the US military apparatus in Puerto Rico and the rest of society. In its domination of an increasing sector of Puerto Rican life, not to mention its total control of a significant area of island territory annexed as bases or bombing ranges, the US military hierarchy (whose Caribbean command-post was shifted recently from Roosevelt Roads, Puerto Rico to Norfolk, Virginia) exerts a decisive proconsular influence over the country's life.

The extent of this Pentagon superordination of Puerto Rican 'self-government' was vividly revealed by the disclosure of the gross violation of Puerto Rico's guarded status in the 1979 Treaty of Tlatelolco. This nuclear non-proliferation agreement between Western Hemisphere governments, blessed by the Carter administration, forbade the location of nuclear weapons of any kind in Puerto Rico. In fact, as Leslie Gelb revealed on 13 February 1985 in the *New York Times*, the Pentagon, without informing the island's ostensible government, was storing deadly B-57 atomic bombs in local bases for deployment in anti-submarine warfare by P-3 aircraft. This embarrassing disclosure (as Gelb explained, one of a long series of deceits involving uninformed 'host' nations) was later officially confirmed by the Pentagon, who admitted that an extensive nuclear arms storage facility existed at Roosevelt Roads Naval Base near the city of Ceiba. Puerto Rican experts, meanwhile, suspect that the nuclear arsenal on the island—in further contravention of treaty obligations—may involve a broad inventory of weapons systems.[14]

Puerto Rico, as much as South Florida, has also become the staging area for rightist paramilitary and 'contra' forces. The large local Cuban exile community, dominating much of the island's retail sector, keeps up a frenzied attack on Cuba and Nicaragua. Partially at the urging of exiles, the Puerto Rican government in

1985 accepted the establishment of a new retransmission station for the 'Voice of America' on the southeastern coast, near Cabo Rojo. This station, in coordination with 'Radio Marti' in Florida, is part of the escalation of psychological warfare which the Reagan administration is conducting throughout the Caribbean.[15] (The government's expropriation of the nearly 2,000 acres required for the station—a very large parcel on this overcrowded island—was countered by vigorous and sustained popular opposition. Cabo Rojo sits astride the strategic Mona Channel between Puerto Rico and Hispaniola, and many local observers fear that this site will eventually find overt military uses as well. Indeed military manoeuvres were recently held near the area and Mona Island—an important nature reserve—closed to visitors.)

Puerto Rico has also been nominated as a new training base for the Contras under the enlarged Reagan aid package. Over the last several years the Contra leaders, with connivance from the local elite, have made open fundraising tours of the country, while the CIA, like the armed forces, has become unusually blatant in its local recruiting tactics. One recent recruitment drive (in the fall of 1985) involved newspaper ads that advised 'wise decisions in international affairs need solid information. The most important decisions are subject to information our enemies hide.' This bizarre understatement was followed by details for applying to the CIA with the high average salaries emphasized.[16]

Rampant militarization, of course, has been contested by Puerto Rican nationalists and progressives; their protests, in turn, have afforded pretexts for increased domestic repression. While the Department of Justice has been somewhat circumspect about the prosecution of political activists in the fifty states (although the recent attack on the Sanctuary movement may signal a reversion, under Attorney-General Meese, to a more aggressive policy), Puerto Rico in recent years has been subject to a new McCarthyism with overtones of police 'death squads' and state terrorism. The most notorious incident, of course, was the Cerro Maravilla affair in 1978, which resurfaced as a major issue in the 1984 elections.

Two young activists at the University of Puerto Rico—Carlos Soto and Arnoldo Rosado—were enticed by a police provocateur to a hilltop, Cerro Maravilla, where they were killed in a police ambush. The official version of events insisted that the pair were trying to blow up a television transmitter and that the police only fired in self-defense. Governor Carlos Romero Barceló pointedly praised the action as 'a blow to leftwing terrorism' and four subsequent investigations—two by the US Justice Department and two by its Puerto Rican equivalent—absolved the police of any wrongdoing. *Independistas*, as well as liberal members of the opposition Popular Democratic Party (which won control of the legislature in 1980), however, refused to accept this account and prompted hearings by the Puerto Rican Senate in 1983. In shocking testimony, two police agents confessed that Soto and Rosado had in fact surrendered, been disarmed and were cold-bloodedly executed while on their knees begging for mercy. The murders were authorized by police intelligence *jefe*, Angel Perez Casillas, and the five-year coverup involved the highest officials in the Romero Administration as well as the FBI.[17]

The ensuing Maravilla scandal was a major factor in the electoral defeat in 1984 of Romero Barceló and his pro-statehood party. Any expectation, however, that the new regime of Hernández Colón and his pro-commonwealth PDP would return to a more conscientious observation of civil liberties has been cruelly disappointed. Because of the purpose that it serves in the larger design of the Reagan Doctrine, the campaign against Puerto Rican nationalism—both at home and in the United States—has continued with relentless energy. Washington's recent effort's to portray a vast Puerto Rican terrorist plot, 'with assistance from Libya and Nicaragua', led to the sweeping raids of 30 August 1985. Across Puerto Rico three hundred heavily armed FBI agents, supported by military units, launched dawn raids on the homes of thirty-six reputed *independistas*. As the Spanish-language press reported, whole communities were put under seige and 'women and children (held) under house arrest for over twelve to sixteen hours'. The homes of well-known artists and intellectuals, including the poet Coqui Stantaliz and the painter Antonio Martorell, were ransacked and manuscripts confiscated, although no arrests were made. Finally thirteen people were extradited to Hartford, Connecticut for their alleged membership in the terrorist group 'Los Macheteros', which is supposed to have masterminded the September 1973 robbery of almost seven million dollars from Wells Fargo.

If comparable raids and intimidation had occurred in Poland or Nicaragua, US press indignation would have undoubtedly waxed to a fever-pitch; as it was, the US media predictably ignored or downplayed the events in Puerto Rico. For his part, Governor Hernández Colón, faced with a general local outcry, could only plead the typical colonial excuse that 'he was never notified' and thus knew nothing about the FBI's plan.[19] Whether the governor was lying or just impotent is less important than the fact that repression has continued unabated since the summer of 1985;

nationalists are still daily harassed and the case of a murdered union leader, Saul Moreno Guzman, is widely rumoured to be a 'second Maravilla' with police complicity.[20]

The current situation in Puerto Rico thus reflects all too well the various facets of actually-existing Reaganism: social polarization, venal entrepreneurialism, hyper-militarization and creeping state terrorism. The challenge to nationalist and left forces in Puerto Rico is to respond to public disenchantment with the Hernández Colón regime, galvanizing new mass campaigns around local democracy, workers' rights and national self-determination. For US progressives, on the other hand, the first challenge is simply to break the silence, as Jessie Jackson did during his primary campaign, and recognize the exceptional importance of Puerto Rico in the global struggle against the Reagan Doctrine.

Contributors

HERB BOYD is a journalist and activist. He has taught most recently at the College of New Rochelle.

ALINE FRAMBES-BUXEDA is on the faculty of the Universidad Interamericana de Puerto Rico and is editorial director of the review *Homines*.

NANCY GUEVARA is a doctoral candidate in sociology at the CUNY Graduate Center.

LEONARD HARRIS teaches philosophy at Morgan State College.

MARK HEROLD is a member of the economics faculty at the University of New Hampshire.

DAVID E. JAMES teaches literature and film at Occidental College.

NICK KOZLOV has taught most recently at Mount Holyoke College in the economics department.

JULIANNE MALVEAUX holds appointments in the Institute for Industrial Relations and the Department of Afro-American Studies at the University of California at Berkeley.

MANNING MARABLE is a professor of political science and sociology at Purdue University. Verso has recently published his two-volume study of Black politics: *Black American Politics* (1985) and *African and Caribbean Politics* (1987).

JAMES A. MILLER is on the faculty of Trinity College. His work focuses on Afro-American culture and critical theory.

CARLOS MUÑOZ, JR. teaches in the Chicano Studies Program at the University of California at Berkeley. His book, *Youth, Identity, Power: The Chicano Generation* will be published by Verso in 1988.

LUCIUS OUTLAW is professor of philosophy at Haverford College.

CAROL A. SMITH teaches anthropology at Duke University.

HORTENSE J. SPILLERS teaches in the English department of Haverford College.

CORNEL WEST is on the faculty of the Yale Divinity School. His book on the genealogy of Western racism is forthcoming in 1987.

Notes

Notes to Chapter 1

1. W.E.B. Du Bois, *The Souls of Black Folk* (Chicago: A.C. McClurg, 1903), p. 3.

2. Edward B. Fiske, 'Ranks of Minority Teachers Are Dwindling, Experts Fear', *New York Times* (February 9, 1969). It is true that a substantial number of middle-class Black students have moved from such traditional careers as teaching into vocations which heretofore were rigidly segregated. For example, in 1970 there were only 378 Blacks who graduated with bachelor's degrees in engineering, less than 1 percent of all engineering degrees granted. By 1985, the figure had increased to 2,041, 2.6 percent of all graduates. See *National Multicultural Banner* (May 1986). However, the dominant trend in most professions since 1980 has been a decline in the numbers of Black graduates.

3. Vernon A. Guldry, Jr., 'Administration Cutting Back On Racial Data', *Black Issues In Higher Education* (December 1, 1985), p. 2.

4. 'Black Democrats Assail Plan', *New York Times* (March 6, 1986); and Phil Galley, 'Democrats, With Little Dissent, Approve New Nominating Rules', *New York Times* (March 9, 1986).

5. Linda F. Williams, 'Black Politics: The Year in Review', *Focus* 13 (November-December 1985), p. 3.

6. Lindsey Gruson, 'In Philadelphia, a Mayor's Career is Called Into Question', *New York Times* (March 9, 1986); William K. Stevens, 'Philadelphia Mayor to Answer Critics', *New York Times* (March 9, 1986); and Stevens, 'Philadelphia Chief Doubts Indictment', *New York Times* (March 11, 1986).

7. Alfonso A. Narvaez, 'Gibson's 16–Year Tenure Garners Mixed Notices', *New York Times* (May 10, 1986); and Joseph F. Sullivan, 'Gibson's Long Struggle Ends, Newark's Continues', *New York Times* (May 18, 1986).

8. Williams, 'Black Politics: The Year in Review', p. 3. Lack of confidence in the performance of many Black elected officials has not meant that electoral participation per se has become irrelevant to most Black workers. The evidence from the 1984 presidential election illustrates that the Black voter registration rate was 66 percent, and actual voter turnout was 58 percent. About 12.2 million Blacks registered and 10.3 million voted in 1984, compared with 8.8 million and 8.3 million in the 1980 presidential elections. About nine out of ten Blacks voted for Mondale, well above Mondale's one-third share in the white electorate. See 'Black Voter Registration, Turnout Improve Dramatically in 1984', *Charleston Chronicle* (May 17, 1986).

9. Manning Marable, *Blackwater: Historical Studies in Race, Class Consciousness and Revolution* (Dayton: Black Praxis, 1981), p. 133; Manning Marable, *Black American Politics: From the Washington Marches to Jesse Jackson* (London: Verso, 1985), pp. 253–254; and Lena Williams, 'NAACP Board Meets At a Time of Troubles', *New York Times* (February 13, 1986). The NAACP asserts that its current membership is approximately 450,000, but most observers place its membership at 150,000.

10. 'Study: Blacks Don't Share Leaders Views', *Ocean State Grapevine* (April 4, 1986).

11. Linda F. Williams, 'Black Political Opinion', *Focus* 14 (March 1986), pp. 4, 9.

12. Williams, 'Black Politics: The Year in Review', p. 5.

13. William A. Ryan, 'Wider, Brighter Rainbow', *Guardian* (April 30, 1986); and Kevin J. Kelley, 'Reorganized Rainbow Takes Halting First Steps', *Guardian* (May 21, 1986).

14. Isabel Wilkerson, 'Minorities' Caucus, Divided, Falters in Albany', *New York Times* (April 26, 1986).

15. Kelley, 'Reorganized Rainbow Takes Halting First Steps'.

16. Citations are from August Meier, *Negro Thought in America, 1880–1915* (Ann Arbor: University of Michigan Press, 1963), pp. 44, 45, 101, 105, 107.

17. 'Boosting the Community: Black Mayors Must Find Other Sources of Income', *Sacramento Observer* (May 15–21, 1986).

18. Alfreda Madison, 'Black Self-Help: Blacks Must Finance Own Recovery', *Sacramento Observer* (December 5–11, 1985).

19. Robert Pear, 'U.S. Urged to End Aid to Businesses Run by Minorities,' *New York Times* (April 8, 1986); Robert Pear, 'Aide to Reagan Challenges Plan by Rights Panel,' *New York Times* (April 11, 1986); Robert Pear, 'Rights Staff Told to Rework Minority Report,' *New York Times* (April 12, 1986); Akinshiju Ola, 'Even Pendleton's Friends Think He's Gone Too Far', *Guardian* (April 30, 1986); and 'NAACP Accuses Pendleton of Out-Reaganing Reagan,' *Charleston Chronicle* (May 3, 1986).

20. Akinshiju Olga, 'What Farrakhan Says—and What's Said of Him', *Guardian* (October 9, 1985); and Dorothy and Bill Doyle, 'Farrakhan Challenges Support for Israel', *Guardian* (October 16, 1985).

21. Marjorie Anders, 'Black Muslim Leader Brings Message to N.Y.,' *Palmetto Leader* [South Carolina] (October 16, 1985); and Doyle and Doyle, 'Farrakhan Challenges Support for Israel'.

Notes to Chapter 2

1. I wish to acknowledge gratefully the following writers and publications for their assistance: The *Guardian*, especially the articles of Frank Elam, Akinshiju Ola, Ben Bedell, John Trinkl and Lynora Williams. Such newspapers and periodicals as the *New York Amsterdam News; Village Voice*, particularly Greg Tate and Nelson George; *Black Scholar; Crisis* magazine; *Black Enterprise; Metro Times* (Detroit); and *Arm the Masses* were invaluable. A substantial body of movement literature was extremely helpful in supplying the day-to-day details of organizations: *Final Call, The Burning Spear, Frontline, By Any Means Necessary, Unity, The National Alliance, Afro-American Liberator, The Militant* and *Revolutionary Worker*. Of the several books I resorted to, those by Lerone Bennett, Howard Zinn, and Manning Marable were continually useful. Finally, my immediate comrades kept me in touch with the movement and reality. Thanks to Ron Lockett, Geoffrey Jacques, Gene Cunning-

ham, Malik Chaka, Bill Bryce, Leni Sinclair, Chuck Bush, Art Blackwell, Ron Williams, Dan Aldridge, Jason Lovett, Kofi Natambu, Katherine Brown and, above all, Elza Dinwiddie. I would also like to dedicate these works to the spirit of two fallen comrades: Rusty and Hayward Brown.

2.   Abu Jamal is currently on death row in Huntingdon State Correctional Institution. He was charged and convicted for the December 1981 killing of a Philadelphia police officer in an alleged shoot-out in which Mumia wound up in critical condition with a bullet in his chest. He had been the target of the Philadelphia authorities from his high school days when he was leader of the Black Panther Party. He was later suspended from school for distributing their literature. Abu Jamal was to become in later years an award winning journalist and broadcaster. His coverage of the MOVE trial in 1978−9 gained nationwide attention. He was president of the Association of Black Journalists in 1981 and his arrest was answered with widespread outrage and protest.

3.   For detailed accounts and analysis of the Washington mayoral campaign and the 1983 March, see Manning Marable, *Black American Politics: From the Washington Marches to Jesse Jackson* (London, 1985), chapter 2 and 4.

4.   See ibid,. chapter 5.

Notes to Chapter 3

*Thanks to my colleagues Mario Barrera and Margarita Melville for helpful suggestions and criticisms of an earlier draft of this work.

1.   See Mario Barrera, 'The Historical Evolution of Chicano Ethnic Goals', *Sage Race Relations Abstracts*, 10, 1 (February 1985), for an historical overview of the various types of Chicano organizations that have emerged in response to racial and class oppression.

2.   *El Plan de Santa Barbara* (Oakland, La Causa Publications, 1969).

3.   *Congressional Record*, 22 April 1969.

4.   *Congressional Record*, 29 October 1971.

5.   Ibid.

6.   Richard Santillan, 'The Latino Community in State and Congressional Redistricting, 1961−1985', *Journal of Hispanic Politics* 1, 1, (1985).

7.   *Con su voto: With Your Vote*, Democratic National Committee Newsletter (Summer, 1984), p. 3.

8.   *Wall Street Journal*, 19 March 1986, p.54.

9.   Ibid.

10.   The sources of estimated Latino votes in the 1984 election vary. The *New York Times* estimated 33% while the Republic Party National Committee estimated 52% voted for Reagan.

11.   Federico A. Subervi-Valez, et. al, 'Capturing the Hispanic Vote: Republican Political Advertising Efforts in the 1984 Presidential Elections', unpublished paper, 1985.

12.   Richard Santillan documents that there has been a steady growth of support for the Republican Party amongst Chicanos since the Nixon Presidency. See his *Latinos in U.S. Politics: 1960 to 1984* [forthcoming].

13.   *Oakland Tribune*, 11 April 1986.

14.   *Dallas Morning News*, 11 February 1985.

Notes to Chapter 4

*This chapter relies heavily on some of my previous work, especially 'Similarities and Differences in the Economic Interest of Black and White Women,' *Review of Black Political Economy* (Summer 1985); 'Low Wage Black Women: Occupational Descriptions, Strategies for Change,' NAACP Legal Defense and Education Fund, 1984; and 'Minority Women in the Workplace' (with Phyllis A. Wallace) in Karen Koziara, Michael Moskow and Lucretia Dewey Tanner, *Women and Work: Industrial Relations Research Association Research Volume* [forthcoming in 1986].

1.   The full title of the Hull, Scott and Smith book (1982) is 'All the Women Are White, All the Blacks are Men, But Some of Us Are Brave: Black Women's Studies'.
2.   Occupational data is classified with varying levels of precision and referred to in terms of the level of precision used in developing an occupational category. Thus, at the 'one digit' level, classification is done by major occupational category. The two digit level represents an intermediate classification, while three digit occupational groupings indicate the smallest divisions. Even at the three digit grouping, it is possible to be more precise abut occupational groupings, since many workers are classified as 'other clerical workers' or 'foremen, note elsewhere classified'. The tables in this paper use the pre-1982 method of classification. Classification changed in 1982, and current Census and Bureau of Labor Statistics data are reported differently. In many cases, the methods of classification are not comparable. See Rytina (1981) for more detail.

Notes to Chapter 6

1.   Philip S. Foner, *American Socialism and Black Americans: From the Age of Jackson to World War II* (Connecticut 1977). Although Foner's other works are not the focus of this article, of particular interest is Philip S. Foner and Ronald L. Lewis, *The Black Worker: A Documentary History from Colonial Times to the Present*, 7 vols. (Philadelphia 1978).
2.   Foner, p. xiii.
3.   Cedric J. Robinson, *Black Marxism: The Making of the Black Radical Tradition* (London 1983).
4.   Orlando Paterson, *Slavery and Social Death* (Cambridge [Mass.] 1982), pp. 77–104.
5.   Paterson, pp. 21–27.
6.   Foner, p. 8.
7.   Ibid, p. 9.
8.   Of the numerous reasons utopianists gave for prioritizing the moral ignominy of wage slavery, few admitted their shared racial identity with whites particularly sensitized them to the condition of white workers.
9.   Foner, p. 14.
10.   Ibid, pp. 17–18.
11.   Ibid, p. 60.
12.   Ibid, p. 58.
13.   Ibid, p. 1.
14.   Ibid, p. 210.
15.   Ibid, p. 210.
16.   Ibid, p. 219.

17. Ibid, p. 302. Also see p. 309.

18. Ibid, p. 366.

19. See Bernard Boxill, *Blacks and Social Justice* (New Jersey 1984).

20. Robinson, p. 1.

21. Ibid, cf. pp. 23, 243, 245–46, 447, 451.

22. Benedict Anderson, *Imagined Communities: Reflections on the Origin and Spread of Nationalism* (London, Verso, 1983).

28. Ibid, p. 15.

29. Robinson, p. 79.

25. Robinson's view of an ontological commitment, or something like it, may help account for why capitalism has both destroyed racial, ethnic, and national identities and simultaneously created new ones with corresponding material interests.

26. Robinson, pp. 451–52.

27. Michael Farbre, *The Unfinished Quest of Richard Wright* (New York 1973), pp. xviii, 67–69.

28. Harold Cruse, *The Crisis of the Negro Intellectual* (New York 1971), pp. 182, 188.

29. Robinson, 435. Wright, 'Blueprint for Negro Writing,' *New Challenge* (Fall 1937), p. 57.

30. Robinson, p. 2.

31. Ibid, pp. 84, 95–241.

32. Ibid, p. 82.

33. See August H. Nimtz, Jr., 'Review, Marxism and the Black Struggle: The "Class v. Race" Debate Revisited,' *Journal of African Marxists* (March 1985), pp. 75–89. This review missed the radical shift Robinson makes in 'The "Class v. Race" Debate.' For a more advanced view that nevertheless takes issue with the exclusion of radical Black traditions rooted in India, Pakistan, and Bangladesh, see Errol Lawrence, *Race & Class* 26, 2, pp. 100–02.

34. See Theodor W. Adorno, *Negative Dialectics* (New York: Seabury Press, 1973); Jürgen Habermas, 'Reconstruction of Historical Materialism,' in idem, *Communication and the Evolution of Society* (Boston: Beacon Press, 1971); and Andre Gorz, *Farewell to the Working Class* (Boston: Beacon Press, 1971).

35. See also Stanley Aronowitz, *The Crisis in Historical Materialism* (New York: Praeger Publishers, 1981).

36. For a discussion of difficulties in perceiving race as a real entity in Du Bois's work, which is similar to perceiving 'Arican people' as a real entity, see Anthony Appiah, 'The Uncompleted Argument: Du Bois and the Illusion of Race,' *Critical Inquiry* (Autumn 1985), pp. 21–37. See also Orlando Paterson, 'The Nature, Causes, and Implications of Ethnic Identification,' *Minorities: Community and Identity*, ed., C. Fried (Berlin: Dahlem Konferenzen, 1983), pp. 26–50.

37. For an analysis of conflicting interests between Black and white women workers, for example, see Julianne Malveaux, 'The Economic Interests of Black and White Women: Are they Similar?' *The Review of Black Political Economy* 14, 1 (Summer 1985), pp. 5–28. For a discussion of various views of racism, particularly interest group theories, see Benjamin P. Bowser, 'Race Relations in the 1980s: The Case of the United States,' *Journal of Black Studies* 15, 3 (March 1985), pp. 307–24.

Notes to Chapter 7

1.   Manning Marable, *Black American Politics: From The Washington Marches to Jesse Jackson* (London: Verso, 1985).

2.   Eric Olin Wright, *Classes* (London: Verso, 1985), p.2.

3.   Marable, *Black American Politics*, p. 50. Black nationalism is a deep-running, complex tradition of great longevity. The literature on this tradition is substantial. Among many works, one might consult John Bracey, Jr., et. al., editors, *Black Nationalism in America* (New York, 1970); Sterlng Stuckey, *The Ideological Origins of Black Nationalism* (Boston, 1970); Alphonso Pinkney, *Red, Black and Green: Black Nationalism in the United States*, (New York, 1976); and M. Ron Karenga, 'Afro-American Nationalism: Beyond Mystification and Misconception', in *Black Books Bulletin* 6,1 (Spring 1978), pp. 7–12. Each of these works provides, in addition, a substantial bibliography on the subject.

4.   The situation is the same for much of social-political theorizing among Black thinkers.

5.   A number of reviews along these lines have been conducted by persons participating in Marxist traditions and by non-(or former) participants critical of them. For example: T.H. Kennedy and T.F. Leary, 'Communist Thought on the Negro,' *Phylon*, VIII, 2 (1947), pp. 116–123; Wilson Record 'The Development of the Communist Position On the Negro Question in the United States', *Phylon*, XIX, 3 (Fall 1958), pp. 306–326; and Philip Foner, *American Socialism and Black Americans* (Connecticut, 1977). For a critical discussion by a Black thinker, see Cedric J. Robinson, *Black Marxism: The Making of the Black Radical Tradition* (London 1983). And for discussions of these issues by black participants in Marxist/Communist organizations, see Henry Winston, *Class, Race, and Black Liberation* (New York 1977); Harry Haywood, *Black Bolshevik: Autobiography of an Afro-American Communist* (Chicago 1978). More recently there is Manning Marable's *Blackwater: Historical Studies in Race, Class Consciousness and Revolution* (Ohio, 1981). Overall, I regard as *required* reading Olivers Cox's *Caste, Class and Race* (New York: 1970) and Harold Cruse's *The Crisis of the Negro Intellectual* (New York 1967).

6.   See Sidney Wilhelm, 'Can Marxism Explain America's Racism?' *Social Problems*, 28, 2 (December 1980), pp. 98–112.

7.   'The [African Black] Brotherhood, or at least prominent members of that organization—[Cyril] Briggs, [Richard B.] Moore and especially Harry Haywood—appears to have provided the Party the immediate ideological stimulus for the development of the Comintern's position after 1928 that Blacks constituted a 'national question' in America.' Cedric J. Robinson, *op.cit.*, p. 300. See, also, Kennedy and Leary, 'Communist Thought on the Negro,' *op.cit.*

8.   Kennedy and Leary, *op.cit.*

9.   See, for example, Mark Naison, 'Harlem Communists and The Politics of Black Protests,' *Marxist Perspectives* (Fall 1978), pp. 20–50.

10.   Note Naison's discussion of such matters in 'Harlem Communists and The Politics of Black Protests'. Speaking of the Communist Party in Harlem during the late 1930s-early 1940s, he concludes: 'Though while the Party remained the most important organized force fighting discrimination in the unions, its actions fell far short of the expectations of black leaders who regarded the continuing marginality of the black poor—and the specter of a permanent class of black welfare recipients—with growing dismay. The increasing tactical conservatism the Party displayed in the face of the desperate plight of working-class blacks helped sow the seeds of a split between the black community and the Left which the Party's abrupt reversals on foreign policy, wartime deemphasis of black issues, and victimization during the wave of postwar repression widened into a chasm.' *Ibid.*,p. 43. A very important

discussion is provided by Cruse in 'Jews and Negroes in the Communist Party,' *The Crisis of the Negro Intellectual*, pp. 147–170.

11. On these challenges to the 'classical position' see Sidney Wilhelm, *op.cit.*

12. Black nationalist literature abounds, and within it are to be found many arguments against Marxist universalism. For an extensive argument that involves a critical historical reconstruction of Marxism and its relations to Black oppression, see Robinson, *Black Marxism: The Making of the Black Radical Tradition*.

13. Cited in David Caute, *Communism and the French Intellectuals, 1914–1960*, (New York: 1964) p. 211.

14. *Ibid.*, p. 97 (emphasis in the original).

15. *Ibid.*, pp. 308–309.

16. The following discussion draws from my 'On "Difference", Marxism and Black Liberation,' an unpublished essay prepared for the 'Gender, Race and Class' Conference sponsored by the Radical Philosophy Association, the Society for Women in Philosophy, and the Committee on Blacks in Philosophy of the American Philosophy Association and held at the Marxist School (151 W. 19th Street, New York), on October 12–13, 1985. See also my 'Race and Class in the Theory and Practice of Emancipatory Social Transformation', in *Philosophy Born of Struggle: Anthology of Afro-American Philosophy from 1917*, Leonard Harris, ed. (Dubuque 1983), pp. 117–129.

17. See 'The Economic and Philosophical Manscripts of 1844' and 'The German Ideology (Part 1),' in *The Marx-Engels Reader*, 2nd ed., Robert C. Tucker, ed. (New York 1978).

18. See Outlaw, 'Race and Class in the Theory and Practice of Emancipatory Social Transformation'.

19. Only because he sees in the proletariat the contemporary, and final, realization of universality, does Marx endow the proletariat with an historical significance and mission ... The universalistic nature of the proletariat does not disappear in Marx's later writings, when his discussion concentrates mainly on the historical causes of the emergence of the proletariat. What was at the outset a philosophical hypothesis is verified by historical experience and observation: the universalistic nature of the proletariat is a corollary of the conditions of production in a capitalist society, which must strive for universality on the geographical level as well.' Shlomo Avineri, *The Social and Political Thought of Karl Marx* (New York 1968), pp.59, 61.

20. (New York 1981).

21. *Ibid.*, p.79.

22. Poulantzas, *Classes in Contemporary Capitalism* (London Verso, 1978); and *Political Power and Social Classes*, (London: Verso 1978) and Wright, *Classes*.

23. *Ibid.*, p. 134, note 27.

24. ' ... the relations of production always dominate the labour process and the productive forces, stamping them with their own pattern and appearance ... This dominant role of the relations of production over the productive forces and the labour process is what gives rise to the constitutive role of political and ideological relations in the structural determination of social classes.' Poulantzas, *Classes in Contemporary Capitalism*, p.21.

25. *Ibid.*, pp. 13–35.

26. For a fuller discussion of the promise of Poulantzas' theorizing for the problem of racism, see my 'Race and Class in the Theory and Practice of Emancipatory Social Transformation,'

27. Wright, *Clases, op.cit.*, p.24.

28. *Ibid.*, p.27.

29. *Ibid.*, emphasis in original.

30. *Ibid.*, p.29, emphasis in original.

31. *The Insurgent Sociologist* 10, 2 (Fall, 1980), p. 12.

32. (Dubuque, 1978).

33. For a well-articulated presentation of the argument that Blacks in the USA comprise an *internal colony*, see Robert L. Allen, *Black Awakening in Capitalist America* (Garden City 1969). Other discussions, pro and con, include: Ron Bailey, 'Economic Aspects of the Black Internal Colony', *The Review of Black Political Economy* 3, 4 (1973), pp.43–72; J.H. O'Dell, 'Colonialism and the Negro American Experience', *Freedomways* (Fall, 1966); William K. Tabb, *The Political Economy of the Black Ghetto* (New York, 1970); Donald J. Harris, 'The Black Ghetto as "Internal Colony": A Theoretical Critique and Alternative Formulation,' *The Review of Black Political Economy* 2, 4 (Summer 1972), pp. 3–33 (a critique of William K. Tabb); 'Capitalist Exploitation and Black Labor: Some Conceptual Issues,' *The Review of Black Economy* 8, 2 (Winter 1978), pp. 133–151; and Stokeley Carmichael and Charles V. Hamilton, *Black Power: The Politics of Liberation in America,* (New York, 1967).

34. Geschwender, *Racial Stratification in America*, p. 262.

35. *Ibid.*, p. 264–266.

36. *Ibid.*, p. 266.

37. *Ibid.*, p.170.

38. Many white workers responded to this influx of Black workers with virulent racism which, in turn, generated a number of forms of Black protest: radical agrarian revolts, an assimilationist-oriented Civil Rights movement, and nationalist separatism. See Geschwender, pp. 193–194.

39. See Outlaw, 'Race and Class in the Theory and Practice of Emancipatory Social Transformation.'

40. 'The bourgeoisie which led the development to capitalism were drawn from particular ethnic and cultural groups; the European proletariats and the mercenaries of the leading States from others; its peasants from still other cultures; and its slaves from entirely different worlds. The tendency of European civilization through capitalism was thus not to homogenize but to differentiate—to exaggerate regional, subcultural, dialectical differences into 'racial' ones.' Robinson, *Black Marxism, op.cit.,* 26–27.

41. As Robinson has noted 'There were at least four distinct moments which must be apprehended in European racialism; two whose origins are to be found within the dialectic of European development, and two which are not: 1. the racial ordering of European society from its formative period which extends into the medieval and feudal ages as 'blood' and racial beliefs and legends. 2. the Islamic, i.e. Arab, Persian, Turkish and African, domination of Mediterranean civilization and the consequent retarding of European social and cultural life: the Dark Ages. 3. the incorporation of African, Asian and peoples of the New World into the world system emerging from the late feudalism and merchant capitalism. 4. the dialectic of colonialism, plantocratic slavery and resistance from the 16th Century forwards, and the formations of industrial labour and labour reserves.' (*Black Marxism*, p. 83)

42. Particularly relevant are the experiences of Richard Wright, W.E.B. DuBois, C.L.R. James, James Boggs (and Grace Lee Boggs), and Harold Cruse, among others. For one discussion of this history, see Robinson's 'Black Radicalism and Marxist Theory,' Part III of his *Black Marxism*, pp. 249ff. *Black Marxism* is a bibliographical treasure of works that discuss the complex but crucial history of American socialism's and communism's dealing with people of African descent. See also Philip Foner, *American Socialism and Black Americans.*

43. On this point, especially, see Harold Cruse, *The Crisis of the Negro Intellectual* (New York: William Morrow, 1967).

44. 'Unfortunately, the relegation of consciousness in the Marxian logic to a reflex of the relations of production and the frequent preoccupation with capitalism as a system determined by its own objective laws and *the* motivating force of historical change, most consistently led to the conclusion that nationalism among working classes was contrary to the historical movement of modern societies. In this sense, nationalism was a backward ideology, often a means of deflecting the class struggle into imperialist wars, and in any case not a fit subject for serious study in its own right since it was merely a politically convenient conduit of other forces and interests ... The dismissal of culture, that is a transmitted historical consciousness, as an aspect of class consciousness, did not equip the Marxian movement for the political forces which would not only erupt in Europe and the Third World but within the movement itself ... What the Marxists did not understand about the political and ideological phenomenon of nationalism is that it was not (and is not) an historical aberration (of proletarian internationalism). Nor is it necessarily the contrary: a developmental stage of internationalism.' Robinson, *Black Marxism* pp. 78, 79.

45. According to Robinson, there was a 'critical contradiction in early American socialist development. The organizing principle was ethnicity while at the same time nationalism, a logical conclusion of ethnicity, endangered and frustrated socialist unity. Ethnicity dominated the movement organizationally, ideologically, conceptually and theoretically.' *Black Marxism*, p. 293.

46. 'There is a kind of progressive Tower of Babel, where we are engaged in building an edifice for social transformation, but none of us are speaking the same language. None understands where the rest are going.' Manning Marable. 'Common Program: Transitional Strategies for Black and Progressive Politics in America,' in *Blackwater: Historical Studies in Race, Class Consciousness and Revolution*, p. 177.

Notes to Chapter 8

1. Although even here the lack of a mass Black audience for avant garde jazz does not discredit other political functions, Kofsky, who has argued the relationship between Black nationalism and modern jazz most thoroughly, quotes Archie Shepp as claiming that jazz is 'anti-war, it is opposed to Vietnam; it is for Cuba; it is for the liberation of the people' (Kofsky, 1970:64). While this may represent the feelings of the musicians rather than the concrete function of the music, still, in its resistance to commodification and its modernist pursuit of its formal possiblities, jazz came closer than any other art form to reconciling negation with populist commitment.

2. In the most extensive collection of essays from the period defining the Black aesthetic (Gayle, 1972), not only is there no section on film, but film is mentioned only three times, in each case to note the absence of satisfactory Black films. Most commentators prefer to reserve the term 'Black Cinema' to productions entirely controlled by Blacks, but admit the unfeasibility of doing so. On Black film as genre, see especially Cripps, 1978:1–13 and Murray, 1973:xi–xv. In addition to providing the best account of the independent Black feature industry of the twenties and thirties, Cripps also records the extraordinary case of the travelling preacher, Eloise Gist: 'she ranged over the South during the great Depression, spreading her revivalist faith through motion pictures shot only for the specific narrow purpose defined by her own faith and spirit. Nowhere from script to screen did any white hand intrude, or any white eye observe. Neither white financing in the beginning nor white appreciation at the end affected her pristine black fundamentalism. Her films were naive, technically primitive, literal depictions of black Southern religious folklore that brought faith to life, much as an illuminated manuscript gave visual life to Christian lore in the Middle Ages' (27). Cripps is naturally interested in Gist as

the best example of a 'pure' Black film; this priority notwithstanding, Ms. Gist's appropriation of the medium for devotional practice and her total integration of it into a life's work is unequalled in recorded film history, although it is approached by the utopian functionalism that history allowed to Vertov.

Taylor claims that a 'new black cinema was born out of the black arts movement of the 1960's' (Taylor:46), but all the examples he gives are from the mid to late seventies, which substantiates my claim (argued further on in this paper) that independent Black film developed out of the educational reforms produced by the Black movement rather than in relation to the movement itself. In addition to the films discussed below, mention must be made of the remarkable *Finally Got the News* (Black Star Productions, 1970), 'the only radical film of the sixties which was made under the direct control of revolutionary working class blacks with the specific purpose of radicalizing other black workers' (Georgakas, 1973:2).

3.   Compare Baraka's essay 'Hunting is Not Those Heads on the Wall' (rpt. Baraka, 1966) where he elaborates the distinction between art-as-artifact and art-as-process.

4.   This is not to argue any radically essential function in the difficulties disenfranchised minority groups have in appropriating advanced technologies. Even an argument, like the one that follows by Black filmmaker Kathleen Collins (*The Cruz Brothers and Miss Malloy*, 1980; *Losing Ground*, 1982), that may appear to imply this, must be understood as designating a socially determined unfamiliarity, and one that in any case had been overcome by the mid-seventies: 'It is very hard to face the gigantic technological achievement—which can be painted white—of this society, which is film, video, the computerized technologies that come out of the handling of image and sound. We as Black people have a reluctance to come to terms with true technology—technophobia. To do good movies you have to solve the technological problems . . . As a race of people we have been intimidated by the technicalism'. (Collins, 81:23).

5.   See especially Cripps, 1978:13–63. Mapp, 1972 excludes from discussion as atypical Black film by Black producers (The Birth of a Race Company, Ebony Pictures and even Oscar Micheaux), but otherwise his is an exhaustive inventory of the changing portrayal of Blacks by Hollywood and independent white productions. Excepting only *The Learning Tree* (1969), *A Raisin in the Sun* (1961) and *Nothing But a Man* (1964), he records unrelieved failure to treat everyday Black life with seriousness or dignity and especially to address the issues of the Black movement.

6.   The tradition of the representation of Blacks by the underground goes back through Ron Rice's *The Queen of Sheeba Meets the Atom Man* (1963), Jonas Mekas' *Guns of the Trees* (1961) and John Cassavetes's *Shadows* (1959), to Lionel Rogosin's *Come Back, Africa* (1959) and Sidney Meyers' *The Quiet One* (1949), where Blacks are typically used as metaphors for white desires or fears. Even an instance of substantial Black control over the pro-filmic like Shirley Clarke's *Portrait of Jason* (1967), sensationalizes and spectacularizes its subject. While together with its use of Black music, from *Shadows* through Michael Snow's *New York Ear and Eye Control*, the underground representation of Black people was sufficiently common that the underground cinema became by default a major moment in Black cinema, that cinema's reproduction in the medium of film of the formal and social qualities of jazz is more significant, and is so in a way that indicates the terms by which a populist Black film style could have developed had the medium stood in a different relationship to Black society. Just as Kerouac and the other beats modelled a literary practice on the spontaneity, improvisation and vitality of the jazz musician, so underground film may best be understood as an attempt to reproduce those same qualities in both pro-filmic performance and in film form. The missing link between the bohemian underground and the lost Black cinema is of course Amiri Baraka/

Leroi Jones. If his *Dutchman* (1967), made in England, had been a popular success, then some of the energy of the revitalized Black theater might have gone into film.

7.   Still, as Mapp notes, Clarke recycles the same stereotypes about Blacks—the vicious criminal, the absent father, the petty thief, the stud—that populate the most racist films (Mapp, 1972:94–95).

8.   *The Murder of Fred Hampton* was especially unpopular. Invoking Godard's distinction between radical filmmaking and the filming of radical politics, *Cineaste* suggested that 'in its portrayal and advocacy of revolutionaries as gun-slinging, death-defying desperadoes [it] will thus be seriously counter-productive' (Crowdus:51). Godard, incidentally, warmly recommended Varda's film at showings of his own very different treatment of the Panthers, *One Plus One*, a film which is itself hardly any improvement upon the conventional image of the Panthers as gun-slinging desperadoes.

9.   Newton ingeniously allegorizes the film's motifs; he interprets the sex scenes as indicating Sweetback's absorption of the community's love, for example, and his silence as a space to be occupied by the voices of the audience.

10.   But these films—*A Man Called Horse* (1970), *Soldier Blue* (1970), *Little Big Man* (1971), and *Tell Them Willie Boy Is Here* (1970)—were little more than 'a facelifting on the old Cowboys and Indians' (Georgakas, 1972:32).

Notes to Chapter 9

1.   Thomas Cripps, *Black Film As Genre* (Bloomington 1979), p. 8.

2.   Donald Bogle, *Toms, Coons, Mulattoes, Mammies & Bucks: An Interpretive History of Blacks in American Films* (New York 1973).

3.   Garth Jowett, *Film: The Democratic Art* (Boston 1976), pp. 338, 346, 452–453.

4.   Daniel J. Leab, *From Sambo to Superspade: The Black Experience in Motown Pictures* (Boston 1975), p. 234.

5.   Bogle, pp. 175–176.

6.   James P. Murray, 'The Subject is Money', *Black Creation* 4, 2 (Winter 1973), p. 26.

7.   Lerone Bennett, Jr., 'The Emancipation Orgasm: Sweetback in Wonderland', *Ebony* (September 1971), p. 16.

8.   For a complimentary critique of *Sweetback*, see the previous essay by David James.

9.   Pearl Bowser, 'Sexual Imagery and the Black Woman in Cinema', in Gladstone L. Yearwood, ed., *Black Cinema Aesthetics* (Athens, Ohio 1982), pp. 42–51.

10.   James P. Murray, *To Find An Image: Black Films from Uncle Tom to Superfly* (New York: The Bobbs-Merrill Company, 1973), p. 111.

11.   Leab, p. 254.

12.   Quoted in Peter Roffman and Bev Simpson, 'Black Images on White Screens,' *Cineaste* 13, 3 (1984), p. 16.

13.   James Monaco, *American Film Now: The People, The Power, The Money, The Movies* (New York: Oxford University Press, 1979), p. 193.

14.   Peter Roffman and Bev Simpson, 'A Soldier's Story: An Interview with Howard E. Rollins, Jr., *Cineaste* 1, (1985), p. 43.

15.   H. Anthony Mapp, 'A Dramatic Success,' *Black Enterprise* (January 1985), p. 29.

Notes to Chapter 10

1.   For a discussion of Black and Latin cultural and political interaction, in relation to hip-hop, see Juan Flores, 'Rappin', Writin' and Breakin': Black and Puerto Rican Street Culture in New York,' *Calalloo* [forthcoming 1986]. See also, John Storm Roberts, *The Latin Tinge: The Impact of Latin American Music in the United States* (New York 1979), for examples of this cultural convergence.

2.   An interesting account is given by Herbert Kohol and John Hinton, 'Names, Graffiti and Culture,' *Rappin' and Stylin' Out*, ed. Kochman (1972), pp. 109–133.

3.   A more detailed description of the graffiti movement and its elaborate techniques may be found in Craig Castleman, *Getting Up: Subway Graffiti in New York* (Cambridge 1982).

4.   The technique of deejaying and the historical background of rap music are detailed by David Toop, *The Rap Attack: From African Jive to New York Hip-Hop* (Boston 1984), and Steven Hager, *Hip-Hop: The Illustrated History of Break Dancing, Rap Music, and Graffiti* (New York 1984).

5.   The origins of *capoeira* are traced to its African predecessor, the foot-fighting traditional among the Bantu of Angola, in Jan Murray, 'Capoeira,' *Contact Quarterly*, 5, 3/4 (1980), p. 29.

6.   A compelling account of this 'decontaminating' process is given by Alfred B. Pasteur and Ivory L. Toldson, *Roots of Soul: The Psychology of Black Expressiveness* (Garden City 1982).

7.   For vivid illustrations of graffiti forms and styles see Martha Cooper and Henry Chalfant, *Subway Art* (New York 1984).

8.   Simon Frith, *Sound Effects: Youth, Leisure, and the Politics of Rock 'n' Roll* (New York 1981).

9.   Cathleen McGuigan, et al., 'Breaking Out: America Goes Dancing,' *Newsweek* (July 2, 1984), pp. 47-52; Kim Watkins, 'Floormasters Break Out,' *Uptown Summer 83* (Summer 1983), p. 3; and Steven Hagar, op. cit.

10.   In addition to the reference in note 9 above, see Dan Cox, 'Brooklyn's Furious Rockers: Break Dance Roots in a Breakneck Neighborhood', *Dancemagazine* (April 1984), pp. 79–81.

11.   See A. Janowitz, *Tabloid* 6 (1982), pp. 50–51. Janowitz reviews Dick Hebdige, *Subculture: The Meaning of Style* (London 1979).

12.   John Duka, 'In Paris a Young Black Society', *New York Times* April 20, 1984.

Notes to Chapter 11

1.   Winthrop Jordan's *White Over Black: American Attitudes Toward the Negro 1550–1812* (Baltimore 1969), remains among the most thoroughgoing analyses of this subject from the point of view of the United States and its colonial antecedents. Part IV, 'Fruits of Passion: The Dynamics of Interracial Sex,' concerns the historical context against which sexual mores were played out. In this 'cultural matrix of purpose, accomplishment, selfconception, and social circumstances of settlement in the New World,' the mulatto child violated the strictest intentions of a binary racial function (p. 167). For Jordan, the situation of mulatto reflects a persistent historicity: the configurations assumed by a cultural phenomenon, or structure of attention, against the perspective of time.

Barbara Christian's *Black Women Novelists: The Development of a Tradition, 1892–1976*(Westport 1980), looks closely at the theme of the mulatta in certain nineteenth and twentieth-century fiction, including that of Frances E.W. Harper, William Wells

Brown, Jessie Fauset, and Nella Larsen. See especially, 'From Stereotype to Character,' pp. 3–61.

Pocahontas's Daughters: Gender and Ethnicity in American Culture by Mary V. Dearborn (New York 1986), explores the specific connection between the thematics of the mulatta heroine in fiction and the act of incest: the denial of paternity and of blood rite to the interracial child creates an ignorance of identity that can redound to the distinct disadvantage of certain lateral kinship relations. Even though Dearborn does not employ Judith and Henry Sutpen as an instance of the fatal unknowing, I think that a case can be made for it. Because they are ignorant of the existence of Charles Bon—their 'Black' brother—incest becomes a distinct possibility for all of Sutpen's children. Drawing out the symbolic and rhetorical resonances of the mulatto theme, Dearborn defines both the fictive character and the historical subject, we infer, as 'a living embodiment of the paradox of the individual within society.' She suggestively describes the 'fictional mulatto' as the 'imaginative conjunction of a cultural disjunction' (p. 158).

The volume of *Critical Inquiry* edited by Henry Louis Gates (12, 1 [Autumn 1985]), does not propose to look specifically at the mulatto/a as an aspect of the problematic of alterity. But the various other issues of the latter explored in the volume are suggestive in a number of ways, particularly Israel Burshatin's 'The Moor in the Text: Metaphor, Emblem, and Silence', pp. 98–119. Burshatin's 'moor', like the mulatto/a', might be viewed as an already inspissated identity before the *particulars* of context have had an opportunity to follow their vocation.

2.   The following list of fictional texts on the mulato/a is not offered as an exhaustive survey. We regard them as impression points that the reader achieves in tracing the career of the subject from Harper's era through the 1930s: *The Autobiography of an Ex-Colored Man* by James Weldon Johnson (New York 1960) with an introduction by Arna Bontemps; *Cane* by Jean Toomer (New York: Liveright, 1975) with an introduction by Darwin Turner. The reader should see specifically the closing section of this powerful work for the tale of Kabnis. Here, the exteriority of the mulatto figure has been revised and corrected into a structure of internal or psychic complication. Further examples include: *Quicksand* by Nella Larsen (1928; rpt. 1969); *Passing* by Nella Larsen (1929; rpt. Arno Press, 1969); *The Chinaberry Tree: A Novel of American Life* by Jessie Fauset (College Park 1969); *Comedy: American Style* by Jessie Fauset (1933; rpt. College Park 1969). The reader can consult the opening section of Barbara Christian's work, op. cit., for a more comprehensive account of the fiction of the mulatto/a. A fine study of Pauline Hopkins, contemporary of Frances Harper, has been done by Claudia Tate, 'Pauline Hopkins: Our Literary Foremother,' in *Conjuring: Black Women, Fiction, and Literary Tradition*, eds. Marjorie Pryse and Hortense Spillers (Bloomington 1985).

3.   The Oxford English Dictionary entry for 'mulatta' situates the term in Spanish. Born of a 'Negra and a fayre man', 'mulatta' in the English lexicon first appears c. 1622. Among its permutations in Portuguese is *mulato*, young mule, or one of a mixed race.

4.   *Narrative of the Life of Frederick Douglass, An American Slave, Written by Himself* (New York 1968), pp. 21–22.

5.   William Faulkner, *Light in August* (New York 1959).

6.   René Girard, *Violence and the Sacred*, trans. Patrick Gregory (Baltimore 1977). Girard's explosive work offers a background against which we might view the fundamental structuration of human community as the deployment of the dynamics of violence and the fear of violent reprisal. By isolating an 'expendable figure', the 'unanimity-minus-one', a community rids itself of various impurities, including guilt. Community also discovers the One Man or Woman (or the substitute) whose elimination would not generate the operations of revenge. Faulkner's Joe Christmas

is perfectly placed to carry out all the requirements of Girard's sacrificial program. Essentially unfathered, Christmas is Everyman/Woman *before* the name of the Father 'cleanses' him/her, or releases from the terrors of 'unculture'.

7.   Trans. Richard Howard (New York 1984); p. 185ff. This interesting conceptual narrative concentrates in the career of the Native American at the hands of the European explorer, but it projects a broader frame of reference that is pertinent to my argument here.

8.   John Irwin's brilliant structuralist reading of incest in Faulkner traces its manifestations in the agency of Quentin Compson. Straddling the narratives of *The Sound* and *the Fury and Absalom, Absalom!*, Quentin reflects his own incestuous urges toward his sister Caddy (*Sound and Fury*) in the narrative that he 'repeats' concerning Charles Bon (*Doubling and Incest/Repetition and Revenge* [Baltimore 1975]).

9.   *Incidents in the Life of a Slave Girl*, ed. L. Maria Child, with introduction by Walter Teller (New York 1973). The economic uses of the African female personality under the onus of captivity are alluded to in Brent's 'Sketches of Neighboring Slaveholders,' pp. 45-53. Not commenting specifically on the mulatta's value, the writer sounds, nonetheless, the profit connections between the female body/sexuality and the oppressive conditions of enslavement.

10.   *Absalom, Absalom!* (New York 1951). References to and direct quotations from the novel are taken from this edition; page numbers are cited in the text.

11.   The informing conceptualization of the relevant paragraph here is suggested by the work of Gayatri Spivak in 'French Feminism in an International Frame', *Yale French Studies* pp. 154–184.

12.   Various aspects of female sexuality in conjunction with history and politics are examined in *Pleasure and Danger: Exploring Female Sexuality*, ed. Carole Vance (Boston: Paul, 1984). My own contribution, 'Interstices: A Small Drama of Words', looks specifically at the grammar of sexuality in relation to African American women's community. The essays here are based on papers delivered at the 'Feminist and Scholar Conference, IX,' held at Barnard College, Spring 1982.

13.   Michel Foucault, *The History of Sexuality: Volume I: An Introduction*, trans. Robert Hurley (New York 1978). Foucault, re-opening the problem of Victorian sexuality, considers the discursivity of his subject. Victorian Europe was not, in his view, a sexually muted culture, but seized instead every occasion to induce and excite discourse about it. Illegitimate sexuality in the historic context he examines becomes one of the 'forms of reality' subjected to a discourse that is 'clandestine, circumscribed, and coded' in reference to the brothel, the mental institution, and other spaces of marginality (pp. 4ff). We would regard the site of the mulatta mistress as a marginalized class of objects erotically configured.

14.   'History is what hurts' profoundly informs Jameson's sense that 'History' is the 'ground and untranscendable horizon [that] needs no theoretical justification.' He offers its inexorability as the fundamental scene against which critical praxis unfolds, against which we gauge the efficacy and completeness of any critical system (*The Political Unconscious: Narrative as a Socially Symbolic Act* [Ithaca 1980]), p.102.

15.   See his *The New England Mind*, 2 vols. (Boston 1961).

16.   The classic account of the tensions engendered between the wish-fulfillment and its prohibitive mechanism is given in Freud's *Totem and Taboo*, vol. 13 of *The Standard Edition of the Complete Psychological Works of Sigmund Freud*, trans. James Strachey (London 1955).

17.   The codification of law that underscores the institution of slavery in the United States is sporadically examined in numerous historical texts. But a work contemporaneous with the final days of the 'peculiar institution' provides not only a detailed reading of the code, but also an instance of a parallel counter-sensitivity that takes on historic appeal in its own right: William Goodell, *The American Slave Code in*

Theory and Practice: Its Distinctive Features Shown by its Statutes, Judicial Decisions, and Illustrative Texts (New York 1853). Apparently the 'runaway slave' was neither rare nor forgotten. The plentiful advertisements describing the person of the fugitive—the model, we might suppose, for the contemporary 'All Points Bulletin' of the Federal Bureau of Investigation and those mug shots that grace the otherwise uniform local post office—argue the absolute solidification of captivity—the major American social landscape, in my view, for two and one-half centuries of human hurt on the scene of 'man's last best hope'. See *Runaway Slave Advertisements: A Documentary History from the 1730's to 1790*, comp. Lathan A. Windley, 2 vols. (Westport, Connecticut 1983).

18. Elizabeth Donnan, ed. and comp. *Documents Illustrative of the History of the Slave Trade to America*, vol. III, 'New England and the Middle Colonies' (Washington, D.C. 1932), p. 130. 'Accounts from an African Trade Book, 1733–1736,' from the Archives of the Newport Historical Society.

19. *Narrative of the Life of Frederick Douglass*, pp. 59-60.

20. (1893; rpt. New York: AMS Press, 1971). All references to and quotations from the novel come from this edition; page numbers are cited in the text.

21. *The Archaeology of Knowledge and the Discourse on Language*, trans. A.M. Sheridan Smith (New York 1972); 'The Discursive Irregularities', pp. 56–64.

Notes to Chapter 12

1. An earlier version of this essay was presented to the faculty seminar on Marxism and Society at Duke University in February, 1985. I wish to thank the following people for helpful comments on the paper: Chuck Bergquist, Don Donham, Brackette Williams, Robert Williams, Margery Wolf, Al Zagarell.

2. For a useful popular description of Guatemala's recent political history that describes the principal actors and goals in the three revolutionary movements since 1944, see Luisa Frank and Philip Wheaton, *Indian Guatemala: Path to Liberation* (Washington D.C.: Epica Task Force, 1984). For a more recent assessment of the current situation in Guatemala, with most insurgent activity neutralized but not entirely controlled, see George Black's 'Garrison Guatemala', *NACLA Report on the Americas* (January/February 1983), and 'Guatemala—the War is Not Over', *NACLA Report on the Americas* (March/April 1983).

3. See George Black's 'Central America: Crisis in the Backyard', *New Left Review* 135 (1982). His analysis contrasts the political groups and struggles in Guatemala, El Salvador, and Nicaragua and describes the main differences of class and state development in the three countries.

4. I use the term *campesino* rather than its usual English equivalent, peasant, to avoid the implication that rural Indians in Guatemala resemble traditional European peasants in any sense. Rural Indians rarely rent or sharecrop land; instead, they tend (since the late nineteenth century) to sole individual proprietorship over small plots. In general, they spend less than 50 percent of their productive time and obtain less than 25 percent of their incomes from agricultural activities of any kind, being for the most part rural artisans or petty commodity producers and traders. (See for further information, note 23 below.)

5. An explanation of the circumstances that led to the retention of Indian ethnic identity in Western Guatemala, as opposed to other parts of Central America, and how these shaped many social and political institutions of Guatemala is given in my 'Local History in Global Context: Social and Economic Transformations in Western Guatemala', *Comparative Studies in Society and History* 26, (1984).

6. See E.P. Thompson, 'Eighteenth-century English society: class struggle

without class?' *Social History* 3 (1978); Perry Anderson, *Arguments Within English Marxism* (London: Verso, 1980), especially Chapter 2; Gareth Stedman Jones, *Languages of Class: Studies in English Working Class History 1832–1982* (Cambridge: Cambridge University Press, 1983), especially Chapter 3. (References to Jones's argument here are to a shorter version published as, 'The Language of Chartism', in J. Epstein and D. Thompson, eds., *The Chartist Experience* (London, 1982), pp. 3–58.)

7.   I refer here to the more 'orthodox' variant of the critical standpoint, first elaborated as an epistemological stance by Georg Lukacs in *History and Class Consciousness* (London: Merlin Press, 1968). A more recent statement of the position can be found in Ellen Meiksins Wood, 'Marxism without Class Struggle?' *Socialist Register* (1983), pp. 239–271. See also her *The Retreat from Class: A New 'True' Socialism* (London: Verso, 1986).

8.   Karl Polanyi, in *The Great Transformation* (New York, 1944), provides one of the best and earliest 'negative' statements of the differing social bases of capitalist and non-capitalist economies. Since that time, a debate has raged in anthropology about appropriate modes of description for non-capitalist economies. Maurice Block's *Marxism and Anthropology* (Oxford 1985), reviews the debate and shows its roots in earlier Marxist thought. Joel Kahn provides a useful critique of the negative position in 'The Social Context of Technological Change in Four Malaysian Villages,' *Man*, N.S. 16 (1982).

9.   Bourdieu, an anthropologist, presents his general position and method in *Outline of a Theory of Practice* (Cambridge: Cambridge University Ptress, 1977). One could argue that the position is much like that of Antonio Gramsci, as he has been interpreted by scholars like Ernesto Laclau in *Politics and Ideology in Marxist Theory* (London: Verso 1977), pp. 138 ff., and Chantal Mouffe, 'Hegemony and Ideology in Gramsci', in *Gramsci and Marxist Theory* (London, 1979), pp. 259–288. See also, Laclau and Mouffe, *Hegemony and Socialist Strategy* (London: Verso, 1985).

10.   Cf., Bourdieu, op. cit., pp. 72–95; and Antonio Gramsci, *Selections from the Prison Notebooks*, edited and translated by Quintin Hoare and Geoffrey Nowell Smith (New York 1971), pp. 323–37.

11.   Thompson, pp. 149, 151.

12.   Ibid., p. 151.

13.   Anderson, p. 43.

14.   Stedman Jones, p. 13.

15.   Ibid., p. 52.

16.   A recent statement of this position can be found in Barry Smart's *Foucault, Marxism, and Critique* (London 1983).

17.   Cf. Gramsci, pp. 365–66, 395–97; Bourdieu, pp. 82–87.

18.   By this I mean the position espoused by G.A. Cohen in *Karl Marx's Theory of History: A Defense* (Princeton 1978). A position closer to my own is developed by Ernesto Laclau in *Politics and Ideology in Marxist Theory*.

19.   Cf. Gramsci, pp. 410–414.

20.   For a more thoroughgoing treatment of the relevant background see the following papers by the author: 'Class and Class Consciousness in Prerevolutionary Guatemala', Working Paper 126, Latin American Program, The Wilson Center (Washington, D.C., 1984); 'Does a Commodity Economy Enrich the Few While Ruining the Masses?' *Journal of Peasant Studies* 11 (1984); 'Labor and International Capital in the Making of a Peripheral Social Formation: Guatemala 1850–1980,' in *Labor in the Capitalist World-Economy*, C. Bergquist, ed. (Beverly Hills: Sage Publications 1984), pp. 135–156; and 'Local History in Global Context: Social and Economic Transformations in Western Guatemala' (See previous citation, note 5).

21.   The basis for these observations about 'objective' class relations in western

Guatemala (where the vast majority of Guatemala's Indians reside) is the following. Between 1976 and 1978, right before the present revolutionary crisis, I spent approximately two and one-half years systematically surveying occupation, production, and class relations in the region. I interviewed 2554 households in 143 different rural hamlets of the region; and I interviewed on occupation and position in production 13,751 male heads of household in 31 different townships in the region. A general report of these findings can be found in my paper, 'Survival Strategies Among Rural Smallholders: A Case Study of Guatemala,' report submitted to the International Labour Office, Employment and Development Department (August 1985).

22. The community of reference for Indians is invariably the township (*municipio*). Of the 325 townships in Guatemala, approximately 150 are mostly Indian; these are located mainly in the western highlands of the country. The township is an administrative entity that lacks pre-hispanic roots, being composed of different *parcialidades* (which do have pre-hispanic roots), aggregated by the Spaniards shortly after the ravages of the Conquest for purposes of controlling the native population. The continuous struggles of the Indians for political and economic autonomy through the channels provided by township administration eventually forged a 'community of interest' in the township. See my paper, cited in note 5 above, pp. 197–200.

23. See Robert M. Carmack, *Historia social de los Quichés* (Guatemala City, 1979), for a discussion of Totonicapan's political activism from the Conquest to the 1970s. There are no published accounts attempting to explain Totonicapan's lack of involvement in the 1978–1982 Indian upheavals. My own hypothesis is that the areas of insurgency were those most affected by the counterinsurgency measures taken by the state, which acted to quell a perceived threat in Indian areas before that threat was even actualized. In some (but not all) cases, the insurgent areas were also those where small armed guerrilla groups were most publicly active; the guerrillas appeared to select the more remote areas or areas where there was heavy dependence on income from seasonal work an plantations. (See Mario Payeras, 'Days of the Jungle', *Monthly Review* 35 [1983].) Thus guerrillas did very little to organize the artisans of Totonicapan, having written them off as 'petty bourgeois.' (See my paper, cited in note 5 above, pp. 219–224.)

24. Guatemala is organized administratively into 22 departments, each with an admininstrative center through which state bureaucrats, invariably Ladinos, oversee local politics. Townships are smaller administrative units whose political representatives were appointed by the central government until 1950, but today have very limited powers. The community of Totonicapan consists of the township of Totonicapan, directed by the town of Totonicapan, which is also the administrative center for the entire department of Totonicapan. As a social entity the township is overwhelmingly Indian. The urban Ladino population, most of it transient, has little stake in Totonicapan as a locality. Their presence in the community, however, has important consequences for Indian social identity. Virtually all Indian townships in Guatemala have at least a handful of Ladino families who mark the ethnic boundary in a local as well as a general sense.

25. The political reforms that accompanied the 1944 'revolution' in Guatemala gave Indians much greater access to economic and political roles outside their community. For a general depiction of these changes see Richard N. Adams, *Guatemala: Crucifixion by Power* (Austin 1970). For a discussion of the consequences of these changes on Indian communities, see my paper, cited in note 5 above, pp. 210–219.

26. For more detailed discussion of the zonal differentiation of Indian townships in western Guatemala, see the works cited in notes 20 and 21.

27. See Smith, 'Does a Commodity Economy Enrich. . . ?'

28. See ibid., pp. 84–89.

29. See Smith, 'Class and Class Consciousness in Prerevolutionary Guatemala,' pp.18–24.

30. For a brief history of Guatemalan views on the links between race and ethnicity, see Roxanne Dunbar Ortiz, *Indians of the Americas* (New York 1984), pp. 110–115. Debates on the issue among Guatemalan intellectuals have broad political implications. See especially Severo Martínez Peláez, *La patria del criollo* (Guatemala City, 1971); and Carlos Guzmán Böckler and Jean-Loup Herbert, *Guatemala: una interpretación histórico-social* (Mexico City, 1970). Guatemalan intellectuals (none of whom define themselves as Indian) all accept that class and ethnicity are largely congruent in Guatemala, but in the mistaken belief that Indians constitute a single 'objective' class (whether peasant, worker, or semi-proletariat). Their main concern is with Ladinos—the class position and consciousness of exploiters who are also exploited. The question is heavily freighted politically because it has to do with which social group in Guatemala, Indian or Ladino, represents the 'real' national identity of Guatemala. The debate thus vitally concerns the nature and future of Guatemalan national identity more than it concerns Guatemalan class and ethnic relations.

31. A sensitive account of contemporary Guatemalan views on race and culture is provided by Joseph Pasini, '"El Pilar," A Plantation Microcosm of Guatemalan Ethnicity,' unpublished Ph.D. dissertation, University of Rochester. Pansini worked as a priest as well as an anthropologist on a large, traditional Guatemalan coffee plantation. He describes in detail the different beliefs about culture and race held by the very different groups (bourgeois [European] owners, Ladino managers, Ladino workers, permanent Indian workers, seasonal Indian workers, and local Indian artisans) who made up the plantation community.

32. My discussion of Indian beliefs about race, tradition, and community is based on fieldwork in Guatemala. But other anthropological accounts, as well as native accounts, provide corroborating evidence. See, e.g.: Kay Warren, *The Symbolism of Subordination: Indian Identity in a Guatemalan Town* (Austin 1978); John Hawkins, *Inverse Images: The Meaning of Culture, Ethnicity and Family in Postcolonial Guatemala* (Albuquerque 1984); Ricardo Falla, *Quiché Rebelde* (Guatemala City, 1983); James Sexton, *Son of Tecun Uman: A Maya Indian Tells His Life Story* (Tucson, Ariz. 1981); Elizabeth Burgos-Debray, ed., *I . . . , Rigoberta Menchu* (London: Verso, 1984).

33. The best sources on the positions taken by the armed opposition in Guatemala on the 'national' or ethnic question and on the proper way of integrating Indians into the revolutionary struggle are the following: *Polemica* (1981–), a publication of the Institute Centroamericano de Documentacion e Investigaciones Sociales (A.P. 174, San Jose, Costa Rica), which publishes many of the political declarations of all four of the armed opposition groups; and *Compañero* (1980–), the International Journal of the EGP (Guerrilla Army of the Poor), which has carried out more public analyses of the Indian question than the other groups (English translations by Solidarity Publications, P.O. 40874, San Francisco, CA). The best available treatment of the Guatemalan left in English is the pamphlet, *Dare to Struggle, Dare to Win*, Concerned Guatemalan Scholars, New York, 1981. Also interesting is the testimony of a Guatemalan guerrilla (member of the EGP), Mario Payeras, 'Days of the Jungle', *Monthly Review* 35 (1983). Unfortunately, these last two sources are now quite dated; no useful analysis of the current situation exists. Payeras, or Comandante Benedicto, and a number of his companions, for example, have separated from the EGP, partly over the 'Indian question', to form a new group.

34. See Smith, 'Labor and International Capital . . . ,' pp. 146–52.

35.   By 'common sense' understanding, I mean roughly what Pierre Bourdieu refers to as 'habitus' or practical consciousness (Bourdieu, op. cit., pp. 72–95) and what Gramsci refers to as 'commonsense' (Gramsci, op. cit. pp. 323–37).

36.   See Smith, 'Local History in Global Context,' pp. 219–224.

37.   On this issue see, e.g., Rudolf Bahro, *The Alternative in Eastern Europe* (London: NLB, 1978); and Michael Burawoy, *The Politics of Production* (London: Verso, 1985).

Notes to Chapter 13

1.   S. Amin, 'The Third World Today and the International Division of Labor', *AMPO: Japan-Asia Quarterly Review* 11, 1, series no. 39 (1979); P. Vuskovic, 'Latin America and the Changing World Economy', *NACLA Report on the Americas* 14, 1 (January-February 1980); G. Helleiner, *A World Divided* (London 1976); J. Leontiades, 'International Sourcing in the LDCs', *Columbia Journal of World Business* 6,6 (November 1971).

2.   Leontiades, p. 19.

3.   Vuskovic, pp. 5–6.

4.   Anwar Shaikh has long been making this point in connection with the theory of economic crisis. Concerning the 'NIDL' hypothesis, some early critics implicitly pointed to the Smithian strains in the theory by referring to the 'internationalization of Babbage'. See D. Jacobson, A. Wickham, and J. Wickham, 'Review Article', *Capital & Class* 7 (Spring 1979). The authors of the present paper have also written a comprehensive critique of the 'NIDL' hypothesis: 'Theorizing the Inconsequential: A Critique of the New International Division of Labor Thesis', unpublished paper. Recently, the 'NIDL' theories have been criticized in R. Jenkins, 'Divisions Over the International Division of Labour', *Capital & Class* 22 (Spring 1984).

5.   M. Herold, 'Worldwide Investment and Disinvestment by U.S. Multi-nationals: Implications for the Caribbean and Central America', unpublished paper; M. Herold and N. Kozlov, 'Autos and Chemicals versus Bras and Calculators: US Multinationals in the Third World', unpublished paper.

6.   See the superb article by Gabriel Palma outlining the similarity in methodological failings of the Russian Narodniks and the twentieth-century dependency theorists: 'Dependency: A Formal Theory of Underdevelopment or a Methodology for the Analysis of Concrete Situations of Underdevelopment?' *World Development* 6, 7–8 (July-August 1978).

7.   Palma, p. 904.

8.   Vuskovic, p. 6.

9.   To indict the MNC is, of course, merely to identify the phenomenon with the cause. Such confusion is evident in F. Clairmonte and J. Cavanagh, 'Transnational Corporations and the Struggle for the Global Market', *Journal of Contemporary Asia* 13, 4 (1983).

10.   J. Annerstadt and R. Gustavsson, *Towards a New International Economic Division of Labor?* (Denmark 1975), p. 11.

11.   A. Cueva, 'A Summary of "Problems and Perspectives of Dependency Theory"', *Latin American Perspectives* 3, 4 (Fall 1976), p.13.

12.   F. Frobel, J. Heinrichs, and O. Kreye, 'The World Market for Labor and the World Market for Industrial Sites', *Journal of Economic Issues* 17, 4 (December 1978), pp. 856–58.

13.   Proximity is not only to be understood in spatial terms, but from the point of view of the crossing of capitals and the maneuvering for markets.

14. A. Shaikh, 'Neo-Ricardian Economics', *Review of Radical Political Economics* 14, 2 (Summer 1982).

15. Shaikh, pp. 76–78.

16. Vuskovic, p. 5.

17. J. Cavanagh and J. Hackel, 'Contracting Poverty', *Economic and Political Weekly* 18, 31 (July 30, 1983), p. 1347.

18. N. Kozlov, 'The North-South Dialogue', mimeograph, University of New Hampshire (February 1979).

19. Vuskovic, p. 14.

20. Given that the degree of appropriability of above average profits—the constant quest of the foreign investor—is much greater in industries producing complex products in complex ways, it is there that one would expect to find the bulk of foreign investment activity, not in the low wage labor assembly and/or labor intensive industries. See S. Magee, 'Multinational Corporations, the Industry Cycle and Development', *Journal of World Trade Law* 11, 4 (July-August 1977).

21. A. Lipietz, 'Towards Global Fordism?' *New Left Review* 132 (March-April 1982); J. Caporaso, 'Industrialization in the Semiperiphery: The Evolving Global Division of Labor', *International Studies Quarterly* 25, 3 (September 1981).

22. A. Shaikh, 'The Current World Economic Crisis: Causes and Implications', unpublished paper; Lipietz, p. 36.

23. Lipietz, p.37.

24. Ibid, p. 44.

25. Ibid, p. 44.

26. F. Vellas, 'Ford Fiesta Spain: A Case of International Investment and Trade', *Journal of World Trade Law* 13, 6 (November-December 1979).

27. 'Mexico Set to Revamp Troubled Auto Industry', *New York Times* (September 15, 1983), p. D1.

28. J. Frieden, 'Third World Indebted Industrialization: International Finance and State Capitalism in Mexico, Brazil, Algeria, and South Korea', *International Organization* 35, 3 (Summer 1981). Although in many respects an apologist for capitalism, Bill Warren was the first to raise some crucial issues regarding Third World industrialization; see his 'Imperialism and Capitalist Industrialization', *New Left Review* 81 (September-October 1973), esp. p. 24.

29. See the *New York Times'* (January 5, 1985) grave warning to the US and other Western nations concerning the dangers of erecting barriers against South Korean steel and color televisions.

30. P. Clawson, 'The Internationalization of Capital and Capital Accumulation in Iran and Iraq', *The Insurgent Sociologist* 7, 2 (Spring 1977), p.70.

31 P. Evans, *Dependent Development: The Alliance of Multinational, State, and Local Capital in Brazil* (Princeton 1979).

32. Herold, 'Worldwide Investment and Disinvestment'.

33. R. Vernon, 'Sovereignty at Bay: Ten Years Later', *International Organization* 35, 3 (Summer 1981), p. 524.

34. M. Doz, 'Strategic Management in Multinational Corporations', *The Sloan Management Review* (Winter 1980), pp. 27–46.

35. W. Kiehel III, 'Playing the Global Game', *Fortune* (November 16, 1981), p.111.

36. Doz, p. 29.

37. Ibid, p. 30.

38. Kiehel, p. 114.

39. Frieden, pp. 407–8; G. Gereffi and P. Evans, 'Transnational Corporations, Dependent Development, and the State Policy in the Semiperiphery: A Comparison of Brazil and Mexico', *Latin American Research Review* 16, 3 (1981), p. 55.

40. Herold, 'Worldwide Investment and Disinvestment'.

41. Ibid.
42. Ibid.
43. Ibid.
44. Ibid.
45. Ibid.
46. D. Nayyar, 'Transnational Corporations and Manufactured Exports from Poor Countries', *The Economic Journal* 88, 349 (March 1978), p. 62.
47. S. Hymer, 'The Internationalization of Capital', *Journal of Economic Issues* 6, 1 (March 1972).
48. S. Rose, 'Multinational Corporations in a Tough New World', *Fortune* (August 1973), p. 56.
49. Other analyses noted that assembly plant exploitation of cheap labor in the Third World was limited to certain kinds of industry and represented a smaller proportion of the recent manufacturing MNCs' operations, the larger part being the expansion of production for the domestic market of a growing number of peripheral nations. See V. Bornschier, *Wachstum, Konzentration und Multinationalisierung von Industrieunternehmen* (Frauenfeld and Stuttgart, 1976).
50. M. Herold, 'Growing Differentiation: Multinational Corporations in the Semi-Industrialized Countries of the Third World', unpublished paper.
51. Herold and Kozlov, 'Autos and Chemicals versus Bras and Calculators'.
52. B. Balassa, 'Export Incentives and Export Performance in Developing Countries: A Comparative Analysis', *Weltwirtschaftliches Archiv* 114 (1978), p. 36.
53. D. Nayyar, 'International Relocation of Production and Industrialization in LDCs, *Economic and Political Weekly* (July 1983), pp. PE-13-PE-26.
54. Herold and Kozlov, 'Theorizing the Inconsequential'.
55. Herold and Kozlov, 'Autos and Chemicals versus Bras and Calculators.'
56. J. Cavanagh and J. Hackel, 'Multinational Corporations in Central America and the Caribbean: International Subcontracting', unpublished paper.
57. Herold and Kozlov, 'Autos and Chemicals versus Bras and Calculators'.
58. M. Herold and N. Kozlov, 'Multinationals in Transitional Societies: Experiences and Lessons', unpublished paper.
59. O. Havrylyshyn and I. Alikhani, 'Is There Cause for Export Optimism?' *Finance and Development* 20, 2 (June 1983), p. 19.
60. Balassa, 'Export Incentives and Export Performance in Developing Countries'; and, more generally, 'Special Issue on Third World Industrialization in the 1980s: Open Economies in a Closing World', *Journal of Development Studies* 21, 1 (October 1984).
61. Herold and Kozlov, 'Autos and Chemicals versus Bras and Calculators.'
62. Ibid.
63. Nayyar, 'Transnational Corporations and Manufactured Exports from Poor Countries', pp. 62, 65.
64. Also noted in R. Jenkins, 'The Export Performances of Multinational Corporations in Mexican Industry', *Journal of Development Studies* 15, 3 (April 1979), pp. 102-3.
65. L. Willmore, 'Direct Foreign Investment in Central American Manufacturing', *World Development* 4, 6 (June 1976), p. 512.
66. Helleiner, 'Structural Aspects of Third World Trade', p. 73; Nayyar, 'Transnational Corporations and Manufactured Exports from Poor Countries,' pp. 63, 65.
67. Helleiner, 'Structural Aspects of Third World Trade', p. 74.
68. Nayyar, 'Transnational Corporations and Manufactured Exports from Poor Countries', p. 65.
69. Frieden, p. 430.
70. World Bank, *World Development Report 1979*, p. 5.

274

71. Herold and Kozlov, 'Autos and Chemicals versus Bras and Calculators'.
72. Although Nayyar, 'Transnational Corporations and Manufactured Exports from Poor Countries', p. 66 and Jenkins, 'The Export Performances of Multinational Corporations in Mexican Industry', p. 67 argue the contrary.
73. Helleiner, 'Structural Aspects of Third World Trade', pp. 72–74.
74. Herold and Kozlov, 'Autos and Chemicals versus Bras and Calculators'.
75. Jenkins, 'The Export Performances of Multinational Corporations in Mexican Industry', pp. 104–5; Fairchild, 'Performance and Technology of US and National Firms in Mexico', *Journal of Development Studies* 14, 1 (October 1977), pp. 14–19.
76. Herold and Kozlov, 'Autos and Chemicals versus Bras and Calculators'.
77. Ibid.
78. Herold, 'Worldwide Investment and Disinvestment'; R. Burbach and M. Herold, 'The U.S. Economic Stake in Central America and the Caribbean', in R. Burbach and P. Flynn, eds., *The Politics of Intervention: The United States in Central America* (New York 1984).
79. F. Halliday, 'Cold War in the Caribbean', *New Left Review* 141 (September-October 1983), p. 6.
80. Willmore, p. 499, citing data from Gert Rosenthal.
81. Herold, 'Worldwide Investment and Disinvestment'.
82. N. Girvan and M. Odle, 'The Role of Transnational Corporations in the Economies of Caribbean Countries', unpublished paper.
83. *Dun's Business Month* (November 1982), p. 39.
84. *Forbes* (February 1, 1982), p. 45.
85. This view is also supported by Nayyar, 'International Relocation of Production and Industrialization in LDCs'.

Notes to Chapter 14

1. See Juan Ramos y Lopez, 'Mas ayuda federal a los municipios—zona de desastre', *El Mundo*, 22 October 1985, p. 3.
2. Cf. Grupo de Economistas CEREP, 'La Crisis Económica de Puerto Rico', San Juan 1984; and Mohinder Bhatia, 'Sound policy comes from diversifying economic base', *The San Juan Star*, 13 October 1985, p. 8.
3. Cf., I. Rodríguez Feliciano, 'Aboga por la privatización de agências como alivio', *El Reportero*, San Juan, 23 October 1985, p. 3; and Tom Dorney, 'Bank head terms P.R. debt Public Enemy No. 1', *The San Juan Star*, 22–24 October 1985.
4. Cf., Julio Muriente Pérez, 'Tránsito millonario de drogas hacia E.U.', *Claridad*, 29 March—4 April, 1985, p.5; Maritza Díaz Alcalde, 'Al Destape la economía subterránea', *El Mundo*, 3 March 1985, pp. 20–21; 2nd 31 March 1986, p. 1; as well as headline stories in the following issues of *El Nuevo Día*: 22 June 1983, 28 June 1985, 23 October 1985, and 2 November 1985.
5. Selling Puerto Rico to Latin America as the 'perfect model' usually involves a large quotient of outright distortion or falsehood. A magnificent example was the recent visit of Dr. Hernan Padilla, the former mayor of San Juan, to Peru, where he testified that 'unemployment did not exist in Puerto Rico'! (See 'Padilla: No existe el desenmpleo en el País', *El Nuevo Día*, 9 February 1985, p. 14.)
6. Cf., Emilio Pantojas García, 'La Crisis del modelo desarrollista y la reestructuración capitalista en Puerto Rico', *Cuadernos de Investigación y Análisis* 9, CEREP, San Juan 1984; Lisette Nuñez, 'Incentivo para el comercia regional', *El Nuevo Día*, 31 January 1985, p. 6; and Juan Manuel Garcia Passalaqua, 'La Caribeñización' *El Nuevo Día*, 29 January 1985, p. 37.

7.   Cited in José A. Castrodad, 'Fija las metas del gobierno', *El Nuevo Día*, 3 January 1985, p. 4. Also see Robert Rivas, 'Hernández Colon Pulls CBI Surprise', *Caribbean Business*, 9 January 1985, pp. 1–2.

8.   Cf. Harry Turner, 'RHC to preach need of 936 funds for CBI', *The San Juan Star*, 28 April 1985, p. 3; Jesús Dávila, 'El Caribe en la órbita de Puerto Rico', *El Mundo*, 5 April 1985, p. 35; Dávila, 'Grenada; satélite de Puerto Rico', *El Mundo*, 6 April 1985, p. 32; and Deborah Ramírez, 'Acevedoff today to plug CBI-936 link' *The San Juan Star*, 24 April 1985, p. 3. On the Deaver connection see *El Nuevo Día*, 18 May 1986, p. 21. Deaver also has business connections with the London-based public relations multinational, Saatchi and Saatchi, which owns Badillo-Compton in San Juan—the agency that handles all public relations for Hernández Colón and the PDP.

9.   Cf. Luis Cabán, 'P.R.: Posible sede del Parlamento', *El Mundo*, 4 May 1985, p. 17; Luis Varela, 'Aponte Pérez quiere isla ingrese en ONU', *El Reportero*, 19 February 1985, p. 4; and Bienvenido Olavarria, 'Acevedo, el hombre de confianza', *El Nuevo Día*, 10 February 1985. p. 6.

10.   This renovated ideological discourse has, at least, three apparent goals. First by identifying Puerto Rico with 'Hispanic America' it seeks, not so much to 'hispanicize' Puerto Rico, as to puertoricanize Latin America: i.e. to project Puerto Rico as the ideal model of development. (This is, of course, a replay of its role in the 1950s.) Secondly, this rhetoric allows Spain a comfortable way to land in America, that is, via Puerto Rico. The third goal is geared towards internal consumption: pro-Hispanic speeches appease popular aspirations without offering anything of substance, a poor surrogate for nationalism.

11.   Cf. Isabel Cinton, 'En San Jóse, abrazos y negocios', *El Mundo*, 15 September 1985, p. 6; Juan Mári Bras, 'La Diplomacia venida a menos', *Claridad*, 25–31 October 1985, p. 31; Richard Walton, 'Costa Rica—A Terrible Sadness', *Mesoamerica* Vol. 4, 10, San Juan, October 1985, pp. 7–10; Rolf Olsen, 'RHC hit by Barrios for supporting U.S. embargo', *The San Juan Star*, 7 May 1985, p. 11; and Luis Torres Negron, 'En marcha planes petroleros para la isla', *El Reportero*, 15 November 1985, p. 8.

12.   Cf. Kal Wagenheim, 'Island Business win more defense dollars', *Caribbean Business*, 21 November 1984, p. 20; and Isabel Cintron, 'Gestionan fábricar en P.R. barcos para ejército de E.U.', *El Mundo*, 9 March 1985, p. 39.

13.   Cf. AP. 'Confirma Roosevelt Roads los ejercicios en el Caribe', *El Neuvo Día*, 7 September 1985; Jesús Dávila, 'En Vuieques tropas Centroamericanas', *El Nueva Día*, 4 September 1985; Luis Torres Negron, 'Mora dice G.N. no ensayó una invasíon en Vieques', *El Reportero*, 6 September 1985, p. 11; and Earl Bousquet, 'Caribbean Militarization Intensifies', *Caribbean Contact*, Barbados, September 1985, p. 5.

14.   Leslie Gelb, 'US Plan for Deploying Arms Wasn't Disclosed to Host Nations', *New York Times*, 13 February 1985, p. 3.

15.   See articles in *Claridad*, 26 July–1 August and 11–17 October, 1985.

16.   'La CIA Busca Candidatos de origen puertorriqueño', *El Nuevo Diá*, 12 August 1985, p. 16.

17.   See Anne Nelson, 'Cerro Maravilla Deaths: Police Cover-Up Rocks Puerto Rico', *NACLA—Report on the Americas*, XVIII, 5, September-October 1984, pp. 9–12.

18.   See 'Pensamiento Critico no será silenciado', *Revista Pensamiento Critico*, (Suplemento Especial), San Juan, July-August 1985.

19.   Fidel Rodríquez Alicea, 'RHC dice que no fue consultado ni por cortesía', *El Mundo*, 3 September 1985, pp. 1–3.

20.   See 'El caso de la Unión de Aeropuertos: Maravilla Inconclusa'. *Revista Pensamiento Critico*, January-February 1986, pp. 21–25.

BLACK STUDIES FROM VERSO

Manning Marable: A THEORY OF BLACK POLITICS. A comparative study of race, class and power in African homelands and the Black diaspora.

'Manning Marable has established himself as one of the most informed and perceptive critics of Black social movements since C.L.R. James.'

Christianity and Crisis

Volume One: BLACK AMERICAN POLITICS: From the Washington Marches to Jesse Jackson.
ISBN 0 86091 816 5

'. . . dense, authoritative, full of enlightening allusion, but always passionate.'

Los Angeles Times

Volume Two: AFRICAN AND CARIBBEAN POLITICS: From Kwame Nkrumah to Maurice Bishop
ISBN 0 86091 884 X

The fate of revolutionary nationalism, including an impassioned and searching analysis of the tragic self-destruction of the Grenadan Revolution.

* * * *

Martin Murray: TIME OF AGONY, TIME OF DESTINY
The Upsurge of Popular Protest in South Africa
ISBN 0 86091 857 2

A careful, well-documented narrative of the popular rebellion combined with an analysis of the politics of the main Black resistance formations, from the ANC to the UDF and the National Forum. An indispensable guide to the epochal struggle of our time.